Where the River Ends

SHAYLIH MUEHLMANN

Where the River Ends

CONTESTED INDIGENEITY IN THE MEXICAN COLORADO DELTA

Duke University Press
Durham and London
2013

© 2013 Duke University Press
All rights reserved
Printed in the United States of America
on acid-free paper ∞
Designed by C. H. Westmoreland
Typeset in Adobe Garamond
by Keystone Typesetting, Inc.
Library of Congress Cataloging-in-Publication Data
Muehlmann, Shaylih, 1979–
Where the river ends : contested indigeneity in the
Mexican Colorado Delta / Shaylih Muehlmann.
pages cm
Includes bibliographical references and index.
ISBN 978-0-8223-5443-7 (cloth : alk. paper)
ISBN 978-0-8223-5445-1 (pbk. : alk. paper)
1. Cocopa Indians—Mexico—Colorado River Delta.
2. Cocopa Indians—Mexican-American Border Region.
I. Title.
E99.C842M84 2013
972'.1—dc23
2013005281

*para Arón Antonio Galindo González y
Ramiro Izayn Martínez Rodelo*

CONTENTS

Illustrations and Maps   ix
Acknowledgments   xi

Introduction   1

Chapter 1. "Listen for When You Get There": Topologies of Invisibility on the Colorado River   25

Chapter 2. The Fishing Conflict and the Making and Unmaking of Indigenous Authenticity   55

Chapter 3. "What Else Can I Do with a Boat and No Nets?" Ideologies of Work and the Alternatives at Home   83

Chapter 4. Mexican Machismo and a Woman's Worth   118

Chapter 5. "Spread Your Ass Cheeks": And Other Things That Shouldn't Get Said in Indigenous Languages   146

Conclusions   171

Notes   181
References   189
Index   215

ILLUSTRATIONS AND MAPS

ILLUSTRATIONS

Figure I.1 Bisected dog   20
Figure 1.1 The Boulder Dam compared to the pyramids   37
Figure 1.2 The world's biggest US flag   38
Figure 2.1 Government official documents fishermen   74
Figure 2.2 "Fish for Sale"   81
Figure 3.1 Soldiers stop in the village for water   99
Figure 3.2 Preparing boat for registration   114
Figure 3.3 Discarded sign in front of the museum   116
Figure 4.1 Women at a fishing meeting   136

MAPS

Map 1.1 Colorado River basin   29
Map 1.2 US-Mexico border area tribal lands   30
Map 2.1 The Upper Gulf of California Biosphere Reserve, Mexican Commission for National Protected Areas (2007)   57

ACKNOWLEDGMENTS

MY GREATEST DEBT is to the many Cucapá families in the delta whose hospitality, kindness, and patience made this research possible. For their friendship and support I would like to extend my deepest thanks to Antonia Torres González, Citlalli Itzel Ruano Torres, María González Portillo, Ruth Guadalupe González González, Noemí Berenice González González, Sol Navil Rodelo Torres, and Juana Torres González. For their wisdom and guidance throughout my fieldwork I thank Inocencia González Sainz, Raquel Portillo Tambo, Onésimo González Sainz, Francisco Javier González Sainz, Colin Soto, and Mónica Paulina González Portillo. For looking out for me more generally I would like to thank Francisco Alejandro Galindo Flores, José Ramiro Martínez Morales, and Francisco Javier González González. For teaching me how to chase rainbows and pronounce words I would like to thank Casca, Neto, Adriana, Suki, Popo, Corey, and Aneth. I am also grateful to Perla, Nieshpak, Nirvana, Casimira, Edith, Andrés, and Margie for their friendship and hospitality.

The Cucapá chief, whom I call Don Madeleno here, was a kind and gentle guide throughout my fieldwork. I am extremely grateful to have had the time that I did with this wise and committed individual. Don Madeleno died of a heart attack in October 2007. His passing represents a great loss to those fortunate enough to have known him.

The faculty in the Department of Anthropology at the University of Toronto offered excellent guidance throughout the course of my doctoral research. I am particularly grateful to Bonnie McElhinny and Jack Sidnell, for trusting me with this project and allowing it to take its own shape. Jack Sidnell has helped shape this project since its very first inception as supervisor for master's work. His conceptual and moral support have carried this project through many awkward stages. Bonnie McElhinny provided incisive and detailed commentary on the initial stages of this manuscript.

The final product, in both narrative form and theoretical scope, has been greatly shaped by her suggestions and criticisms.

Michael Lambek, Valentina Napolitano, Gavin Smith, Tania Li, Monica Heller, Bruce Miller, and Sandra Bamford offered critical commentary at various stages of my research. I am also grateful for the comments I received from scholars at other institutions at different stages of this research, including Benedict Colombi, Les Field, Alexander Dawson, and David Rojinsky. My cohort at the University of Toronto also provided intellectual and moral support throughout the early stages of this project. I would like to thank Lori-Anne Théroux-Bénoni, Emma Varley, Zoë H. Wool, Janet McLaughlin and Abigail Sone.

Max Ascrizzi, Sally Vernon, and Anna Kramer read and offered comments on drafts of this manuscript. I would also like to acknowledge the friendship and support of Terese Bressette, Mike MacLean, Jake Fleming, and Jana McQuilkin. Joshua Barker was a consistent source of advice throughout the early stages of this research. Conversations with Jonathan and Nancy Barker also helped refine the scope of this project. Several other individuals provided crucial moral support at different stages in the writing of this manuscript including Anne Marie and Pat Owens, Joe and Lynn Ascrizzi, Maddie and Billie Stanton, Donna Sartonowitz, Jimmy Ryan, Maureen Ryan, and Lee H. Merrick.

Many of the environmentalists working in the Colorado delta were a source of encouragement during my fieldwork in Mexico. I am grateful to Guadalupe Fonseca Molina, Alejandra Calvo Fonseca, Francisco Zamora, and Osvel Hinojosa Huerta. Their dedication to the environmental revival of the delta and to finding ways to improve the quality of life for residents of the area was a consistent source of inspiration for me during my fieldwork. Edith Santiago-Serrano opened her home to me when I first arrived in Mexico and provided consistent technical and moral support throughout the course of my fieldwork. Conversations with Mark Lellouch consistently reinvigorated my research program. Joaquín Murrieta has been an important interlocutor throughout the course of this research. His work, motivation, creativity, and dedication had a huge impact on this project.

Part of this manuscript was completed during a summer writing residency at the School of Advanced Research (SAR). The network of scholars and associates integral to this program offered advice and encouragement at a critical moment in my writing process. I am particularly thankful to

James F. Brooks for his perceptive commentary and continued encouragement. My cohort at SAR was also a source of lively feedback and friendship, particularly Kristin Dowell and Rebecca Dolinhow. Further revisions of this manuscript were completed during a postdoctoral appointment at the University of California, Berkeley, where William F. Hanks, provided extremely valuable encouragement, as did Cristina Giordano, Chelsea Blackmore, Mia Fuller, Marco Jacquemet, and Terra Edwards. Finally, my colleagues and students at the University of British Columbia have provided encouragement during the final stages of revision, and particularly Carole Blackburn, Julie Cruikshank, Patrick Moore, Kiley Hamlin, John Barker, and Felice Wyndham. Thanks also to my students Meredith Diane Mantooth and Danielle Good for their help editing the manuscript.

I'm very grateful to Valerie Millholland, my editor at Duke University Press, for her encouragement and support of this book project. I also owe many thanks to Duke's anonymous reviewers who read and provided detailed commentary on the manuscript through various rounds of review. The research for this book has been funded by various institutions at different stages including the Social Sciences and Humanities Research Council (SSHRC), the Wenner-Gren Foundation for Anthropological Research, the International Development Research Centre (IDRC), the Ethel-Jane Westfeldt Bunting Fellowship, the Centre for the Study of the United States at the University of Toronto (CSUS), the University of Toronto and the Ontario Graduate Scholarship.

Finally, Gastón Gordillo's tireless editorial assistance, insightful feedback, and unfailing support were crucial for the completion of this project. Rachel Ryan Muehlmann provided relentless moral and editorial assistance. Scott Ryan Muehlmann sang along and always reminded me to celebrate. Robert Muehlmann and Patricia Ryan read every word and offered enduring humor and encouragement.

INTRODUCTION

ALTHOUGH MAPS STILL show the Colorado River running from the Rocky Mountains to the Gulf of California in northern Mexico, today the river no longer reaches the sea. While I conducted most of the fieldwork for this book in a Cucapá village in the now-dry delta of the river in Mexico, I began my research upstream in the green mountains of the state of Colorado in the United States. This is where the river's headwaters rush up from under the hard earth and begin a 1,450-mile run. I started my journey there because I wanted to arrive at the end of the river with a sense of where it came from, and a sense of the history of how this quintessentially American river now fails to reach the sea.

From Colorado, I followed the river across the Glen Canyon and Hoover Dams, the first of the big dams to be built on the river. I followed the river to Lee's Ferry, where the annual flow of water is measured in order to be divided among the seven states and two countries that depend on it. I stopped in Las Vegas to examine the artificial waterfalls and light shows at the large casino-hotels. Then I traveled past golf courses and swimming pools and through the Grand Canyon and the lush Imperial Valley.

Finally, I drove across the US-Mexico border, where the wide empty fields of the Imperial Valley meet the tall barbed-wire fence that defines sections of the borderlands. Directly across the border the river's water trickles to a stream. This is the most unequal international border in the world, a geopolitical barrier that while seeking to stop people from going north also, as we shall see, prevents water from flowing south. Now, all that remains of the Colorado River is a dried-out riverbed, whose cracked and saline surface is a potent reminder of the river that once fanned out in the Mexican Colorado delta. Beyond the fence at the border lies the bustling city of Mexicali. In contrast to the wide fields and highways just north of the border, Mexicali emerges as a huddle of low, cramped buildings and makeshift *tiendas* (stores). Rows of dental clinics offer reduced prices to medical tourists. Past the frenetic traffic, the smog, the roundabouts, and the urban density, the city splays out into huge expanses of factories, smoke billowing from bristling outcrops of towers.

With the river no longer available as my guide, I followed Route 5, the only tarred road that runs north–south between the Mexican states of Sonora and Baja California, connecting Mexicali to the interior of the Sonoran Desert. On this road, the traffic flows to and from the coastal town of San Felipe and beyond to Puerto Penasco. Buses run at all hours transporting workers from the nearby *colonias* to work in the factories, also known as *maquiladoras*.[1] In the winter, caravans of Americans pass on their way down to the coast, which has become a popular destination for those seeking to winter in warmer locales. Past the factories, the road winds through small colonias huddled close outside of Mexicali's city limits and congregated along drainage routes and passes into green farmlands where fields of cotton, onions, *nopales*, and wheat stretch out beneath the blue desert sky. Finally, the road narrows to a bumpy two-lane concrete path. It passes the invisible *línea de compactación* (line of compression), where irrigation ends and green fields converge with empty expanses of desert.

This is not the kind of desert that is decorated with saguaro cacti and splashes of blooming flowers. This is the most unvegetated zone of the Sonoran Desert. When traveling south through this desert, one sees on the left in the distance the black volcanic mountain named Cerro Prieto that juts conspicuously out of the flat desert, northwest of the Cerro Prieto Geothermal Field, the site of a large power plant complex. In the creation myths of the Cucapá people, the original inhabitants of the Colorado River delta, this mountain is the center of the earth and the source of the power of creation. The Cucapá chief, Don Madeleno, often recalled how the "white men" laughed at their myths, emphasizing that this mountain is now home to a multi-million-dollar electricity plant with four geothermal steam generators that light up the entire valley of Mexicali and parts of California. He pointed out that now no one denies the power that emanates from that place.

Finally, the road catches up with the cascading peaks of the Sierra Cucapá and winds around its rocky inclines. There, just beyond the shade of rocky peaks, sits the Cucapá village where I would spend a year living and carrying out the majority of my research. The village is flanked by the

Hardy River to the east and the Sierra Cucapá to the west. The Hardy River, a tributary of the Colorado and the only water from the river that still reaches the area, consists primarily of agricultural runoff from the Mexicali Valley. Local residents fish in the Hardy River, and in the summer children bathe and swim in its murky shallows. Past the village, the river moves on in a shallow rivulet, finally connecting with the mouth of the former Colorado River at the Gulf of California. Locals call that place, where the meager Hardy and gusts of groundwater meet the sea, *el zanjón*,[2] the fishing camp of the Cucapá people.

In this book, I examine how these people have experienced and responded to the disappearance of the river on the former delta and the attempts by the Mexican state to regulate the environmental crisis that followed. For generations local people relied on fishing as one of their primary means of subsistence, but in the last several decades this practice has been severely constrained by water scarcity and Mexican government restrictions. As a result of the 1944 water treaty between the United States and Mexico, 90 percent of the water in the Colorado is diverted before it reaches Mexico. The remaining 10 percent is increasingly being directed to the burgeoning manufacturing industry in Tijuana and Mexicali (Espeland 1998). Since 1993 the Cucapá people have been legally denied fishing rights in the delta under the Mexican Federal Environmental Protection Agency's fishing ban and the creation of a biosphere reserve.

While the Cucapá have continued to fish in the Gulf of California at the zanjón, they are facing increasing pressure to stop from federal inspectors and the Mexican military. As part of this conflict, the Cucapá's "authenticity" as an indigenous people has been repeatedly challenged by state officials. Like many indigenous groups in Mexico, the Cucapá people no longer speak their indigenous language (Cucapá) and are highly integrated into nonindigenous social networks. Despite pressure from the National Human Rights Commission, the government has maintained that the Cucapá's fishing practices, and their relationship to the territory in question, are not sufficiently "indigenous" to warrant preferred fishing rights. In the last several years, the situation has escalated in a series of intense negotiations among the Cucapá people, human rights lawyers, and federal and state environmental officials (Navarro Smith 2008; Navarro Smith, Tapia, and Garduño 2010).

In this book, I trace a path through a series of institutions and sites central to the water conflict at the end of the Colorado River: from the huge dams upstream in the United States to the dried-out riverbed of the Colorado delta, from the archives of the Bureau of Reclamation to the homes of Mexican and Cucapá fishermen in Baja California, from the president of the biosphere reserve's office in San Luis Río Colorado, to the disputed fishing grounds where Mexican marines and environmental officials often far outnumber illegal fishermen. In tracing this path I introduce a series of people and describe their everyday practices: environmental officials discussing multiculturalism, fishermen and fisherwomen strategizing the composition of their crews, NGO workers mapping traditional lands, neighbors gossiping about gender roles, indigenous fishermen forfeiting their nets in exchange for trafficking illegal drugs up the river, and scientists counting birds and fish. Combining analytic techniques from linguistic and political anthropology, I examine how local people use symbolic and material tools, including maps, indigenous swearwords, surveys, and traditional legends, as a means to negotiate dramatic environmental and structural change and to reflect on what this change means and who is responsible.

Research Trajectory

In the summer of 2005, I attended the Arizona Water Summit in Flagstaff, Arizona. It was an unusual event because it brought together scholars, water engineers, and members of Arizona's indigenous tribes.[3] It was striking to witness the diversity of approaches to water management and conservation that emerged from this motley combination of people. Panels ranged from topics such as irrigation techniques, traditional ecological knowledge, water management, and policy approaches. After one well-attended panel on water resource management that was particularly laden with technical terminology, Vernon Masayesva, a respected Hopi elder and leader, approached the podium during the question period. He delicately took the microphone, fumbling to adjust it to his shorter stature, and then said firmly, "The thing you people don't understand is that we don't manage water; water manages us."

I set out thinking that I would examine the dispute over the last stretches of the Colorado River by analyzing precisely the juxtaposition that Vernon Masaysva was pointing out in his comment. I intended to look at how people were talking about water, how water was being discursively constructed in different ways by different groups involved in the conflict. This was the relevant question upstream, where I did two months of research. The controversy in the southwestern United States polarizes around the way engineers and ranchers conceptualize and talk about water and how the Colorado River's indigenous groups, at least traditionally and often strategically, conceptualize it.[4] These debates were centered around whether water is sacred or a commodity, whether we "manage" water or water "manages" us, and who gets to decide these matters in the first place.

When I crossed the border and reached the Cucapá village where I would carry out my fieldwork, however, the debate shifted onto entirely different grounds. I found that people were hardly talking about water at all. Instead, the terms of crisis were centered around a lack of work. "There is no work here" was a common comment among residents. When I would ask why there was no work, people tied the issue directly to the fact that the Colorado River no longer reached them and further understood this by noting that the United States had "stolen" most of this water. But this was not the way the conflict was articulated when I was not leading the conversation. Instead, the majority of people narrated the injustices carried out by the Mexican government by placing restrictions on their fishing. Perhaps it did not seem surprising to them that the United States would "steal" so much water. Instead, the outrage was felt around the fact that the Mexican government would not let its own people work. Therefore, local people pointed to another level on which the fishing conflict was playing out. Instead of situating the fishing conflict in a discourse of environmental crisis, they shifted the terms of the debate onto the conditions of poverty that made feeding their families the ultimate priority.

This analytic move, refocusing attention from the environment to the social conditions of poverty, led me to my current research focus. Environmental conflicts are not just struggles over natural resources. They often become a terrain on which other ideological conflicts play out. The water conflict at the end of the Colorado River has been as much about struggles over class hierarchy, language politics, and what constitutes indigenous identity as it has been about who gets access to water and fishing rights. Debates about the conservation of the river have become a battleground for conflicts over how cultural difference should be recognized and what constitutes that difference in the first place.

This conflict at the end of the Colorado River is certainly not an isolated environmental phenomenon; it is indicative of a worldwide crisis of water scarcity. A recent United Nations report stated that water quality and management is the overriding problem of the twenty-first century (UNDP 2003). Indeed, stories of water shortages and conflicts in Israel, India, China, Bolivia, Canada, Mexico, and the United States have recently appeared in major newspapers, magazines, and academic journals across the globe. Conflicts have erupted over the building of dams, the privatization of public sector utilities, and binational water agreements (DuMars et al. 1984; Shiva 2002; de Villiers 1999; Ward 2001).

While water scarcity is increasingly a problem that is being felt across the world, it manifests itself in particular local meanings and struggles. In this book, I analyze the measures taken by a group of Cucapá people to maneuver through the complex structural and political changes they have experienced over the last several decades as fishing, their main form of subsistence, has become both environmentally untenable and criminalized by the state as a measure of environmental management. I examine the strategies that many local people employ to subsist and transform their lives under conditions of profound environmental and economic change as well as extreme power asymmetries. Therefore, this book explores the intersections between environmental conflict and the production of collective identities. I show how in the context of the water crisis in the Colorado delta, identity is articulated and contested through various forms of struggle, while at the same time social systems of difference are reproduced through contestations over natural resources.

A number of authors have come to explain how local processes of identity formation have been connected to broader systems of signification through the concept of "articulation" (Clifford 2001; García 2005; Li 2000; Nelson 1999; Yeh 2007). Drawn from Stuart Hall, this concept is used to denote a double meaning: the way that groups come to express and enunciate particular collective political identities and also how they manage to connect these expressions of identity to wider discourses and social forces.

My work is guided by this theoretical framework, but departs from it by attending specifically to situations in which articulations fail. That is, rather than focusing on when and where articulations do or do not happen, the ethnographic case I analyze here explores an instance where articulations are specifically unhinged from the historical conjunctions that might otherwise make them possible. Cucapá activists have so far been unable to connect their discourses to the wider discourses of the state involving environmental sustainability and indigenous connection to the land. In other words, they have failed to successfully articulate their claims for traditional fishing rights with the state because, despite their efforts, they are not seen as indigenous enough.

My analysis also differs from recent ethnographic interest in articulation in relation to the double meaning that Hall emphasizes. "To articulate" means "to utter, to speak forth, to be articulate" as well as to connect (Hall's example is the way a trailer connects to a truck [1996: 53]). In this book I focus as much on the first sense of the term (as enunciation and expression) as I do on the arguably more political moment in which a connection to a wider context can take place. I am equally interested in exploring the processes by which certain discourses and expressions are rendered inarticulate—the process that often makes the unhingings possible in the first place. For example, I examine contradictions that emerge around gender ideologies as they are expressed in a local context, and I analyze the tensions in expressions of gendered indigenous identities. Additionally, in examining how the Cucapá's authenticity is often judged based on fluency in an indigenous language most people no longer speak, I analyze the way they are constructed as culturally inarticulate by outsiders. That is, I focus precisely on an instance where *not* being understood, as a result of speaking an exotic and inscrutable indigenous language, would be the expression of identity ironically capable of articulating with wider contexts of language politics. Thus in this book I am interested in the failure of articulation in both senses of the term.

The Fieldsite

The village where I lived in 2005–2006 is the home of the largest population of Cucapá people in Mexico with approximately two hundred residents. Approximately one thousand Cucapá (Cocopah) tribal members live in Somerton, Arizona, and several hundred more live in the Mexicali Valley in the Mexican states of Sonora and Baja California. There are, of course, conceptual difficulties with identifying a group under such an ethnic label (the difficulties of which are a central topic of this book). I use the term "Cucapá" because it is the way that people routinely self-identify. Cucapá people are Mexican citizens as well and often identify as such. However, in contexts where people would make a distinction between indigenous and nonindigenous residents of the area they use the word "Mexican" to refer to individuals of nonindigenous descent.[5]

Before the 1980s, many of the Cucapá families that are currently located in Baja California lived in scattered, semi-permanent homes along the banks of the Hardy River. After major floods in the late 1970s and early 1980s destroyed most of these homes, the government donated materials to rebuild the houses that were damaged and designated the current village as the site, largely because it is at a slightly higher elevation than other points along the river. The settlement comprises approximately forty houses,[6] a small medical clinic, a primary and secondary school, a dilapidated building bearing the sign "Cucapá museum" (which contains a display case full of beadwork), and a small and long-abandoned *caseta de policía* (police booth), which now serves as junk storage.

The roads in the village are made of loose, sandy gravel. Barbed-wire fences roughly cordon off areas around people's homes, but they are generally twisted down so that they can be stepped over or spread apart to be squeezed through. Scattered throughout the backyards one can see stripped bed frames, used as chairs or piled with blankets, holes dug out with garbage loosely piled within them, or metal barrels where the garbage is burned. Most homes have outhouses that are made out of thin metal or plywood. Potable water is held in storage tanks outside the houses. Approximately every fifteen days, a truck comes from Mexicali to sell potable water and refill these tanks.

The climate of the Colorado River delta is characterized by extremes. In my first twelve months there, there were more than twice as many earthquakes as there were rainfalls. Temperatures between May and October are extremely high, often over 110 degrees Fahrenheit, and winter nights are often very cold, reaching the low 30s. In the broad delta basin, invisibly split by the San Andrés Fault and ravaged by saline waters, there is very little evidence of the river that once fanned its delta across this land.

During my ethnographic research I stayed with the Martínez family. The mother, Ana María Martínez, invited me to stay with them not long after we met. Ana is the daughter of the chief, Don Madeleno, and was married to Cruz Antonio Martínez, with whom she had three children in their late teens: twin eighteen-year-old daughters (one of whom was several months pregnant) and a nineteen-year-old son.

During my fieldwork, several dynamics in this family and in the village profoundly shaped the experience of living there and doing research. One was the effect of drug addiction on the household where I was staying, and the other was a rivalry between two of the prominent families in the village. Ana's husband, who had a strong presence in the home (as he does in the pages that follow), was addicted to crystal methamphetamine (*cristal* in Spanish) the first four months I was living with them. This was something that I came to realize somewhat belatedly. Ana's impatience with him was my first indication of what was going on. When he came in the house acting noticeably different, she would offer him food. He would refuse and she would keep offering. I later learned that he always denied his use to her and, indignant at his dishonesty, she would punish him by drawing inordinate attention to the drugs' effects, for lack of appetite is a sure sign of use. During these times, she would cast knowing glances across the table in my direction. She did not want me to think she was fooled. But of course, it was I who had been unaware, and thus I came to understand the cause of his erratic behavior.

I was completely unfamiliar with the nature or effects of cristal and was initially quite agitated by this aspect of my living situation. My first few weeks in Ana's house were incredibly stressful because of the presence of Cruz, whose manner I found very disconcerting. As a result of a case of strabismus (a condition that results in crossed eyes), it was difficult to know when he was speaking to me, which was compounded by the fact that he often spoke at a remarkable, drug-induced speed. I was originally concerned about how erratic or dangerous his behavior might be. My worries about Cruz subsided not long after getting to know him better. He was embarrassed by his addiction and tried to hide it as much as possible, and despite his sometimes unpredictable behavior, his remarkable qualities as a person quickly became evident.

While Cruz's addiction slowly splintered the ties among Ana and their family, another division had an equally unsettling effect on research conditions in the village more generally. During my fieldwork a rivalry between two of the most prominent Cucapá elders was a constant source of tension. Don Madeleno, the Cucapá chief, and his sister Doña Esperanza were distinctly alienated from each other during this time. In addition to long-standing personal conflicts, a central tension between Doña Esperanza's and Don Madeleno's families was a land conflict over Cucapá territory.

The Cucapá's struggle for water follows decades of struggle for the legal title to their lands. After the formation of the international border in 1853, the Cucapá who found themselves in the United States retained their lands. But on the Mexican side people were incorporated into the hacienda system, whereby large tracts of land were titled to landowners who were given rights to the labor of its inhabitants. At the beginning of the twentieth century, the Colorado River Land Company, a US land syndicate operated out of Los Angeles, acquired most of the land in the Colorado delta (also known as the Mexicali Valley). The land was worked by tenant farmers, most of whom were Chinese immigrants, as well as local Mexicans and some Cucapá families. This land was then appropriated by the Mexican state during the agrarian reform that followed the 1910–1920 Mexican Revolution (Dwyer 2008; Gómez Estrada 1994).

In 1936, under the Mexican president Lázaro Cárdenas (ruled 1934–1940), the Cucapá people were granted an ejido, land communally run by local people but owned by the state (Krauze 1997: 352).[7] Kelly (1977) documents how the ejido system failed for the Cucapá people, citing poor direction on the part of Mexican officials and growing distrust and lack of interest among many Cucapá. In the 1940s, those Cucapá people living on the ejido gradually left work as laborers and fisherman (Gómez Estrada 1994; Kelly 1977: 13). Several Cucapá people also suggested that many of the residents were bribed off their ejido lands by nonindigenous local people. Currently, only a few Cucapá families live on the ejido, which is about twenty miles north of the village to which most families have moved.

After years of demanding land from the Mexican federal government, a fight led by Don Madeleno, in 1976 the Cucapá were finally given the rights to communal ownership of 143,000 hectares (375,500 acres) of their traditional land (Gómez Estrada 2000; Sánchez 2000). But due to the environmental degradation the region has been through, this land is not irrigable or farmable. Furthermore, ultimately some people, such as Don Madeleno's family, were excluded from the lands granted in legal title. One reason for this exclusion was a fissure between different levels of government that was created when traditional chiefs were recognized by the Mexican government after reforms in the 1970s. This created two official leadership positions with overlapping powers: the *comisariado ejidal* (or *comisario*), the existing authority on agrarian issues, and the traditional chief, representing the indigenous group more generally.[8]

Doña Esperanza, Don Madeleno's rival, is closely associated with the comisario, and she and her family have legal land rights to traditional territory. Meanwhile, Don Madeleno and his supporters have been fighting to reallot land rights for years, but the negotiations are progressing slowly. A representative of the Comisión Nacional para el Desarrollo de los Pueblos Indígenas (CDI)[9] whom I interviewed suggested that despite the conflict the issue of land rights has created, the legal value of this title is questionable, since the land is communal and thus cannot be sold or even divided among individuals. Therefore, he thought that title to land involving those 143,000 hectares was more "symbolic" than anything else.

The attitude of Esperanza's daughter, Manuela, toward her own land rights exemplified the "symbolic" value that the representative from CDI referred to. She occasionally brought up her land rights as if they were evidence of her superiority to the other rival group. For example, one day she commented, "Madeleno's family doesn't even have land rights!" I asked if Thalia, Manuela's sixteen-year-old daughter, had legal land rights, and Thalia promptly responded that she did not because she was underage but also that she did not want them. When I asked her why, she said, "Because they're good for nothing but fighting over!" Since her mother protested Thalia's answer, I pressed Manuela on what they were good for in her opinion. After hesitating, she finally repeated, laughing, "Well, they're good for fighting over!"

However, Don Madeleno explained that the fight over land title between these two factions is not just "symbolic" but has exacerbated economic inequalities between members of the group. The legal land title has allowed the titled members to rent out sections of land for gravel extraction, an activity that has become a lucrative business in the border region, where it is used for building roads. Proceeds are shared among those with title but not among the rest of the people recognized as Cucapá in the region. Don Madeleno also explained that if laws change such that communal land could be sold, following the privatization trends that have sped up in the last decades in Mexico, this could be catastrophic for those without title.

For the most part, younger people did not directly involve themselves in the conflict between the two families. Although the divides were clearly visible on a social level, they did not affect what kinds of projects younger people worked on, or the composition of their fishing crews. In fact, the youth there felt a general sense of exasperation about the conflict and many expressed the opinion that the tension between the families was a result of jealousy about who was involved in what project and who was benefiting from the social support extended to the Cucapá people.

While issues over land title pitted families against each other, conflicts over the river and fishing rights pit local people against the state. Particularly for younger generations, the fishing conflict seemed to unite them more easily across internal divides, creating a sense of shared, collective opposition against the federal imposition of fishing restrictions (see Navarro Smith 2008). For this reason the fishing conflict, as we shall see, has also become an important context in which local people have contested state ideologies of what constitutes indigenous identity.

Multiculturalism and the Political Terrain of Indigeneity

I completed this research during a unique political and historical moment for indigenous people in Mexico. After centuries of discrimination on the grounds of ethnic difference that resulted in high levels of cultural assimilation, government policies have in the last decades shifted to encourage multiculturalism. While previous state programs, implemented since the revolution, had identified indigenous groups in order to receive certain forms of support, the goal of these programs had always been eventual assimilation (Dawson 2004; de la Peña 2006). Therefore, the Cucapá people now share a political circumstance with many contemporary indigenous people around the world, who increasingly face both the older pressures to assimilate and, simultaneously, more recent pressures to perform otherness. These contradictory demands create paradoxes of recognition (Povinelli 2002) that have been documented elsewhere and yet manifest themselves differently among groups in distinct historical contexts (Cattelino 2008; Clifford 1988; Field 1999; Gordillo 2011; Gustafson 2009).

In Mexico during the first half of the twentieth century, and largely due to the political impact of the revolution, national policies and class-based organizing encouraged indigenous people to self-identify as *campesinos* or peasants (Jackson and Warren 2005). Campesinos constituted a political category meant to represent a distinct social class with common interests and grievances, related primarily to issues of land. They were seen as a key element in the struggle for land reform that would be the cornerstone of Mexico's social revolution (Boyer 2003). Nationalist ideologies of mestizaje that were popular during and after the revolution emphasized cultural and biological mixing as opposed to ethnic difference and further discouraged politicized indigenous identification (Alonso 2004; Jackson and Warren 2005; Knight 1990). Even the ideological movement of *indi-*

genismo within the Mexican state, which ostensibly celebrated multiculturalism as a government policy, maintained that the full extension of citizenship to indigenous peoples would ultimately come through assimilation (de la Peña 2005).

A crucial component of state formation in postindependence Latin America has been the capacity of governments to define what it means to be indigenous and to create the conditions for this specific political identity to emerge within the nation (de la Peña 2005: 718). As I discuss in detail in chapter 2, the shift from policies of indigenous assimilation to a program of multiculturalism in public discourses during the 1980s and 1990s represented a significant change in the conditions under which indigenous groups interact with the state.

This shift can be understood as the result of political and ideological changes. Beginning in the 1980s, strong international pressure came to bear as environmentalism and human rights advocacy gained momentum. The concept of "indigenous people" gained legitimacy in international law with the creation of the United Nations (UN) Working Group on Indigenous Populations (WGIP) in 1982, which created a space for grassroots movements to gain more direct access to the UN (de la Peña 2005; Gray 1996). In addition, under pressure from the International Monetary Fund (IMF) and the World Bank, many Latin American states agreed to adopt neoliberal reforms, which resonated with discourses on diversity, community solidarity, and social capital (Sieder 2002).

It has generally been assumed by scholars and activists that neoliberalism and multiculturalism are divergent projects. This is partially due to neoliberalism's notorious celebration of the economic individual as the quintessential autonomous subject (Kingfisher 2002; Peters 2001) and the related idea that the neoliberal program calls into question collective structures that might be obstacles to the logic of the pure market (Bourdieu 1998; D. Harvey 2005). Recently, however, a growing number of authors have drawn attention to how discourses and policies of multiculturalism in fact form part of the larger neoliberal project in Latin America and beyond (Comaroff and Comaroff 2009; Hale 2005; Martinez Novo 2006; Sieder 2002; Speed 2005). In this book, and especially in chapters 2 and 5, I draw on this body of work to analyze how the seemingly counterintuitive pairing of neoliberalism and multiculturalism in Mexico has created political conditions in which ethnic difference is foregrounded as a way of denying certain rights to marginalized groups who do not look or act "indigenous enough."

The shift to policies encouraging ethnic self-identification has also benefited many indigenous communities in Latin America because it has created a political climate and the legal grounds to argue for territory and rights to natural resources. The indigenous movement has succeeded in forming political parties in Bolivia and Ecuador. Successful indigenous and popular mobilizations in Cochabamba, Bolivia, in 2000 forced the government to cancel plans to allow the Bechtel Corporation to sell water to local people (Laurie, Andolina, and Radcliffe 2002). The Zapatista uprising in Chiapas in 1994, protesting the oppression of indigenous peoples in Chiapas and the signing of the North American Free Trade Agreement, was able to force the government and Mexican public opinion to recognize the marginalization of indigenous communities in the country (N. Harvey 1998; Ramírez Paredes 2002). Furthermore, constitutional reforms have occurred across Latin America recognizing the multicultural character of these nations.

These successes, however, depend on performing indigenous identity according to a definition imposed on indigenous communities by nonindigenous actors. Article 2 of the Mexican constitution uses the following criteria to define indigenous people: they must be descendants of the people who lived in the same territory at the beginning of colonization, and they must preserve their own social, economic, and cultural institutions. The criteria also specify that indigenous people's awareness of their indigenous identity should also be considered (although, in practice, this last criterion is rarely emphasized).

Many Cucapá people I spoke with experience this shift in policy emphasis to preserving indigenous identities as a profound contradiction. After centuries of discrimination on the grounds of ethnic difference, government policies now encourage indigenous self-identification and, indeed, require the Cucapá to identify as "indigenous" in order for their claims for certain rights and resources to be seriously considered. People negotiate this contradiction by identifying with categories of indigeneity unevenly and ambiguously. Indigeneity and identity, more broadly, are also authenticated and contested at the community level in complex ways that may not align with national criteria. What constitutes "Cucapá identity" is also highly contested. Local articulations of identity develop a particular gender ideology in opposition to "Mexican machismo" and trace an ancestral inhabitance, and a history of fishing, on the river from before colonization.

Throughout this book, I examine how many Cucapá people, by realigning the ways they connect to the nation and their own unique historical and political circumstances, have come to identify themselves in a particular way that both engages and critiques national and international discourses on indigeneity. In other words, this book explores indigenous identity not as a preexisting entity but as a set of historically and politically constituted practices and idioms that emerge through processes of engagement and struggle (Baviskar 2005; de la Cadena and Starn 2007; Field 2008; Li 2000; Miller 2003; Niezen 2003).

Research Setting and Methodology

In your interviews you should ask the older people if the US ever asked if it was okay with us that they took all the water from the river up there. I bet they never asked.
—PABLO

The fieldwork on which this book is based primarily took place over twelve months in 2005 and 2006. While I focus on the events that transpired during this period, my narrative is also informed by subsequent and shorter fieldwork periods in the village as well as surrounding communities where I did research in northwestern Mexico in 2007, 2010, and 2011. In the first phase of my fieldwork in the United States, I interviewed ranchers, water engineers, and government officials. I stayed at a ranch in Colorado, toured the major dams and reservoirs, and interviewed guards and tour guides. As noted above, I also attended the Arizona Water Summit in Flagstaff, as well as a tribal water summit and interviewed tribal members and leaders from the Navajo, Cocopah, and Hopi nations. In the United States I also completed the bulk of my archival research. I visited the offices of the Bureau of Reclamation and the Colorado Plateau special archival collections at the University of Arizona, Flagstaff, and San Diego.

In the Colorado delta in Mexico, I participated on fishing trips, government make-work programs, fishing meetings, meetings with the fishing cooperatives, and meetings with their lawyer and conservation organizations. I attended scores of social gatherings, including birthday parties, funerals, and baptisms. I also volunteered for some of the local river association's projects—planting trees, testing water quality, and counting birds and fish—and with a mapmaking project carried out by a binational NGO based in Tucson, Arizona. Finally, I also visited the archives at the Universidad Autónoma de Baja California and the National Archives in Mexico City and attended the World Water Forum in Mexico City in March 2006.

After some initial and awkward attempts at conducting formal interviews in the village, I gave up on this method for the first few months of fieldwork. I found that people would give nervous and confused answers to basic questions. The technique of waiting for topics to come up naturally in conversation and expressing my curiosity in these contexts was more effective. I learned later that structured interviews were closely associated with interactions with government officials in relation to the registration and confiscation of fishing licenses as well as the monitoring of fishing more generally. This was perceived as a distinctly hostile genre of communication (see also Briggs 1986).

Five or six months into my stay, however, friends and neighbors started asking why I had not interviewed them yet. They knew I was interviewing officials and NGO workers, and it had come to signify the research I was "doing" in ways that my informal participation and presence in their daily lives did not. One day a man I did not know very well came to our house very early in the morning and yelled for me to come out, announcing, "I've come for my interview!" I took this incident as my cue to attempt interviews once again and began actively interviewing people. As I was much more familiar to local residents by then, the interactions were much easier.

Although I never found that interviews were particularly useful as a method of gathering information, they functioned as a way to remind people that I was doing research and as a way of engaging people with whom I would not otherwise have easy contact.[10] My interviews also took on an unexpected role as a conduit for social information to move more generally. People were extremely interested in whether their answers were similar to others' and would often suggest that so-and-so might disagree on a given point. As Pablo's comments in the epigraph of this section indicates, the interviews also became proposed pathways through which interviewees asked questions of their own.

Because drug abuse and illegal activities are a feature of everyday life among many of the people I describe, I have taken care to obscure identities, both renaming the individuals and at points merging or separating identities to further complicate possible attempts to identify them (particularly in chapter 3). The disadvantage of this method is that it also obscures the trajectory of life histories and undermines the complexity of the individual characters who shared parts of their lives with me. The majority of people I talked to or interviewed explicitly on this subject felt that my concerns were highly exaggerated and volunteered to share their identities. "Come on, Shaylih, how many people do you seriously think are going to read this thing?" was a common response to my worries about anonymity. In other cases, people felt my anxieties were unfounded because they had already spent time in jail for the experiences they described.

Nonetheless, the pervasive nature of racist stereotypes that amplify the participation of poorer populations in illegal activities has led some authors to avoid writing about these experiences of vulnerable groups altogether (see Nader 1972). While this has been a common academic response to the frustration of writing about the deprivation of the poor, more recent work on poverty and violence has convincingly argued that to avoid writing about suffering denies its very existence. I therefore agree with Bourgois when he writes that "sanitizing suffering and destruction" makes one complicit with oppression (2002:12; see also Goldstein 2003). Scheper-Hughes (1992: 27–28) made this point eloquently when she wrote that "not to look, not to touch, not to record, can be the hostile act, the act of indifference and of turning away."

Layout of the Book

In the chapters that follow, I analyze the ways contemporary invocations of identity, particularly in relation to the fishing conflict, shape the formation of political subjectivities as well as modes of livelihood. Starting from a focus on the particular confrontations and encounters engendered by the fishing conflict over the Colorado River, the chapters are loosely thematized around how the idioms of ethnicity, nationalism, class, gender, and language have shaped the way that locals have negotiated the dramatic structural, ecological, and discursive transformations that have characterized life there over the last few decades.

In chapter 1, I analyze how maps, literature, and media coverage collude in a representation of the Colorado River that erases the delta and its inhabitants in northern Mexico and how people experience the material effects of these discursive occlusions. I also examine how the discursive constructions of the river legitimated radically unequal distribution of water rights. I continue by analyzing a controversial mapmaking project that attempts to redraw the map of the Colorado delta and the Cucapá territory. In particular, I focus on the politics of this project, exploring the tension between the way in which places are represented on maps and in oral histories.

In chapter 2, I analyze how the Cucapá fishing cooperatives' arguments for fishing rights in the delta have been facilitated and constrained within the terms of current environmental discourses. I examine how local environmental NGOs and government bodies have both aligned themselves with the Cucapá people through various projects and refused to support their environmental claims by imposing measures of authenticity to which the Cucapá do not fully conform.

Chapter 3 explores how people maintain a minimum standard of living under the pressures of structural and environmental changes and in a context in which their primary subsistence activity, fishing, has been criminalized. I examine the rise of narco-trafficking as one economic alternative produced by these constraints and argue, furthermore, that some people see narco-trafficking as a form of resistance to US and Mexican domination, albeit a multidimensional resistance shaped by internal politics.

In addition to negotiating the terms of authenticity imposed on them, local people also engage in contentious debate over what constitutes Cucapá identity. In chapter 4, I explore how local struggles over this identity are established and contested, especially in connection to gender relations. I focus on a particular view of gender that emphasizes women's power and is often articulated in opposition to Mexican machismo. I follow the conflicting historical narratives on the establishment of women's primacy in the social and political sphere and consider how the ideology of gender that emerges from these narratives forms the basis for a wider cultural identification and symbolic resource.

In chapter 5, I analyze the use of swearwords by the younger generations of Cucapá speakers. I argue that this vocabulary functions as a critique of, and a challenge to, the increasingly formalized imposition of indigenous language capacity as a measure of authenticity and as a formal and informal criterion for the recognition of indigenous rights. I examine how, for the youth, indigenous identity is located not in their indigenous language but in an awareness of a shared history of the injustices of colonization and a continuing legacy of state indifference.

These chapters are also structured to reflect on certain methodological concerns that emerged during my research. Throughout my fieldwork, I paid attention to the moments when people identified a discourse as ideological or a political structure as oppressive, and the questions that guide each chapter attend to these identifications. For example, why would elders push paper maps away when asked to identify places and instead locate places in historical legends? What does it mean when an environmental official states that the fishing conflict is not about the environment but, rather, about social difference and authenticity? Why would a local drug smuggler argue that fishing regulations are not about fishing but, rather, about "the war on drugs"? And what can we learn from an instance when a man forgets everything about his personal history and the entire village claims that this is not the result of amnesia but a symptom of changing gender relations?

These sorts of gestures and attitudes form an implicit guide to my analysis. Of course, in the process of identifying what a process or event is "about," social actors, in multiple levels of interpretation, privilege their own terms of debate and subjugate other voices. I am not arguing that those we study have a more privileged position from which to identify the "real" or that by paying attention to the kinds of gestures we will be pointed to "the truth." Instead, I bring the analytic move itself into focus. This shifts attention to how certain interpretations become dominant, and what these interpretations highlight and erase. By observing how debates are moved onto another "terrain" (Mani 1998; McElhinny 2007), one achieves a vantage point from which to understand how people are experiencing their own lives and the structures through which they navigate their worlds.

The Lines That Follow

During the first months of my fieldwork, there were no white lines to mark the edges of the sides of Route 5, which led to and from the village. This made driving through the desert at night extremely treacherous. Finally, in November 2005 the municipality of Mexicali painted white lines on the side of the road. From the village, we watched the trucks and

20   Introduction

FIGURE I.1 Bisected dog. Photo by author.

workmen move down past us, tracing the edges of the road with their paint machines. Later that day, a rumor circulated that there was a disturbing sight to be seen a few miles north. I drove there with my camera and took this picture: a dead dog at the side of the road and a fresh white line of paint bisecting its still-warm carcass (see figure I.1).

The scene evoked outrage and a lot of talk from residents in the area. When the dog was finally pushed aside, the photograph that I had taken and subsequently printed out replaced the scene on the side of the road as a focus of indignation. The owner of a nearby construction company, who had heard about the photograph, wanted copies to give his political connections in the municipality so that the negligent workers might be rooted out and punished. The photograph circulated in the village as well, passed around by friends and family. Don Madeleno, the Cucapá chief, heard about the photo and asked for a copy. When I brought him the five-by-six-inch print, he held it up and said, "You see? This is what our government is like." In a place where dogs are not particularly respected animals, it was notable to see how this image nonetheless came to symbolize for local people the negligence of the Mexican government in its disregard for life and flagrant disrespect toward them.

In the months that followed, I often found myself reminded of that line over the dead dog on the road. I thought back to it in reference to other lines that bisected the delta of the Colorado River in similar strokes of reckless inattention. One of the lines that inscribes the delta's landscape is about fifteen miles north of the village; it is the line that marks the end of legally irrigable land and separates those with the means to pursue agriculture, those north of that line, from those without the means, to the south. It is called the *línea de compactación*. South of this line, all water rights were suspended in 1970 in response to the increasing pressure that water scarcity was having on agriculture in the region. This marks the end of viable agricultural lands in the Mexicali Valley and the beginning of non-irrigable desert.

The most significant line slashing through the Colorado delta, however, is the international border between the United States and Mexico. Prior to the setting of the border, indigenous peoples in this region had territories (with relatively flexible boundaries between neighboring groups) that stretched into what today are two different national geographies. In those days, Cucapá villages extended into what are now California and Arizona in the United States and Sonora and Baja California in Mexico. These territories and the previous patterns of separations between settlements were certainly not taken into account when the border was drawn up. The treaties and agreements that set the international boundaries between the nation-states of North America were negotiated and signed by the colonizers alone (Firebaugh 2002: 160).

These Cucapá villages were first split by the border delineated in the 1853 Gadsden Purchase following the US-Mexican war (1846–1848), which resulted in Mexico losing control of much of what is today the southwestern United States.[11] At this time, however, the border did little to physically separate these groups or impede movement across the line. It was only in the late 1930s that the Immigration and Naturalization Service (INS) began reinforcing border controls on the American side of the border. Luna Firebaugh (2002) argues that heightened border controls affected the Cucapá people earlier than other transborder groups because they were located adjacent to a primary river crossing and because control of the Colorado River was crucial to the US government (Firebaugh 2002: 167; see also Tisdale 1997).

Currently, most Cucapá people living on the Mexican side are not permitted to cross over into the United States at all. It is almost impossible for them to get visas, especially given that most people do not have other forms of documentation, such as birth certificates. Many families that were separated by the border have very little contact with each other. As a result of the different experiences and sociopolitical relations created by the border, the disparity in the quality of life between the Cocopah people in Arizona and the Cucapá living in Mexico is extreme. The Cocopah in the United States were granted water rights to the Colorado River, have large agriculture tracts, and also run a successful museum and casino (Tisdale 1997).[12]

Therefore, the border replaced local territorial divisions and movements with a dividing line derived from state bureaucratic structures that had few practical ties to the original inhabitants of the region and that was opposed to the patterns of kinship and birthplace on which prior local boundaries were based. Foucault (1995) writes of such lines when he describes the type of rationality behind the bureaucratization of rule. He posits that these forms of markings and divisions are the modern form of disciplinary rationality. Discipline is a technology of traces—visible marks, inscriptions, and imprints. For Foucault, discipline works by division. By dividing wholes, it divides up space and movement into smaller and smaller fragments, subjecting each fragment to intense and extensive scrutiny. Disciplinary rationality takes things that are not visible and makes them observable and measurable by dividing constellations into innumerable points of illumination. These actions specify surveillance and make it functional (Foucault 1995: 174).

Whereas Foucault's lines regulate, control, and survey, however, the lines I have described in northwestern Mexico appear far more reckless. Instead of simply dividing and subjecting an object to scrutiny, they inscribe over and erase, ignoring previous spatial sensibilities and divisions. It is not so much that these lines break up wholes but that they vandalize them. From the ground, these lines appear to slash the landscape in gestures of disregard. The lines derived from state administrative structures and mechanisms such as irrigation laws, municipal paint crews, and federal international treaties, trod heavily over the daily practices of people who trace different routes and boundaries on this landscape.

In this book, one of my objectives is to examine ethnographically these locally constituted routes and boundaries as well as the conflicts and tensions they create with the state-sponsored routes outlined above. This will lead me to other, less publicly visible kinds of places and traces: the traces of drug trafficking through the desert, the notches on the roads to prevent the landing of cargo planes, the tracks of soldiers trying to rout them out. I will also trace lines on maps and the routes crisscrossing the landscape in the historical legends told by elders. In the next chapter, I trace a line that bisects scores of maps of the region yet no longer reaches the delta or the Cucapá people: the Colorado River.

CHAPTER 1

"LISTEN FOR WHEN YOU GET THERE"
Topologies of Invisibility on the Colorado River

We are here. We eat, we dance, we fish.
Here we are and we still live.
No éramos, somos. (It's not that we were, we are.)
—DON MADELENO

DON MADELENO OFTEN REPEATED the refrain "We're still here." The first time I heard him say this, I interpreted it as a triumphant declaration of survival. In this instance, Don Madeleno was narrating the history of the Cucapá people in the delta: a history of war, conquest, disease, water scarcity, the criminalization of fishing, and the rise of the narco-economy. After everything his people had experienced, they were still there carrying on with their lives.

I heard Don Madeleno use the phrase in this sense on many other occasions: in interviews, at festivals, and in informal conversations. Because it was part of his personal narration I was struck when I first heard him use the phrase in a much more literal sense in the context of maps. Every so often I would bring Don Madeleno a map of the delta from books or archives to elicit his reactions to these representations of the land he knew so well. Every time I brought him a map we went through the same routine: he would look over the page slowly and meticulously and start pointing to all of the places it was missing. He would comment on whether or not the map showed the Cucapá village, the fishing grounds, and the Sierra Cucapá. He would also bring up the places that were almost always missing—Las Pintas, Pozo de Coyote, and a dozen other sites important to Cucapá history. Then Don Madeleno would irritatedly declare, while pointing at the absent places, "Estamos aquí" (We are here). Once or twice he went on to emphasize his point by saying, "Somos aquí" (We *are* this place).

In this context, "We are here" took on a meaning that is central to the issues I explore in this chapter. What Don Madeleno meant was that while you would not know it from looking at any official map of the area, the Colorado delta is a terrain rich with the traces of his people's presence: their places, stories, and history. And by saying "Nosotros somos aquí" he invoked an even stronger connection to place, drawing on the distinction in Spanish between the two verbs for "to be": *ser* and *estar*. Whereas *estar* is used to describe the current state of something and is almost always used to describe a location in space, *ser* is used to describe the unchangeable nature of something. By emphasizing "*somos* aquí," Don Madeleno was arguing that his people were not just occupying the delta but that they *were* the delta and that their very being was inseparable from that space.

This statement is not just a strategic invocation; it is also indicative of Don Madeleno's personal experience of the changing landscape. He was born on February 16, 1934, one year before the construction of the Boulder Dam (later renamed the "Hoover"), the first of the large dams on the river. His life has spanned exactly the time frame in which the Colorado River has been siphoned off from the lower part of the delta where his village is located. Since the first dam went in, about eighty dams and diversions have been built on the rivers of the Colorado watershed (Reisner 1993: 40). In the process, the flow of the Colorado to the delta and the Gulf was completely cut off.

In this chapter I analyze how maps, literature, and media coverage collude in a representation of the Colorado River that erases the Colorado delta and its inhabitants in northern Mexico. Therefore, this chapter provides the historical background and upstream context for why the river no longer reaches the sea. I argue that the rhetoric around the construction of these dams, and in particular the central concept of "beneficial use," promoted a particular water logic that carries through to present-day politics. Whereas in later chapters I examine how people experience the material effects of this water logic, in this chapter I examine how they experience the political and ideological erasure that results from it. In doing so, I trace a landscape that has been made invisible in representations of the river. This is a landscape filled with the places people navigate on a daily basis—their homes, the river, *el monte* (the bush), el zanjón (the fishing grounds)—as well as the places at a greater distance but still intimately connected to everyday routes in and out of the village: Cerro Prieto, nearby colonias, and el Valle de Guadalupe.

The narrative will also visit, if only in stories, places that no longer exist: colonias wiped out by floods; fishing grounds long evaporated as a result of the dams upstream; the Colorado River itself, now whisked off in canals along the border. And we visit the places that feature in legends and creation myths: where Coyote first shared water with the people, the mountain of the eagle where the spirits go after death, the mountain range that a giant carved into the shape of houses and windows. I conclude by analyzing a mapmaking project that attempts to redraw the map of the Colorado delta and the Cucapá territory.

The Mirage on the Map: The Makings of a River without a Delta

The idea that space is *made* meaningful is familiar to anthropology, which has long recognized that the experience of space is socially constructed. Several authors have pointed out that a key concern in the politics of place making is the question of who has the power to make spaces and what is at stake in the process (Braun 2002; Gordillo 2004; Gupta and Ferguson 1992). This is a particularly important consideration in the context of environmental disputes, which construct places in specific ways. Constructions of place that focus on nature, regardless of whether this focus is in nature's "defense," can participate in colonialist erasures of native people from political geographies (Braun 2002). These erasures are often accomplished through powerful representations of place, which are used to legitimate specific institutional policies and practices (Carbaugh 2001; McElhinny 2006; Mühlhäusler and Peace 2006; Myerson and Ryden 1996). Maps, media coverage, and educational materials on the Colorado River are a vivid example of exactly such strategic representations.

Gupta and Ferguson (1992) have emphasized that "the presumption that spaces are autonomous has enabled the power of topography to conceal successfully the topography of power" (8). Tsing (2000: 330) has voiced a complementary concern by pointing out that the recent fascination with global flows obscures the material and institutional components through which powerful and central sites are constructed. The dangers of both an assumption of autonomy and fluidity in spatial imaginaries is apparent in the case of the Colorado delta. Here a discourse of free trade, migration, and movement has obscured the very real friction that the border creates: the river barely makes it down across the border to Mexico, and migrants are increasingly prevented from making it up across the border to the

United States. Ironically, this very friction is facilitated by a parallel assumption of autonomy. The lands and people across the border in Mexico are over and over again represented as a blankness on maps from agencies in the United States and are rarely mentioned in many of the major literary and historical works on the Colorado River.

Before exploring the geographies made invisible by the representations of global flows, it's helpful to look at how those powerful sites and flows became constituted in the first place. This is the central question that guided my archival research upstream in the Bureau of Reclamation in Boulder, Nevada, and the Cline Library's archive on the Colorado Plateau in Flagstaff, Arizona. In these archives, I sifted through dozens of documents on the construction of the dams and the litigation of the Colorado River: water compacts, explorers' accounts, treaties, and educational as well as promotional pamphlets. The archival material I analyze here was published in the decades around the Boulder Canyon Project, which was completed in 1935. Most of these documents were produced in association with the Bureau of Reclamation, an agency under the US Department of the Interior. The Bureau of Reclamation oversees water resource management, specifically the oversight and operation of water diversions, and hydroelectric power generation projects that the bureau has built throughout the western United States since the beginning of the twentieth century.[1]

Because maps are the most obvious representations of land and water, I paid particular attention to them. The two defining features of maps of the Colorado River are that they show the river running through land it no longer reaches and that they almost always represent the river as the lone detail south of the border, running through a featureless and vacant landscape (see map 1.1). By showing the river flowing where it no longer exists, these maps deny the fact that the Colorado's water is almost entirely appropriated for use in the United States and that the strongly diminished flows that cross the border are appropriated by the Mexican border manufacturing or agricultural zone. The blankness represented south of the border also implies that it does not matter if the water does not reach there anyway, since there is ostensibly no life in the area. Note that in map 1.1, all of the major dams, reservoirs, states, and state lines in the United States are represented but that none are represented in Mexico. These features depoliticize the overuse of water upstream both by obscuring the extent of overuse as well as providing a potential justification for this water not reaching Mexico.

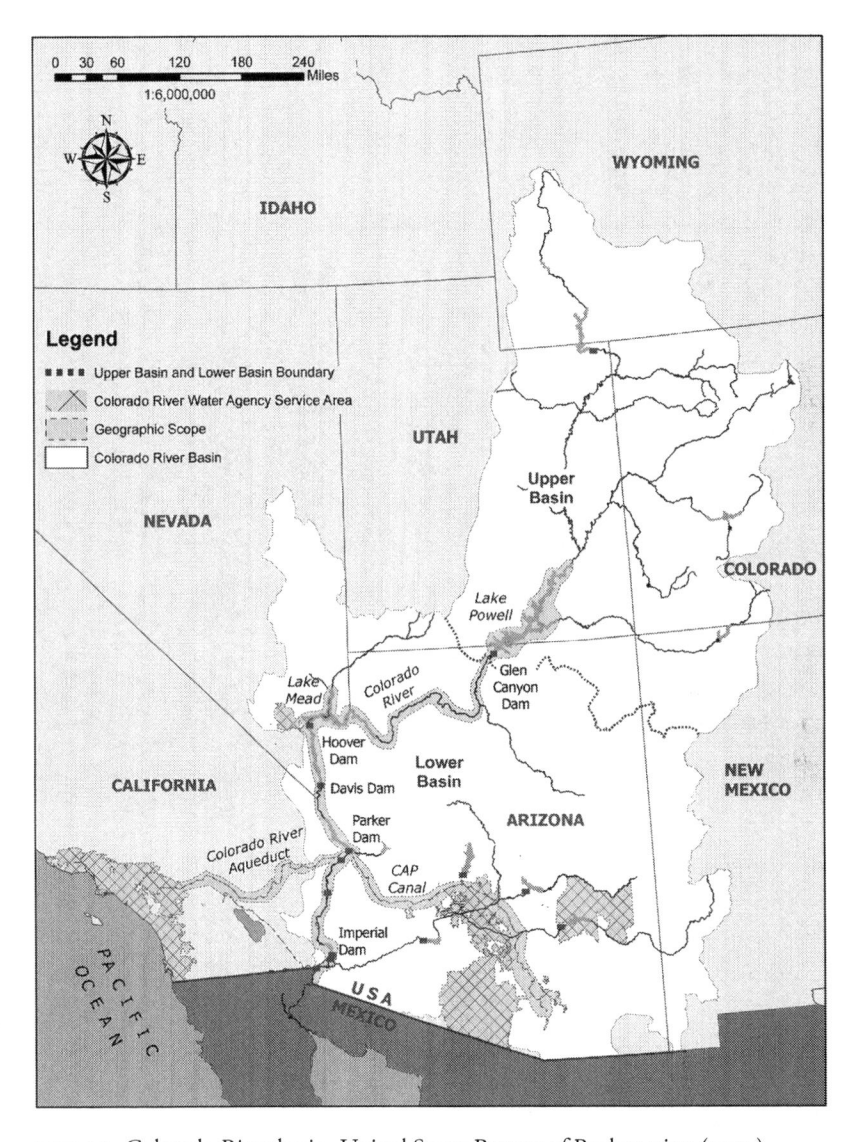

MAP 1.1. Colorado River basin. United States Bureau of Reclamation (2007).

30   Chapter One

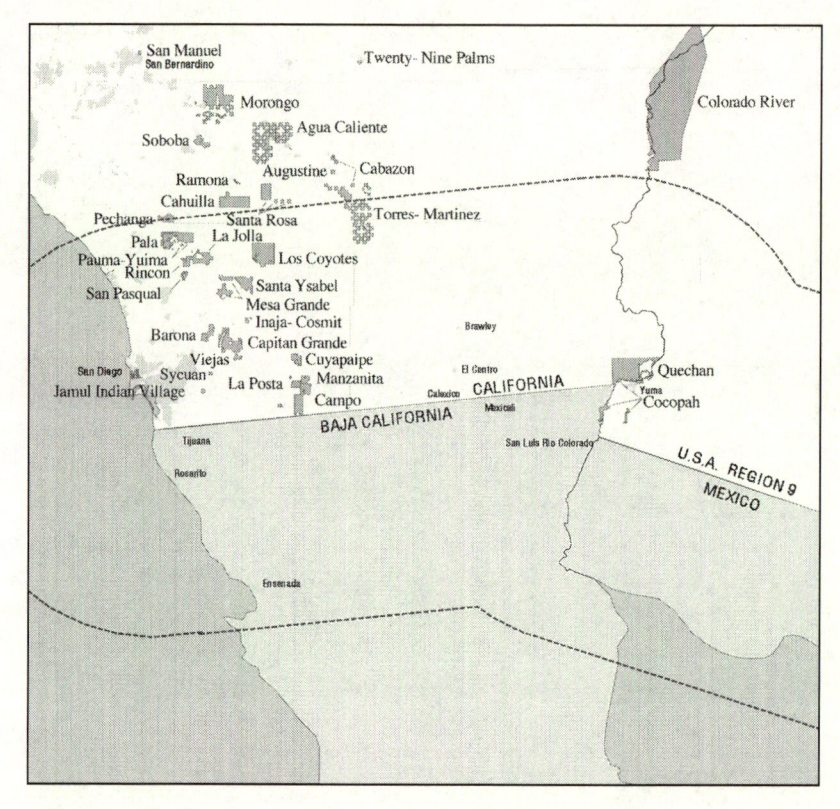

MAP 1.2. US-Mexico border area tribal lands. Environmental Protection Agency (1998).

The consistency of these features on maps from the Boulder Dam Commission, the Department of the Interior, and the Bureau of Indian Affairs illustrates the extent to which the Bureau of Reclamation has defined the geography of the American West. Other agencies concerned with the distribution of water follow suit in their representation of the river. For example, the Environmental Protection Agency (EPA) published a map of tribal lands along the border that also showed conspicuously little detail below the border (see map 1.2 [Environmental Protection Agency 1998]). What is even more striking is to find the river represented as reaching the sea by an agency concerned with environmental degradation. Federal environmental agencies have certainly no jurisdiction across international territories, but as many environmentalists have pointed out, ecosystems do not obey borders, hence environmental problems cannot be treated in national isolation (Kiy and Wirth 1998).

The material effects of these representations are that they underwrite decades of policy that effectively cut off the delta, both literally and graphically, from the rest of the river in the process of its development upstream (Fradkin 1981). As Bergman has argued (Bergman 2002), since the Hoover Dam was completed on the Colorado River in 1935, the delta has been a "blind spot" in the American imagination.[2]

Maps are a particularly obvious case of how representations of place can be used as instruments of persuasion and power rather than impartial tools of reference (Hanks 1999b; Wood and Fels 1992). However, maps are not the only tools that experts use to represent the river in particular ways and for particular purposes. Engineers and ranchers in the United States draw on an expert discourse, colloquially identified as "waterspeak." *Waterspeak* is famous along the Colorado River for its extensive and often opaque vocabulary. For example, a common unit of measurement for the river is an "acrefoot," or 326,000 gallons (approximately enough water to sustain a family of four for a year). Another common term is "waterdebt," which refers to when one country or state has used more than its allotment of water ("waterdebt" is measured in "acrefeet").[3]

At a tribal water summit in Flagstaff, Arizona, in August 2005 that brought together tribal members along the Colorado River in the United States, several people argued that waterspeak itself forms an exclusive discourse which controls access to the river. In the summit dialogue and in my interviews with some of the attendees, it was repeatedly expressed that waterspeak constitutes an exclusive language understandable only to water engineers, lawyers, and ranchers. Indeed, waterspeak is further legitimated by the legal framework through which the river is allotted, a framework known as the "Law of the River": a massive collection of treaties, compacts, and court decisions stipulating the conditions under which water is distributed.

One of the most interesting and prevalent concepts found in the intricate vocabulary of waterspeak is the idea of "beneficial use." Peter Culp, an environmental lawyer, argues that this is the unifying concept in the Law of the River (2000). According to the Bureau of Reclamation, "beneficial use" is the use of a reasonable amount of water necessary to accomplish the purpose of appropriation without waste. The uses that are considered beneficial according to the Colorado Compact are "water applied to domestic and agricultural uses," where domestic use "shall include the use of water for household, stock, municipal mining milling industrial and other like purposes" (quoted in Culp 2000: 14).

It is important to clarify how "waste" is used in this context. In most parts of the United States, "wasting water" refers to using too much water or using water for frivolous purposes (e.g., long showers, golf courses). On the Colorado River, however, "wasting water" refers to letting any drop escape human use. "Wasted water" is water *not* diverted out of the river and used. Another important aspect of the concept of "beneficial use" is that an exclusive set of uses is delineated as "beneficial." Significantly, water used to maintain ecological habitats is not included; indeed, it was not until recently that environmental groups have lobbied for environmental considerations to be stipulated with water allotments.

The principle of "beneficial use" and the idea that any drop not used is "wasted" are reflected in the blank space we find on maps, emphasizing that water really would be wasted if it reached the barren land void of a civilization across the border. This logic can also be traced to the rhetoric around the construction of the first dams on the river.

As the Colorado River Flows Merrily out to Sea . . .

[In] no part of the wide world is there a place where Nature has provided so perfectly for a stupendous achievement by means of irrigation as in that place where the Colorado River flows uselessly past the international desert which Nature intended for its bride. Sometime the wedding of the waters will be celebrated, and the child of that union will be a new civilization.
—WILLIAM ELLSWORTH SMYTHE (1900: 293–294)

When the preceding passage was written in 1900, the building of the great dams on the Colorado River was just beginning to be imagined, but the idea that the river would be "useless" past the international border was clearly already firmly established. One of the ways the concept of "waste" was articulated in the early literature on the Colorado River was through the idea that nature, left to its own devices, was inherently wasteful. For example, in "The Story of a Great Government Project for the Conquest of the Colorado River," an informational pamphlet published by the

Boulder Dam Association in 1928, the Colorado River was characterized in the following way: "Today the Colorado, on the one hand, is an ever increasing flood menace and, on the other, a notorious waster of its precious cargo of water so desperately needed in that region through which it passes" (Boulder Dam Association 1928: 1).

The idea here that the river wastes its own water simply by letting it flow its course is replete throughout the literature on the dams. William Smythe (quoted in the epigraph for this section), who was the chairman of the National Irrigation Congress in 1900, further develops the idea of nature's wastefulness by way of an economic metaphor: "dark, deep water [flows] uselessly to the ocean past an empire that has waited for centuries to feel the thrill of its living touch. It is like a stream of golden dollars which spendthrift Nature pours into the sea" (Smythe 1900: 288).

By suggesting that Nature is "spendthrift," spending "money" extravagantly and wastefully, Smythe elaborates another important sense of "waste" by drawing on the analogy between water and money. Versions of this metaphor are still rampant in the West. A famous saying in the southwestern United States is that "in the West, water runs uphill towards money," and metaphors of water as "liquid gold" or as a "liquid asset" are strikingly naturalized among many residents of the Colorado's watershed.[4] Therefore, Smythe's metaphor foregrounded the controversy on the river over whether water should be treated as a commodity, owned by individuals, or a commons, that communities have rights to (Reisner 1993; Shiva 2002; Worster 1992).

This passage from Smythe also emphasizes a sense of "waste" that is often elaborated directly in reference to Mexico. After the 1944 Colorado River treaty many of the southwestern states were resentful that 10 percent of the river was allotted to Mexico. The sentiment was that Washington had "given away" their water and, furthermore, that it would be wasted on Mexico. Therefore, the resentment was not simply over the fact that the river's water would flow past the region but also that it flowed into a "foreign country" whose population was, and is to this day, racialized as lazy and incompetent.[5]

In 1949, as California and Arizona were feuding over water allotments, *Western Construction News* printed an article titled "The Colorado Is Flowing Merrily out to the Sea, While Arizona and California Play Tweedle-Dum and Tweedle-Dee." The article expressed outrage at the negligence of these two states for becoming caught in a cycle of constant combat with each other. The authors also urged that in the "United States, threatened by an unfriendly world . . . harmony and unity are essential" (Server 1949: 2). The implication here was that the states' internal feuding left the water resources vulnerable to "unfriendly" usurpation by Mexico.

It is noteworthy that "flowing out to sea" was how the water was imagined once it got to Mexico (instead of being used for agriculture or fishing, for example). Furthermore, the idea that the river would carry on in its wastefulness "merrily" implies a character of ignorance that was often emphasized in portrayals of the river as inept and clueless in the early literature on the dams. In this rendition it was up to "man" (henceforth without quotations) to put nature to some use. The trope of man as an improver of wasteful nature is frequent in the original propaganda for the construction of the major dams on the Colorado River. In *The Colorado Conquest*, David Woodbury establishes this way of viewing the dams on the river by the following set of comparisons:

> When nature is disclosed at some magnificent task it is the habit of imaginative men to interfere and show her how to do the job a better way. Sometimes this impulse converts mountains into statues, at others it suggests a concrete lip to prevent Niagara falls from wearing itself away. On rare occasions such dreams succeed and nature is made an ally and a friend. (Woodbury 1941: 5)

In this passage, we find again the image of nature as self-destructive without the intervention of "man." Niagara Falls would "wear itself" away without the human prosthetic of the lip, and the Colorado River would waste itself all the way to the sea without the dams to hold it back.

The reference to nature as "her" in the passage above points to the ambivalently gendered dimension of this discourse on the river. When "nature" is represented in these texts as an abstraction, it is often distinctly feminized as docile, merry, or inept (see Ortner 1974). This stands in contrast to another strain of this discourse, which emphasizes the river's vicious, masculine character and in turn glorifies the magnitude of man's success in its conquest. This was most bluntly put in a promotional publication for the Boulder Canyon Project produced by the Boulder Dam Association. This pamphlet explained, "The boulder canyon dam is being planned to command the meanest, most savage, wickedest river in the world" (1930: 2). Particularly in the planning for the Boulder Canyon Dam, which was the first major dam on the river, there are countless references to the Colorado River as a "national menace." In an account of the Spanish captain Hernando de Alarcón's first voyage up the waters of the Gulf of California in 1540, the Bureau of Reclamation declared that "since that distant day when Alarcon first gazed upon the Colorado, this untamed river has been the natural enemy of man" (Bureau of Reclamation 1920: 5).

In some cases, the "vicious" character of the river is endowed with further agency through implications that the river had malicious intentions. For example, Herbert Corey (1923), writing on behalf of the Boulder Dam Commission, described this maliciousness in relation to the plight of riverside inhabitants before the construction of the major dams as follows: "The frightened dwellers in the flat lands build levees frantically. Little, thin, weak levees of soft dirt, heaped up like mud pies. The river has accepted this restraint for a year or so, chuckling to itself" (Corey 1923: 2).

The image of the river chuckling (or smiling) to itself while planning to wreak its havoc on unsuspecting river dwellers, clearly invoked in Corey's account above, is another common image in the promotional literature for the dams. Woodbury describes how

> fifteen generations of men and women were those others, who, without knowledge or resources, would not give up the fight. With high courage and endless patience they returned again and again and for four hundred years repeated their heartbreaking attempts to live by this vicious river which smiled until men trusted it and then turned and destroyed them. (Woodbury 1941: 5)

The intentionally destructive nature of the river was often underscored through reference to its inherently corrupt moral character, often drawn in parallel to the "dirtiness" of the silt-filled waters. In the same article quoted above, sponsored by the Boulder Dam Commission and "desirous of furnishing authentic information regarding this project," Corey elaborated on the river's moral inferiority: "It is a dirty river morally as well as physically. It seems to have the malign intelligence of a rogue elephant. Other rivers overflow their banks of course. But they have some sense of decency. The Colorado has none" (Corey 1923: 2).

The specter of imperiled lives and property in the face of the malicious force of the river implied in this passage was also invoked in *The Menace of the Colorado*, written by Mulford Windsor some thirty years after the construction of the Hoover Dam (1935) and only several years after the

Glen Canyon Dam (1964). Windsor explains that the dams represent "the heart of humanity responding to a just call for succor. The safety of women and children is threatened: homes and towns and cities are in the path of destruction; an agricultural empire faces extinction" (Windsor 1969: 2). With the river representing a force as destructive and malevolent as this, the conquest of the river by man carried particular dramatic and heroic appeal. This heroism is aptly captured in Woodbury's account.

> For a hundred and fifty thousand centuries the Colorado River has been steadily cutting a gash in the American continent, splitting its way to the sea through mountain and desert and plain. Not even the granite backbone of the earth itself has been able to interrupt this river's downward progress for so much as a single hour. . . . Now, suddenly, the relentless action has halted. The whole great span of the river's geological history has reached a dead end. In five little years the minute hand of man has reached into that open gash and stoppered it with a dam. (Woodbury 1941: 3)

Here again we find the magnitude of the manly accomplishment of the dams highlighted. The reference to the river as a "national menace" also points to the national significance of the project of building the Boulder Dam. In addition to the frequent reference to the river as a "national" menace in the literature in support of the Boulder Dam Project, a common rhetorical tactic also compared the dam to other national monuments.

Herbert Corey's comparison is particularly evocative:

> By comparison with the dam—the enormous stupendous cyclopean dam which is being planned by the United States Reclamation Service for the Boulder Canyon of the Colorado River—the pyramid of Cheops is a rockpile in the desert. The Panama canal shrinks. The Suez Canal is a mere trickle of water. The Assuan dam, which waters part of lower Egypt, is little more than a shovel and wheelbarrow affair. The Washington monument is a milepost. The Boulder Dam is for tomorrow. I am breathless—. (Corey 1923: 1)

These kinds of comparisons became part of the official rhetoric of the dams. Indeed, in 1937, the Bureau of Reclamation published *Boulder Dam: A Book of Comparisons*, a picture book that compared the Boulder Dam with other national monuments around the world. Among other examples the book boasted that "two earth and rock replicas of the largest pyramid in Egypt could be built with all the material excavated to anchor the sides and the base of the Boulder dam" (see figure 1.1).

Topologies of Invisibility on the Colorado River   37

TWO EARTH AND ROCK REPLICAS OF THE LARGEST PYRAMID IN EGYPT COULD BE BUILT WITH ALL THE MATERIAL EXCAVATED TO ANCHOR THE SIDES AND THE BASE OF BOULDER DAM

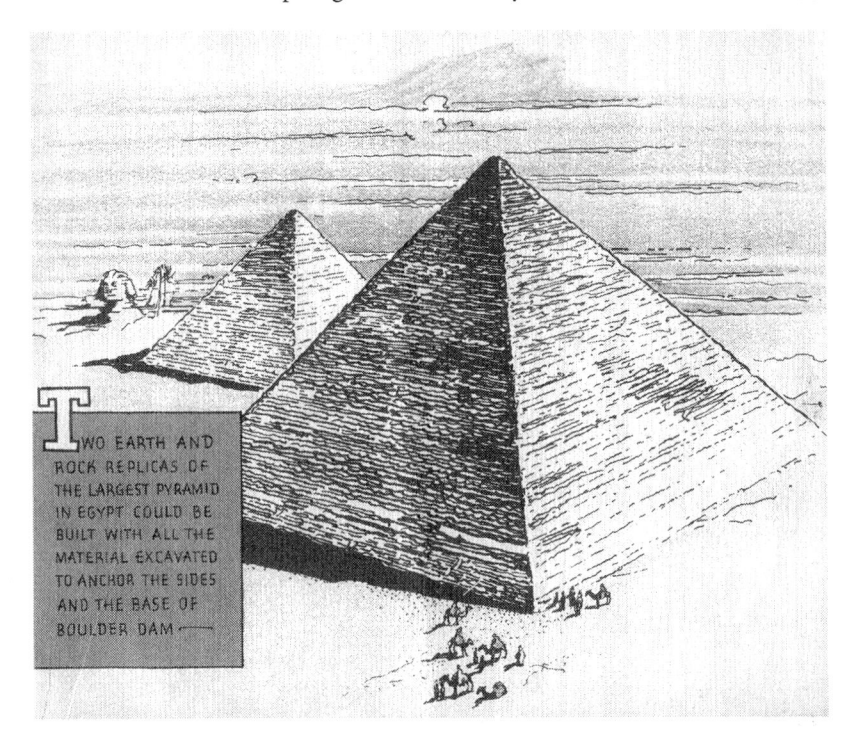

FIGURE 1.1. The Boulder Dam compared to the pyramids. United States Bureau of Reclamation (1937).

The nationalism associated with the Hoover Dam can be attributed to the era in which it was constructed—the Great Depression. The Hoover was built in extreme temperatures, under perilous conditions, and by laborers who were paid at minimal wages. Families moved from far away for the work the dam offered, sleeping in barracks built against the cliffs upstream from the site. The Hoover Dam was the pinnacle of an aggressive dam-building philosophy to which the United States ascribed during the late 1800s and early 1900s. In the early twentieth century, when dams were built mostly to power the mills of the Industrial Revolution, they were also symbols of power and technical progress.

In this context, the Hoover Dam is an example of what David Nye (1994) has termed the "technological sublime." Nye argues that from the very beginning of American history, technology was seen as a way of projecting US moral and political superiority in the world. As Nye writes:

FIGURE 1.2. The world's biggest US flag. United States Bureau of Reclamation (1996).

> The sublime was inseparable from a peculiar double action of the imagination by which the land was appropriated as a natural symbol of the nation while, at the same time, it was being transformed into a man-made landscape.... The sublimity lay in realizing that man had directly "subjugated" matter, and this realization was a collective experience. (1994: 37)

By Nye's account, the Hoover Dam can be understood as promoting a sense of nationalism and a popular identification with the state by subjugating the river in a collective enterprise. This nationalist identification was perhaps expressed most literally during the 1996 Olympic Torch Relay, when a US flag that measured 255 by 505 feet (78 by 154 meters) was hoisted on cables across the Hoover Dam (see figure 1.2).

The dam is a particularly spectacular example alongside those canals, railroads, bridges, dams, skyscrapers, and factories that were symbols of America's modernity and grandeur (see Barker 2005 for a similar case of techno-nationalism in the Indonesian context). The sheer architectural garishness of these dams was a point of pride for exactly this reason. In my tours of the Hoover and Glen Canyon Dam the guides recited impressive figures of how much concrete the construction of the dams required. I learned, for instance, that there is enough concrete in the Hoover Dam to pave a two-lane highway from San Francisco to New York and enough in the Glen Canyon Dam to build a four-lane highway stretching from Phoenix, Arizona, to Chicago, Illinois.

Finally, the logical outcome of the national project to conquer the menace of the Colorado was to tame the river. Woodbury's description of the river postconquest is explicit in this regard: "The river is docile now and does only what it is told to do. Its mighty strength no longer consumes and destroys; it builds. It has turned a broad wasteland of sand and sage into a garden; it is lighting and watering a new civilization" (Woodbury 1941: 3).

The general metaphor here is that the havoc of the river and its destructive character is transformed by man into a useful and productive force to strengthen the economy. However, a more specific metaphor about citizenship also emerges in the context of the nationalistic discourse around the dam. For example, in 1923 Corey wrote that "the boulder dam will be but the cutting edge of the plan which is ultimately to change the Colorado River from an outlaw into a hard-working member of a riverine society" (Corey 1923: 7). Therefore, the dam is more than a national monument; it is also the disciplining force that turns the river into a good citizen of the nation.

An examination of the various strains of this discourse reveals several unifying tropes. First the river, in its natural state, is so unwieldy and inept that it cannot do its own job; it is wasteful. The fierce, savage, conniving river must be tamed by man. The conquest of the Colorado River involves capturing it, harnessing it, and teaching it how to do its job better. When the river is conquered, it is finally transformed from a morally corrupt savage outlaw with no decency into a hard-working citizen.

The Savagery of the Colorado

Reclamation
2. b. The action of reclaiming from barbarism.
—*Oxford English Dictionary* (2d ed.)

After pulling together the various themes of this discourse, the parallel between the conquest of the river and the conquest of the American Indian is striking. All the connotations of the word "savage" as it was used by state agents to refer to American Indians are apparent in the representations of the Colorado River: uncultivated, barbaric, offensive, fierce, and uncivilized (McGee 1901; Powell 1888). The "benevolent" aim of the conquest of native populations, like the conquest of the river, was also to civilize them, tame them, teach them better manners, and ultimately turn them into productive citizens of the nation.

Therefore, one way of interpreting this discourse is by seeing the conquest of the river as a metaphor for prior forms of conquest. The river was as wild as the natives who lived on its banks (see Gordillo and Leguizamón 2002 for a similar metaphor in the case of the Pilcomayo River and the indigenous groups in Argentina and Paraguay). Captain Richard Pratt, one of the founders of the American Indian residential school system, invokes this metaphor in his famous phrase "Kill the Indian, and Save the Man" (Bess 2000). This phrase draws attention to the imagined parallels between the river and indigenous people. While Pratt was speaking on the education of American Indians, the idea that "civilizing" the "savages" involved taming them, and eradicating something essential about their character, was central. For both the Indians and the river, taming their wild ways was crucial to teaching them to be productive citizens.

The Indians, like the river, are what stood in the way of civilization. Examining the belief that the American Indian was an exemplar of savagery, the opponent of civilization and of the European settlers in North America, Roy Harvey Pearce wrote:

> Our civilization, in subduing the Indian, killed its own creature, the savage . . . it has not been able entirely to kill the Indian, but having subdued him, no longer needs or cares to. Still, it might be that there will always be somebody who needs to be subdued . . . savages standing in the way of civilization. (Harvey Pearce 1953: 243–244)

Pearce suggests that civilization always requires its semiotic foil, in this case savagery, in order to establish itself. American Indians have represented both a physical obstacle and a moral impediment to the complete conquest and control of the continent. In the arid land of the American Southwest, the river also came to represent that which civilization would overcome. As Nye suggested in the quotation above, the river represented for European settlers the "subjugated matter" in the same way that the Indians represented the force to be subdued in order for modern civilization to be realized.

By tracing the notion of "beneficial use" back to some of the seminal publications on the river, we have followed this notion through an implicit narrative that associates the conquest of the river with the conquest of the native groups that populated its banks. Given this parallel that was made between the savagery of the river and that of the American Indians, it is worth noting that this literature rarely mentions the prior inhabitants of the river's banks who *had* managed to live by the river despite its unpredictable nature. The Cucapá people, for instance, moved across the delta, fished, and farmed according to the flooding of the river for centuries before the building of the dams upstream (Colombi 2010). But after the compacts and the Law of the River were established, their access to the river was severely limited.

But the concept of "beneficial use" also directly impacted the access indigenous groups in the West had to the Colorado River because it has been a central conceptual device in limiting the water rights of the native tribes that historically inhabited the watershed.

The principle of "first in time, first in right," which underwrites the seniority of water rights on the river, should theoretically have resulted in indigenous groups having the most senior water rights to the Colorado because they had been there the longest. But the legal allocations of water under the 1922 compact constituted only "paper rights," or water allocations that exist only conditionally; they did not grant actual access to the water until it could be proved that the allocations could be put to "beneficial use." This severely limited the extent to which tribes could access water by imposing a set of conditions for water use. In cases where there was an insufficient infrastructure in place to put the water to "beneficial use," tribes would not have "wet" water rights. Holders of "paper rights" (also referred to as "reserved" or "conditional" rights) are also required to prove "due diligence," which means being able to demonstrate to the water court that they are making efforts to construct the facilities necessary (such as ditches or reservoirs) to apply the water right within a reasonable time.

In its 1963 decision in *Arizona v. California*, the US Supreme Court determined the Colorado River rights of Arizona, Nevada, and California and also quantified federal reserved rights of the five reservations along the lower Colorado: Chemehuevi, Cocopah, Colorado River, Fort Mohave, and Quechan (Fort Yuma). Therefore, while these five reservations were granted "reserved rights" of approximately 900,000 acrefeet of water in total (Checchio and Colby 1993), many other native tribes in the United States, including the Walapai and Havasupai in Arizona, were not granted rights to the river.[6] None of the indigenous groups in Mexico were granted rights to the 10 percent of the Colorado River allotted to the Mexican federal government.

The Second River

The conquest of the river and the taming and ordering of its flows meant that every single drop of the river was eventually allocated and controlled. The Colorado River now boasts the superlative of being the most litigated river in the world. The Law of the River has produced a virtual river, and it is this "second river" that determines access to the actual Colorado River. Commenting on this abstraction, Bergman writes, "It is a separate river, a textual river, a river of words that stretches back over a century in time. First we created a language that defined and controlled the river, and then that language transformed the river into a simulacrum of itself, a vast plumbing system" (Bergman 2002: 21). In this way, the Law of the River provides a particularly troubling example of what scholars have called "second nature," a concept which highlights the ways that nature is socially produced and shaped by political, economic, and social processes (Lefebvre 1991; Marx, Engels, and Riazanov 1963; Cronon 1991; McDermott 2005). More specifically to this context, Escobar (1999: 7) characterized second nature as the ensemble of social institutions that regulate the exchange of commodities, including the nature(s) produced by humans.

The material effects of this assemblage on the Colorado watershed, and especially on the delta, have been dramatic. For millions of years, the entire flow of the river reached the delta. Before the dams, the delta consisted of more than 2 million acres of wetlands where the river flowed toward the Gulf of California; it was the nexus of an ecological web that provided subsistence for the residents of the region and habitat for wildlife and marine fisheries in the Gulf. It also formed a link in the Pacific Flyway for birds flying north from Central America (Jenkins 2007). Now, as a result of the exploitation of the river in the United States, the Colorado has one of the highest rates of species extinction and endangerment on the continent (Bergman 2002: 29). In fact, the joke along the river is that there are only two species on the river's entire watershed that are not endangered: engineers and lawyers (Bergman 2002: 163).

Therefore, it is evident that the concept of "beneficial use," as it is woven through these archival materials, has allowed for certain discursive and material occlusions. These erasures primarily include indigenous people and the environment. This is partially accomplished by the way the idea of "beneficial use" is taken up in certain representations of the environment: the river, represented as a malicious savage, and the delta, represented as a barren land. This case exemplifies how verbal and graphic descriptions of land and place vary according to peoples' position in a political dispute (Carbaugh 1996; McElhinny 2006) and how descriptions of place also vary according to their location in prior political geographies. The delta also provides an example of how places are differently constructed according to their relationship to other sites.

Gordillo (2004: 3) has argued that places are always produced in tension with other geographies. Indeed, the way the Colorado delta was imagined and made invisible in the early twentieth century can be seen in revealing contrast to representations of another site on the Colorado River several hundred miles upstream. At the same time that the Colorado delta was being erased from the American imagination, the Grand Canyon was being hailed as a national icon.

In *How the Canyon Became Grand*, Stephen Pyne (1999) analyzes how the Grand Canyon was first found by European explorers and then disappeared from Western imaginings for another 250 years. Pyne shows how geologists helped construct the Grand Canyon as a monument, much like the Hoover Dam, to challenge built monuments in Europe. Unlike the Hoover Dam, however, the Canyon, while it certainly already existed in the physical environment, was constructed through ideas, words, images, and experiences. Therefore, instead of tracing a geological history of the canyon through faults, rivers, and mass wasting, Pyne examines another set of processes: "geopolitical upheavals and the swell of empire, the flow of art, literature, science, and philosophy, the chisel of mind against matter" (1999: xxi). Pyne shows how these were the processes that determined the shape of the Canyon's meaning and distinguished this place from hundreds of other competing landscapes.

The Grand Canyon was one of the earliest of North America's "natural wonders" to be visited by Europeans (along with Yellowstone, Yosemite, etc.) when Spanish conquistadors came to the south rim in 1540. Furthermore, the Colorado was mapped long before the Lawrence, Columbia, and Mississippi and appeared on European maps by the mid-sixteenth century, dominating North America on the Gastald map of 1546. But interestingly, as Pyne points out, there is "no indication of a great arroyo along the river's inland channel" (1999: 6). He argues, therefore, that while the Canyon was one of the first places in the interior of North America to be visited and mapped by Europeans, it was also one of the last to be celebrated as a "wonder" (4). This is why the Grand Canyon was not so much revealed as created. "More than once the Canyon was missed entirely or seen and dismissed. Then, with the suddenness of a summer storm, American society in the mid-nineteenth century mustered the capacity and the will to match its discovered opportunity and transformed land into place and place into symbol" (Pyne 1999: xiii). Thus, in the mid-nineteenth century the Canyon was transformed from a scene "as alien to western civilization as the plains of Mars or the craters of Mercury" to an "exemplar of geology, an epitome of historicism, a talisman of landscape art, and an icon of American nationalism" (Pyne 1999: 38). As a final testament to its transformation, in 1903 President Roosevelt took the train on the newly constructed railroad along the rim and said it was one of the "great sites every American should see." In roughly forty years (1869–1882), the canyon had become "grand" (Pyne 1999: 38). Interestingly, the Grand Canyon and the Hoover Dam are both sometimes referred to as "the Eighth Wonder of the World," in comparison to the Seven Wonders of classical antiquity.

The monumental importance that the Grand Canyon was to have in the American landscape came to public attention in the 1950s and 1960s, when it was named as the site of the last of the great dam projects on the Colorado. In 1968, public opposition blocked the construction of the Marble and Bridge Canyon dams, which would have flooded parts of the Grand

Canyon between the Hoover and Glen Canyon dams. David Brower, a champion of the early environmental movement in the United States, and the Sierra Club mounted a national campaign against the Grand Canyon dams. A famous moment of this campaign was when David Brower placed a full-page ad in the *New York Times* in June 1966, asking, "Should we also flood the Sistine Chapel so tourists can get nearer the ceiling?" The major public outcry that ensued succeeded in stopping the construction of the dams.

Meanwhile, the delta of the river lay relatively forgotten during the construction of all the major dams upstream. Because there was very little consultation with Mexico on the construction of the dams, the archival record in the United States only ever mentions the delta in passing. Not surprisingly, there is no parallel to the promotional and educational literature examined here in archival records in Mexico. Today the delta covers less than one-tenth of its original area, expanding across 150,000 acres south of Mexicali and north of the Gulf of California. Much of what comprised the upper region of the delta is now irrigated farmland, while the formerly vegetated lower reaches of the delta are now mud or salt flats.

It has only been within the last decade that an environmental movement in the delta has started protesting the damage done by water scarcity. The Defenders of Wildlife and the Center for Biological Diversity, along with other US national environmental and animal welfare organizations, including the Sonora Institute, filed suit on June 28, 2000, in the US District Court for the District of Columbia. Also among the plaintiffs were four environmental groups in Mexico, including the Asociación Ecológica de Usuarios del Río Hardy y Colorado (AEURHYC—Ecological Association of Users of the Hardy and Colorado Rivers). The lawsuit demanded that the Bureau of Reclamation consult with the US Fish and Wildlife Service on the status of wildlife in Mexico's delta and the effects of river management on those species (Bergman 2002). The plaintiffs argued that the Endangered Species Act had been violated with respect to protected species in the Colorado delta. In 2001, the Sustainable Water Project Tour, organized by Living Rivers (an environmental group in the United States), brought the issue of the delta to the basin's seven states with the rallying cry "One Percent for the Delta!" (i.e., demanding that 1 percent of the water of the Colorado reach the delta). More than 130 groups representing 12 million people from the United States and Mexico joined the campaign. Despite the publicity this project gained for the delta, in March 2003 a federal court finally rejected the claims of the lawsuit, finding that under the terms of the 1944 Treaty and the Law of the River, the Department of the Interior has no discretion to release additional water to Mexico.

As I examine in detail in chapter 2, while the environmental movement has made the ecology of the delta more visible, it has also erased local indigenous populations by often portraying the Cucapá people as yet another endangered species. The human geography of the delta, the places navigated on a daily basis, and the significance of these places for local people was therefore a topic I was particularly interested in pursuing when I reached the delta to begin my ethnographic fieldwork.

"Listen for When You Get There":
Redrawing the Map of the Colorado Delta

NGO worker (at a mapmaking meeting):
    What is the most important place on Cucapá land?
PEPÉ (raises his hand with a wry smile):
    Mi casa (My home).

After conducting archival research upstream on the river, compiling maps and documents, and attending meetings at water summits and the Bureau of Reclamation, I finally arrived in the delta with a set of questions: What is the alternate landscape that residents of the delta know? How do they experience the material effects of the discursive erasures accomplished upstream? I quickly came to learn that local people certainly do not see their landscape as a dead or featureless space at the end of the river; rather, they see it as a land filled with places that tell a distinct local history. And these are places that cannot be found on any map drawn up by the Bureau of Reclamation. These were the places that I wanted to learn about and document.

My principal method for approaching these questions was to bring people maps, as I had done with Don Madeleno, and ask them about the places that were not represented on them. To my surprise, however, unlike Don Madeleno, the majority of elders refused to engage with my maps at all. Esperanza, a seventy-four-year-old woman with whom I was particularly close, was especially uncomfortable about my solicitations for her to identify places on the maps. One day I brought her a map of the delta and asked her to show me where the mountain range she called "Las Pintas" was located. It was a place she had already described on several occasions. However, when I unfolded the map of the delta and asked her to point to Las Pintas, she refused to even look at the map. She gently pushed it away, looked out past the road south to the desert, and launched into the following story.

> There was a giant once named *mat-kakáp*. Every day the giant would traverse the land of the delta. He started at Cerro Prieto [the site of the creation myth where Sipa and Komat emerged from the water], then he walked around the Laguna Salada [an old fishing grounds now completely dry], Tres Pozos, and all the way up to the north to the Canyon of Guadalupe. After that, he would pass up around what is now Yuma, Arizona, going around crossing the high desert and the Colorado River, then down below the Sierra Cucapá, south to Las Pintas, repeating this same journey every day.
>
> Every day he would pass a Cucapá child playing below Las Pintas, and he would watch her. He kept passing and carried a little stick with him with a ball on the end and he would hit the mountains with it as he went. In one of these journeys he kidnapped the Cucapá child and hid her in the canyon of Guadalupe. Years passed in which the giant wandered the Colorado delta collecting food for the child. And as he wandered he continued to hit the mountains with his stick.
>
> That's how the mountains look the way they do, shaped like houses with windows. Have you seen this in the morning when the light comes in? This is how Las Pintas were made. This is how he made the doors, the windows, *las ramadas* [shelters]. You see how beautiful they look in *la mañanita* [early morning] as the sun rises and enters. The giant, yes, mat-kakáp, that means "he who cuts the earth," like an engineer that cuts the earth.
>
> And the child stayed with him and grew older and then the child became fat as the giant continued *dando vueltas* [making his rounds]. Every day he traveled his route around *la sierra* [the mountains]. And then the giant died, he was lost that way [*se perdió así*]. But the parents searched for the child and finally found her in the cave ready to give birth. They brought her back to where Lucía [Esperanza's cousin] lived and they did a ceremony to help her give birth. She gave birth to twins who became little giants. As they got older the first giant did the father's journey, around his route through the delta everyday until he got lost and died. Then the second child did the father's journey until he also got lost and died. And that's where the story ends.

Esperanza went on to describe how she had told one of her grandchildren this story and he did not believe her. "Then one day we were fishing in the Laguna Salada . . . and I said look there at the mountains. Look at how they are my child, like I told you. And *se quedó clavado en el cerro*" (his eyes locked on the hill).

Felix Coto, an elder from the Cocopah reserve in Somerton whom I interviewed on another occasion, suggested that this story, which he had also heard as a child, represents vulnerability in the face of the power of the delta's landscape. He said that it was the environment that killed the giant and the twins. The giant who helped shape the mountains was "lost" to them in the end. According to this interpretation, this legend foreshadowed the current socioeconomic situation, where a delta that people like Don Madeleno feel connected to in an essential manner now has its residents entirely at its mercy.

Coto's interpretation struck me as particularly interesting in relation to the comment that Esperanza made about how the giant "cut the earth like an engineer." On first hearing this analogy, it struck me as opaque: it was unclear to me why Esperanza would associate engineers with "cutting the earth." However, Coto's interpretation reminded me that for many local people engineers are associated, more than anything else, with the large dam constructions upriver in the United States. Like the giants in the story, engineers in the United States have remade the delta in ways that have held its residents captive, like the kidnapped child, to the dramatic changes of the landscape.

What is particularly interesting about this story for our purposes here, however, is what Esperanza was doing with her story, rather than what she may have been relaying with it (see Schegloff 1997; Sidnell 2000). It is noteworthy, for example, that she told me this story when I showed her a paper map. Esperanza refused to locate Las Pintas on the map; instead she located it in a story and in a description of the places she knew I was already familiar with. She narrated the physical landscape in order to provide direction and context for the location, instead of tracing it on the map. I found myself in similar situations with other elders. They would motion the map away (or ignore it all together), look out into the desert, and launch into a story about the place that I asked about.

For instance, I once brought a map to Barbara, a Cucapá elder who lived with her son not far from the main village, and asked her to show me where Hutpa Niuaha was, a place she had already told me many stories about. She had fished in Hutpa Niuaha with her husband when he was still alive and also with her sister. She was tremendously nostalgic about this place. However, like Esperanza, Barbara ignored the map and instead told me a story about how one day Coyote went wandering in the desert.

> He was wandering below Wishpa [the mountain where Cucapá souls go after death], in the desert out past Las Pintas, and eventually he became very thirsty under the hot sun. And so it was to his great delight that he happened upon a beautiful spring in the middle of the desert. The water was cold and fresh and clear. It was better than the water that comes from the *garrafón* [drinking water bought from trucks]. Then Coyote decided to share the water with the Cucapá people. He took them to the spring.

Barbara explained that is why they call the spring "Hutpa Niuaha," glossed as "Agua del Coyote" (Coyote's Water). She specified that "it's not Pozo de Agua [Water Spring], as the Mexicans say." Instead they use the name that gives credit to the original discoverer who showed the spring to the people. The fact that Coyote shared the water was a significant element of this story. Coyote is an enduring figure often featured in American Indian oral traditions (Bright 1993; Bunte 1980, 2002; Malotki and Lomatuway'ma 1985); he is often portrayed as a trickster, a wanderer, and a survivor (Carroll 1981; Lévi-Strauss 1963; G. McDermott 1994). In some appearances, as in Barbara's story, Coyote also takes on the role of hero (Segal 2000). Don Madeleno added on another occasion after recounting the same story, "I don't ever kill the Coyote, even if one comes prowling near my house."

The literature on language and place is useful in delineating the ways in which understandings of the Colorado River delta are locally articulated in these examples (Basso 1996; Bender and Winer 2001; Feld 1990; Frake 1996a, 1996b; Sidnell 1997). Basso's *Wisdom Sits in Places* (1996) is particularly relevant to the interactions I describe here. Basso analyzes Western Apache place-names from the greater Cibecue region in a community quite close to the Cucapá in northern Arizona. He demonstrates how places linked to traditional stories about historical events are used to illuminate the consequences of immoral conduct. In contrast to the view of proper names as having meaning solely in their capacity to refer, Basso argues that the use of place-names in interaction has particular values and functions (1996: 76). Apache constructions of place reach deeply into other cultural spheres, including conceptions of wisdom, notions of morality, politeness, and tact in forms of spoken discourse and certain conventional ways of imagining and interpreting the Apache past.

The use of place-names that Basso describes is similar to that in the case

I explore here because it shows how thoroughly contextualized places and place-names are within wider systems of local meaning as well as culturally specific communicative routines. Basso shows that place-names are not simply labels for physical locations but also deeply embedded in systems of cross-generational communication that underscore conceptions of morality and history. As is true of historical discourse and legends more generally, history is closely associated with a detailed system of place-names that is known, by and large, only to the residents of this community (Briggs 1988). The place-names Basso analyzes, which are compact sentences such as "Widows Pause for Breath" and "Men Stand above Here and There," condense the moral message of the associated narrative and ground it on a unique location.

The stories that Basso analyzes are different from the set I examine here in the emergent quality of the performance—the way in which the elders display the available communicative resources for an audience and within a particular context (Bauman 1977). In the cases I describe, the emergent quality of the performance results from my bringing a map and asking people to locate a site on it. The resulting dislocation of the performance from the social context in which these stories would otherwise be told prevents a full analysis of how these stories might be performed in other contexts and for audiences other than myself. However, the set of performances I witnessed through these interactions is revealing in other ways. The communicative routines that emerged from them provide a telling example of how maps locate places in ways that are not always commensurable with other ways of understanding place.

Charles Briggs (1986) explores the methodological problems that occur when interviewers nonreflexively impose their own communicative norms on speakers whose expectations stem from other traditions. By introducing these two-dimensional maps as modes for eliciting place-names, I was doing just that—assuming that a shared communicative routine would emerge with the elders in the way that it had with Don Madeleno. Fortunately, Esperanza's redirection of the event allowed for her own "communicative routines to work their way into the interview situation" (Briggs 1986: 28).

I began to better understand these communicative routines, and the discomfort I encountered locally around maps, when an NGO conducting a participatory mapmaking project of the delta began working in the area. The project, called "Mapeo Comunitario" (Community Mapping), was meant to design and implement mapping techniques to "promote conservation, understanding and respect" for the indigenous lands of the Sonoran Desert (Sonoran Institute 2007). The initiative followed in a recent trend of community mapping that attempts to use "community-created" maps as political and development tools (Chapin, Lamb, and Threlkeld 2005; Chase Smith et al. 2003; Herlihy and Knapp 2003). The technique has been influenced by what Nancy Peluso (1995), in the Indonesian context, has termed "counter-mapping," a way of representing space that is often hailed as encouraging the recognition of boundaries drawn before conquest that are not represented on conventional maps.

As a result of my interest in place-making, I was enthusiastic about this project and volunteered on every level of its initial planning. The project seemed to have political potential because of the ongoing struggle over the fishing grounds at the mouth of the river. Whether these grounds were actually "traditional" was commonly disputed in fishing meetings with government officials. Part of the problem with the Cucapá's fishing cooperative's legal claims to the fishing area was that they did not have the kind of documentation or expert knowledge that would establish their long-term occupation of the area. In other cases, indigenous land claims have indeed been legitimized by locally constructed maps (Chapin, Lamb, and Threlkeld 2005). While the members of the NGO conducting the project hesitated to admit the potential political uses of these maps and instead focused on their potential for cultural recovery, during the 2006 fishing season the advantages of making such a map seemed clear to members of the local fishing cooperative. A map would provide them with additional documentation on which to base their legal claim over the contested fishing grounds.

For these reasons I was disappointed when many of the elders, after attending the first meeting for the mapmaking project, refused to participate. When I asked Esperanza why she was not interested, she explained that she thought the project was a good idea but she did not want to be involved. One of her reasons for this was that she was illiterate. She explained that she felt excluded from the PowerPoint presentations and the maps displayed by the NGO members. She felt embarrassed because she could not follow the representations the way the younger people could.

The contrast between the ways the mapping project was hoping to "map" traditional land and the way Esperanza identified these locations reveals some of the distinctly local ways that the delta's landscape is invoked among Cucapá elders. Ethnographers working in contexts where oral traditions are prominent have recorded similar expressions of dissonance between other ways of rendering the land. For example, Julie Cruikshank describes a First Nations elder from the Yukon Territory commenting to a group of scientists at a conference on regional history, "you people talk from paper. I want to talk from Grandpa" (Cruikshank 2005: 76). Similarly, Basso quotes one of his informants as commenting that while "white men need paper maps, we have maps in our minds" (1996: 43). While Esperanza had less of a sense of authority in her opposition to the paper and PowerPoint of the mapmaking meetings, her dismissal of the paper map in exchange for a beautifully rendered oral account resonates with this statement. Esperanza felt alienated from the project not just because she is illiterate but also because it did not account for the type of spatial sensibility Esperanza was fluent in. For Esperanza, locating places was an aural/oral process, as opposed to a purely visual one (see also Feld 1990).

While Basso's work helps illustrate the local ways that people construe their land and render it intelligible, it also foregrounds a set of problems that arise for making sense of just such local renderings. Basso's work has been critiqued both for overlooking the role of power relations and history in the making of senses of place (Gordillo 2004: 4) and for failing to fully contextualize these local ways of place making within ongoing disputes about native land claims in the United States (McElhinny 2006).

The experience of the Cucapá elders raises the question of how to make local ways of space making intelligible to the decade-long legal battle to secure the rights of the Cucapá people to their traditional fishing grounds at the mouth of the Colorado River. The stories that elders told me about places in the delta and their dismissal of maps also has practical implications for countermapping projects. If the political potential of maps rests on representing local senses of place, and if local senses of place cannot be straightforwardly translated into maps, then the allegedly political efficacy of mapmaking projects is necessarily compromised and becomes a relatively hollow pursuit.

Pamela Bunte and Robert Franklin (1992) have explored the ways that cultural differences in thinking and speaking about topography and directions can have concrete implications for land conflicts. They examine depositions and trial testimonies in order to understand the cultural, linguistic, and communicative style dimensions of the problems that arose during a land claim dispute. In the course of the trial, specific linguistic and cultural aspects of San Juan Paiute concepts of location and direction led to interpretation difficulties and mutual misunderstandings. One of the Paiute elders who acted as witness was not accustomed to conceiving of an area of land through the schematic framework of maps, with their totalizing bird's-eye perspective and decontextualized distances and cardinal directions. Instead, he used directions from his own point of view, the view of one who experiences a terrain directly (1992: 20, 26).

Bunte and Franklin describe how, with their help, the Paiute lawyers worked with the elders and the court to find a mutually intelligible set of terms through which to communicate about the space in question. On one level, Bunte and Franklin do what Basso's work has been critiqued for neglecting to do; they place Paiute ways of thinking about space in the context of contemporary land conflicts and show some of the tensions that arise when these spatial imaginaries come into interaction with nonnative institutions (see also Richland 2008, 2011). However, in the case I describe, it is questionable whether a process of translation or reaching a level of "mutual intelligibility" would be enough to effectively incorporate, and do justice to, local renderings of place.

The more fundamental incommensurability between aural renderings and visual representations of place leaves us with a more disturbing conundrum. Paper maps become another way of colonizing local landscapes and transforming them into two-dimensional, silent objects. They may correct conventional maps by representing places that were absent before, but in the process, the stories that local people tell about them are silenced. The stories that Barbara, Esperanza, Don Madeleno, and many other elders told me problematize the attempts to encode local knowledge about place in conventional maps.

In May 2006, I raised these concerns at a meeting with the advisers of the mapmaking project at the casino on the Cocopah reservation in the United States, attended by the director of the project and some of the elders from the reservation. I suggested that there might be a way to include this sensibility, those verbal descriptions of place, into the final representation of the map, with the idea that this proposal might also accommodate the elders. While the director was fairly dismissive of my suggestion, Felix Coto, one of the elders in attendance, approached me after the meeting. He told a story about a time when he was a child traveling with his father on the reservation. It was a pitch-black night, and he was scared because they could not see where they were. His father comforted him by explaining that they would know when they arrived by listening to the wind in the trees and by listening to the river. "That's how you tell," he said. "You listen for when you get there."

While Felix did not explicitly answer the question of how to accommodate the elders' senses of place in the case of the Mexican Cucapá, he was nonetheless affirming that if we wanted to know where the places were, we really would have to listen to the stories. He also emphasized the distinction between looking and listening for places. Felix's mention of "listening to the river" reminded me of how frequently Cucapá elders in Mexico recollected with nostalgia the roar of the Colorado River. Therefore, Felix's story also suggests that we could also listen to the places that are not on the landscape anymore. When we look at maps of the southwestern United States and Mexico, we see the river. But from the former riverbed in Mexico, all one has to do is listen to know that the river is no longer there.

CHAPTER 2

THE FISHING CONFLICT AND THE MAKING AND UNMAKING OF INDIGENOUS AUTHENTICITY

Si has bebido agua del Colorado,
una gran historia corre por tus venas.
(If you have drunk of the Colorado River,
a great history runs through your veins.)
—Mexican proverb

A GROUP OF EIGHT Cucapá men and women crowded into their lawyer's office on a sweltering summer afternoon in Mexicali. Andrés Rivioli, the lawyer who handles the Cucapá's fishing conflict with the Mexican federal government, began the meeting by denouncing the government for denying the Cucapá access to their ancestral fishing grounds. He said that by criminalizing their fishing, the state was effectively committing "cultural genocide" on its own people. The lawyer was referring to the federal biosphere reserve that was created in 1993 in the delta to protect its struggling ecosystem. Since then, Cucapá fishers have been denied access to their fishing grounds, now cordoned off within the limits of the protected area. While they have been granted permits to fish upstream, those areas have very few fish and are not seen as a viable source of livelihood.

Rivioli, the lawyer, is a large, broad-shouldered man with a slightly overbearing countenance. He had a talent for impassioned and effective speeches about the Cucapás' situation. He took any opportunity to relay his message in meetings for reporters and in private conversations with the fishing cooperative's members. The lawyer's diatribe about the injustices suffered by the Cucapá people was a familiar opening to his meetings with the fishing cooperative. Unlike at previous meetings, however, on this occasion the lawyer moved on to propose some of the reasons that the Mexican government had banned the Cucapá's fishing in the first place, despite a decade of protests, a constitutional promise, and pressure from the National Human Rights Commission: they were not adequately performing their indigeneity. In addition to advising that they wear traditional grass skirts and go back to living in *cachanilla* huts (made of mud and roofed with arrowweed), he told the group that they had to speak their indigenous language if they wanted their government to take them seriously as Indians.[1] "How is the government even supposed to know you're Indians?" he concluded, pointing to one of the women. "You dress and speak like Mexicans!"

I glanced around the room at the circle of people, mostly women, he was referring to. They looked shamed by his remarks. The lawyer's accusation was particularly striking because that day the fishing women were not clad in their usual mud-caked jeans and long-sleeved shirts, the standard wear during the fishing season to protect against the blistering sun and muddy inclines. Instead, they wore floral blouses and looked clean and carefully put together: an effort, no doubt, intended for their trip into town and to show respect for their lawyer.

This incident foreshadowed what I came to learn was a more general critique by officials of the legitimacy of Cucapá claims to an indigenous identity. The conflict over the Cucapá people's rights to fish corvina (*Cynoscion xanthulus*, Mexican saltwater sea bass) in the government-protected ecological reserve is a debate deeply intertwined with issues of indigenous authenticity, hegemonic assumptions about cultural and ethnic difference, and state-sanctioned rights granted on the basis of such differences.

In a departure from the past, when indigenous groups throughout the Americas were denied rights if they resisted cultural and linguistic assimilation (Díaz Polanco 1997), in the last several decades identifying as indigenous has become an important means of legitimating claims to natural resources (Chapin, Lamb, and Threlkeld 2005; Conklin 1997; Graham 2002; Hathaway 2010; Jackson and Warren 2005; Li 2000). In chapter 5, I examine how the Cucapá's linguistic practices have been negotiated through this political paradigm. In this chapter, I examine how the fishing conflict with the Mexican federal government has been shaped by these same political circumstances.

The environmental movement in Mexico has also been a critical platform for neoliberal interventions because it imposes particular constraints on how environmental rights and resources should be distributed. In the

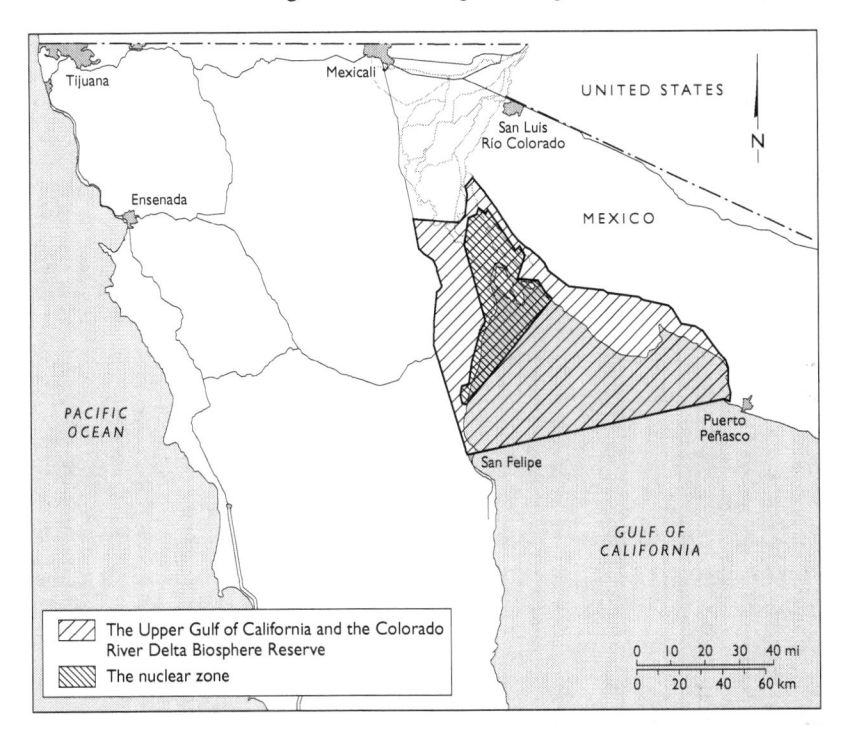

MAP 2.1. The Upper Gulf of California Biosphere Reserve. Mexican Commission for National Protected Areas (2007). Credit: Bill Nelson

following pages, I show how different actors invoke and deploy environmental discourses in the Colorado delta. I focus my analysis on a series of fishing meetings, government documents, and NGO reports I examine how the Cucapá's arguments for fishing rights have been facilitated and constrained by current environmental discourses that impose implicit measures of indigenous authenticity on them. I argue that environmental struggles do more than align preexisting groups with and against each other. The struggles themselves have shaped the political boundaries of the Cucapá community by constituting what membership means and how alliances are formed.

Neoliberalism, Multiculturalism, and Indigeneity

As noted by several authors, the neoliberal project encompasses both economic restructuring and new practices of governance, including the transfer of state responsibility for mediating social conflict to civil society and the encouragement of forms of "self-regulation" for certain groups (Inoue 2007; Speed 2005). On the US-Mexico border, the North American Free Trade Agreement (NAFTA) has been the most obvious manifestation of the economic restructuring of neoliberalism and the subsequent rise of export-oriented development, specifically with the increasing presence of assembly plants (*maquiladoras*) owned by US corporations in the border region.

These reforms also imported ideological changes encouraging a move toward official multiculturalism. Under pressure from international agencies and in preparation for NAFTA, Article 2 of the Mexican constitution was altered to recognize Mexico's "pluriethnic composition," and multicultural policies were introduced encouraging "cultural recovery" (Hale 2005; Sieder 2002). These reforms were intended to further integrate Mexico within the new neoliberal global order (Speed 2005: 35).

Despite the simultaneous rise of narratives focused on neoliberalism and multiculturalism, some observers, as noted, have seen them as antagonistic projects. This view has been particularly apparent in some parts of Europe, where conservative, neoliberal governments have been lukewarm or even hostile to embracing multiculturalism vis-à-vis immigrant populations. For example, in countries such as the Netherlands and France, recent political debates about immigrants have shifted away from the celebration of multiculturalism and toward highlighting the need to "integrate" these groups within the national mainstream (Bjornson 2007; Fassin 2005).

In Latin America, the perceived contradiction between neoliberalism and multiculturalism has been fueled by high-profile cases where policies espousing economic liberalism, free trade, and privatization triggered the rise of political movements that have challenged and openly criticized neoliberalism in the name of "indigenous rights." The Zapatista movement in Mexico or the rise to power of Evo Morales in Bolivia are probably the clearest examples of this trend (Postero 2007; Ramírez Paredes 2002). Finally, the assumption that trends of neoliberalism and multiculturalism run counter to one another is also due to the fact that scholars who have explored the ideological effects of neoliberalism have often focused on the particular notion of the individual it propagates, which assumes a self-contained rational actor who stands in tension with the collective notions of group membership often associated with indigenous groups (Ellison 2006; Ferguson 2007; Inoue 2007).

A growing number of authors, however, have challenged the view that neoliberalism and multiculturalism necessarily stand in tension with each other, especially in Latin America (Hale 2002, 2005; Martinez Novo 2006; Sieder 2002; Speed 2005). Shannon Speed (2005), for example, argues that one of the main differences between neoliberalism and earlier forms of liberalism is precisely that the emphasis on the individual as the primary social actor has been reduced. In the neoliberal period, the need for multiculturalism results from the minimization of the role of the state and from the impulse toward the self-regulation of different sectors of society. Speed cautions that if we continue to see the neoliberal state as a project that advances "individualism," it is easy to arrive at the misleading conclusion that all groups pushing for collective rights are necessarily anti-neoliberal (Speed 2005: 46; see also Armstrong-Fumero 2009a).

Therefore, theorists have increasingly noted that multicultural policies form part of the larger neoliberal project in Mexico and beyond (Postero 2007; Povinelli 2002). The simultaneous introduction of neoliberal reforms and multicultural policies in many Latin American states has been explained in various ways. Some scholars have argued that multicultural policies were implemented to overcome a crisis of legitimacy or were introduced in response to international pressures (de la Peña 2005; Jackson and Warren 2005; Sieder 2002) or to avoid ethnic conflict (Yashar 1998). Others have explained the introduction of multicultural policies in neoliberal regimes as a form of cooptation (Stephen 1997) and some, more optimistically, as a deeper change reflecting democratization (Hernández Castillo 2001).

Other scholars have argued that multiculturalism is more fundamental to the project of neoliberalism in Latin America (indeed, Hale's term "neoliberal multiculturalism" [2005] was intended to signal this). Rachel Sieder (2002) argues that Mexico's neoliberal government has embraced multicultural policies because they are a way to recalibrate mechanisms of control. For example, as indigenous groups have started asserting more independence, the state has been able to intervene in new ways, under the banner of human rights and multiculturalism (see also Hale 2002, 2005).

Martinez Novo (2006) provides an example of these recalibrations from Baja California, where she argues that state institutions do not perceive the national projects of economic liberalization and ethnic projects of cultural recognition as contradictory. Instead of repressing indigenous identity or interpreting it as a challenge to their interests, government officials and chamber of commerce members sought to support a particular understanding of "Indianness" that they perceived as akin to their goals. For example, Martinez Novo describes how tourism and other economic interests such as commercial agriculture for export benefit from the reinforcement of Indian identification by keeping indigenous day labor cheap.[2]

Environmentalism and Indigenous Politics

Recent work in anthropology has examined how environmental movements can be exclusive, favoring the interests of some groups over others (Haenn 1999, 2002; McElhinny 2006; Zerner 2000). This is particularly true in the case of protected areas, which have often alienated natural resources from local users (Brosius and Russell 2003; Doane 2007; Kaus 1993; Toussaint 2008; Walley 2004; West, Igoe, and Brockington 2006; Wolmer 2003). And work on fisheries specifically has shown that government restrictions that do not take local livelihoods into account often fail to be successfully enforced (McCay 1984; Vásquez León 1999).

Anthropologists and other scholars have also drawn attention to the ways in which environmental discourses both incorporate and erase indigenous subjects by assuming a natural relationship between indigeneity and environmental sustainability (Bamford 2002; Braun 2002; Chapin 2004). Since the 1980s, indigenous people have been key symbols and sometimes key participants in the development of a transnational environmental ideology and discourse that has promoted an image of the "ecologically noble savage." These Western environmental ideologies have discursively located authenticity and purity in indigenous peoples, presenting the latter as dwelling according to nature, outside modernity, and resistant to global capitalism. Environmentalists have used these discourses as leverage for their own projects (Brysk 2000; Conklin and Graham 1995; Graham 2002; Mathews 2008, 2009), and NGOs and indigenous groups have sometimes benefited from the unlikely alliances they have forged (Conklin 1997; Greenough and Tsing 2003; Mathews 2009).

Yet as I noted in the introduction, little systematic attention has been paid to cases in which these same articulations are not successful and actually suppress demands for indigenous rights. In our case, the way that indigeneity has been foregrounded ultimately constrains access to environmental resources among vulnerable groups such as the Cucapá. In short, this is a story in which indigeneity and environmentalism did not fully "articulate," in part because of the neoliberal assumptions about multiculturalism and indigeneity at play in the fishing conflict.

In the Colorado delta, essentializing images of indigenous people popularized in environmental discourses have resulted in ambivalence among NGO workers, government officials, and the local public about how to situate the Cucapá people in the environmental crisis. This ambivalence manifests itself in two incommensurate portrayals of the Cucapá, both of which allude to a notion of authenticity: a romanticized version, derived directly from mainstream environmental discourses; and a "corrupted" version, created when the romanticized portrayal proves contradictory and untenable. The romanticized version, often produced by conservation NGOs, portrays the Cucapá as "guardians of the river" and highly capable natural conservationists who "worship" the nature at risk of disappearing. At its worst, this view imports a series of related stereotypes about indigenous people along the lines of what the lawyer described in the opening vignette (that "real" Indians speak indigenous languages, live in mud huts, and wear traditional clothing). While the romanticized version sometimes presents the Cucapá as victims of environmental degradation, it more often portrays them with even less agency. In fact, as I will show in the following, extreme versions of this view go so far as to describe them as yet one more endangered species that needs to be defended by conservation efforts.

When people do not live up to these stereotypes, their perceived indigenous purity is defiled and a portrayal of their corruption emerges. Local NGO workers and officials working in the field were quick to point to the Cucapá's environmentally destructive practices: burning and dumping garbage, fishing endangered species, and using tightly woven nets that catch baby fish. Often working closely with the Cucapá, environmentalists also saw the deprivation they experience: the domestic violence, drug addiction, and poverty. The ambivalence toward the role of the Cucapá people in the environmental crisis arises from what many local Mexicans and NGO workers perceived as a glaring contradiction between the idealized place of indigenous people in some environmental rhetoric and the more complex reality in the field.[3] At its worst, this portrayal identifies the Cucapá as the perpetrators of the environmental damage in the delta rather than the victims.

The Fishing Conflict: "We Will Fish Here Forever"

When I began my fieldwork in August 2005, the corvina fishing season was to begin only six months later, so my introduction to the issues that faced Cucapá fishers was a series of meetings with different governmental representatives, lawyers, human rights officials, and NGO members over those first months. I was also well briefed on the dynamics of this conflict through local newspaper coverage. The claims by the Cucapá's fishing cooperative to their fishing grounds hinged on a long-standing connection to place with an emphasis on indigenous identity and ancestral lands.

I started attending fishing meetings before I had a chance to become close with all the fisherpeople and gain their trust. At one of the first major meetings, I arrived early to make sure I could find the room in the Mexicali hotel where the meeting was held and to set up my recording devices. Then the officials from the Commission for Indigenous Development (CDI) filed into the room and set up their laptops and projectors. Some of the Cucapá fishing families also arrived, trailed by children running around the room and climbing onto the cookie table. I felt awkward being there, even though the president of the fishing cooperative had given me permission to attend. It seemed to me that everyone was slightly suspicious of me, wondering whose side I was on.

Just before the meeting was about to commence, the head delegate for CDI entered the room. He took one glance around the motley assemblage of people and then fixed his gaze on me, immediately recognizing the anomalous presence. He proceeded to walk directly over to where I was sitting and began questioning me. I introduced myself as an anthropologist doing research with the Cucapá people, and right away he asked who I was affiliated with. I explained that it was my own research, but he pressed on asking about my local affiliation, insisting that I had one when I explained again that I was there independently. Finally, he asked for my passport, which I did not have on me, and proceeded to talk quickly and confrontationally about permissions and affiliations until, noticeably distressed, I explained that I was still getting used to speaking Spanish and that I did not understand everything he was saying. This seemed to comfort him and he left me alone, waving me off with his hand and walking away.

Rattled by this confrontation, I noticed that the fisherwomen had started smiling over at me and shaking their heads knowingly and in disapproval of the delegate's display. When we returned to the village after the meeting, I learned their interpretations of the incident as we sat around the table in Adriana's kitchen eating beans and tortillas and drinking instant coffee. Adriana, who was the president of the fishing cooperative at the time and the chief's daughter, spoke more openly with me than she had before.

"That was really clever how you said you couldn't understand him," she said, misidentifying my communicative breakdown as strategy. She was very sympathetic that they had treated me so abrasively and explained that they did so because they did not want me there to witness "how they treat the Indians." From that moment on, Adriana was quick to claim my presence as their guest at fishing meetings. It was as if the delegate's public display of irritation at my unannounced and undocumented presence was a de facto voucher for my trustworthiness. What the members of the Cucapá fishing cooperative wanted was a witness and this chapter is intended to fulfill that potential.

While I focus primarily on a core group of fishers, it should be noted that not everyone in the village where I did research belongs to the fishing cooperative.[4] The Cucapá people who live in this village constitute a very diverse group and have responded to the environmental and fishing crisis in different ways. Some former fishermen and women reject local ideas that the Cucapá people will "fish forever" (an idea espoused by many in the cooperative) and have become more integrated in the local formal and informal economies: working on farms or on road-building projects by the government, collecting and selling scrap metal, or working in the narco-economy, which has taken a strong hold of the region (as we shall see).

Regardless of their subsistence strategies, however, there was markedly uniform agreement that the federal government's denial of their fishing rights was an affront to their identity, autonomy, and livelihood. As a result, the conflict served to sharpen the boundaries between local groups (especially between indigenous and nonindigenous fisherpeople) and to strengthen a sense among Cucapá people that they shared a common identity in opposition to the abuses of the Mexican government.

In the last several years, the fishing conflict has escalated in a series of intense negotiations among the fishing cooperative, human rights lawyers, and federal and state environmental officials. In 2002, after nine years of conflict, Adriana, president of the Cucapá fishing cooperative, made a complaint to the Human Rights Commission of Mexico. In the recommendation that resulted from the commission's investigation, the council declared that the fishing restrictions were violating the Cucapá's human rights (Waisman, Lichtinguer, and Arroyo 2002). The report is one of the main avenues of appeal that people have against the fishing restrictions. It recommended that a solution to the conflict be negotiated that would allow the Cucapá people who fish to continue to practice their traditional economic activity. This report is routinely cited by their lawyer and by the more politically active fishermen and women. It will also be the basis for further appeals to the International Human Rights Commission. Yet as this book goes to press nearly eleven years after the report, the Mexican government has yet to respond to its recommendations. Indeed, on my first day in the biosphere reserve at the beginning of the 2006 fishing season, there were twice as many environmental officials and marines trying to enforce restrictions as there were Cucapá people trying to fish.

While the Human Rights Commission's recommendation was based on national and international laws regarding indigenous rights to resources and the practice of "traditional customs," local environmental officials have been able to bypass these legal stipulations by questioning the legitimacy of the Cucapá people's claims to an indigenous identity in the first place, much as the lawyer suggested in the opening vignette.

Where Does the River Become the Sea?
Claiming a Place at the End of the Colorado

The debate over the Cucapá's fishing rights revolves around three key themes: whether the fishing grounds at stake were actually "traditional"; the extent to which fishing, and in particular fishing for corvina, is "a Cucapá custom"; and whether the Cucapá's fishing techniques are adequately "indigenous" in character. The last of these themes, a certain conception of how indigenous people should fish, has come to take primacy in the current legal dispute over the river.

The Cucapá fishing cooperative argues that they have a long-standing historical connection to the delta. Archeological and ethnohistorical evidence suggests that their ancestors had a presence in this area for thousands of years.[5] Indeed, the Cucapá people are locally known as the "people of the river" as a result of their association with the Colorado. The controversial fishing camp at the center of the debate, el zanjón, is the location of their traditional grounds and is off the shores of their ancestral land.

Environmental officials used the logic of the Cucapá's "ancestral land tenancy" to argue against the cooperative's claims. They agreed with the premise that a long-standing connection to place should afford indigenous people certain rights but suggested that the zanjón is not exactly the Cucapá's ancestral grounds. Several officials from the Mexican Federal

Agency for Environmental Protection (PROFEPA) told me that since "Cucapá" means "people of the river," this alone was proof that the zanjón was not ancestral, because it is located where the river "meets the sea." Some Cucapá fishers counterargued that the only reason the corvina came to lay eggs in the zanjón was because of the freshwater, thus proving that the area was still the river, not quite the sea yet.

Other critics of the cooperative's claims argue that even if the zanjón is their traditional grounds, corvina cannot be their "traditional fish" because it is not a native species; it only started to spawn in this area quite recently. Martha Rodríguez of Sonora's Environment and Sustainability Development Commission (CEDES) argued that corvina did not start coming up into the zanjón until after the El Niño floods in the 1990s. She claims that there is no previous record of corvina migrating to the area (though Navarro Smith [2010] argue that there is indeed a historical record of this species' presence).

But according to Víctor Ortega, the director of the biosphere reserve, the primary reason the Cucapá's case was rejected was because their fishing techniques were considered both "unsustainable" and "unindigenous." He said: "If they fished with spears or bows and arrows it would be a different story. But the Cucapá fish with very large nets on *pangas*" (small boats with outboard motors). The issue was not with the equipment per se, for Cucapá fishers use boats and nets that are smaller than those used in many of the surrounding nonindigenous fishing communities. Yet Ortega believed that the fact they did not use canoes, for example, significantly undermined their claims to "indigenous fishing rights." He argued, "They don't just fish to feed their families. They sell the fish! It would be fine if they just fished to feed themselves as Indians did traditionally." Ortega was referring to the fact that the Cucapá fishers sell the fish in nearby cities such as Ensenada and Mexicali or to buyers who come to the village.

It may appear that Víctor Ortega was making an ecological argument against the environmental impact of Cucapá fishing in the reserve. This is, in fact, an argument that has often been used against Cucapá fishers. Article 49 of Mexico's general law of ecological balance and environmental protection states that in "nuclear zones" (the centers) of protected areas it is prohibited to exploit any species. However, it also specifies that limited exploitation of these zones is permitted as long as it does not affect the overall "ecosystem balance." There is ample scientific evidence that the Cucapá fishing cooperative's yields alone are not substantial enough to affect the ecological balance of the reserve. Several investigations carried out by the Universidad Nacional Autónoma de México and the Centro de Investigación y Estudios Superiores de Ensenada have shown that the Cucapá fishing cooperatives' yields account for less than 3 percent of the total extraction in the zone, with the rest of the extraction from nonindigenous fishing cooperatives (Alarcón-Cháires 2001). Indeed, when I pressed Ortega on this issue, he agreed that the issue was not the number of fish extracted (though this was clearly the legal matter from the environmental standpoint). He went on to say that it would be different if they were going to fish quite a bit and then salt the fish (he motioned to me at this point, "like the way they do in Canada with salmon") and eat it later—in the winter, for example. Ortega's concern was not environmental but social: he did not think Cucapá fishers qualified as having differential rights.

While Victor Ortega expresses a purist version of the discourse on indigenous people existing completely outside of capitalism, recent strains of environmental activism take as their point of departure that human beings are fundamentally economic creatures (West 2005; Zerner 2000). Organizations like Conservation International (CI) have implemented programs that attempt to incorporate indigenous people into economic markets through sustainable entrepreneurship and ecotourism projects (Bamford 2002). Many such projects have been initiated in this area, such as training guides to run boat tours of the river and developing projects with local *artesanas* (artists/craftspeople) to sell traditional crafts. Nonetheless, this more recent strain of conservation philosophy retains the fundamental ideology of indigenous people as resistant to global capitalism by specifying that their participation in the market is sustainable. It continues to exclude indigenous groups from participating in local economic markets.

The particular argument against the Cucapá fishers having differential fishing rights that Ortega expressed in my interview draws directly on recent environmental discourses, which portray indigenous people as resistant to, and existing outside, capitalism and as natural allies of conservationists. By this logic, evidence that indigenous people do not conform to given stereotypes also functions to disqualify them as properly "indigenous" and exclude them from the constitutional guarantees of their right to livelihood and to practice their customs (see also Cattelino 2008). This is not the way it is laid out in the Mexican constitution. Nowhere does it state that in order to receive differential rights indigenous people have to conform to expectations of being "natural conservationists" (see Conklin and Graham 1995; Krech 1999).[6] While this stipulation is not written in national law, it is powerfully underwritten by current global discourses on the environment and indigeneity. In fact, as many have argued, current discourses on ecopolitics that invoke a particular incarnation of the "noble savage" were born in the transnational environmental movement (Ramos 1994). Mainstream environmentalism constructs the threat to the environment in a way that prescribes the particular set role that certain actors, particularly indigenous people, should play (Bamford 2002; Braun 2002; Brosius 1997, 1999; Escobar 1996, 1999).

For example, Braun (2002) has analyzed how a discourse of indigeneity dovetailed with environmental politics on Canada's west coast in the 1980s and 1990s. He describes how the campaign to save the rainforest on Clayoquot Sound on Vancouver Island made First Nations people visible, but only by incorporating them within the terms of antimodern preservationist politics. This left the First Nations in British Columbia with limited options, since participating in the region's resource economies means they risk losing what many non-natives consider their authentic indigenous culture and, as a result, their right to speak for their lands as indigenous peoples in the first place.

The discourse of the ecologically noble savage has become so powerful that legal conflicts for the Cucapá have sometimes played out as if those stereotypes were legal terms of recognition. This particular notion of indigeneity has not always been a feature of environmental discourses. Until recently, environmental advocacy focused solely on protecting nonhuman aspects of ecosystems, and the presence of any type of people tended to be seen as an obstacle to environmental preservation (Hecht and Cockburn 1990: 27). As environmental philosophy shifted to emphasize "sustainable development" rather than strict preservation, an ecological rationale for defending indigenous people emerged. Conklin and Graham (1995: 698) examine how during the 1980s environmentalist NGOs began to promote local equity and the preservation of local cultures as a central component of development planning.[7] It was at this time that "Indians—formerly seen as irrelevant to economic development—now were championed as the holders of important keys to rational development" (Conklin and Graham 1995: 698). In this form the discourse of the ecologically noble savage has particular political appeal, as it allows for the assumption that native peoples' views of nature and ways of using natural resources are consistent with the goals of conservationists.

Perhaps precisely because of the global cachet of current environmental discourses, the Human Rights Commission's report, which recommends that the government support the Cucapá fishing cooperative's claims, appeals as much to ideas of indigenous sustainability as it does to legal frameworks. The commission's recommendation cites Article 2 of the Mexican constitution, which recognizes that Mexico is a pluricultural nation. It also cites the International Labour Organization (ILO) Convention No. 169 concerning Indigenous and Tribal Peoples in Independent Countries, which Mexico ratified in 1990.[8] This convention states the obligation of governments to recognize, protect, and respect the values and practices of indigenous people and, in particular, their spiritual and cultural relation to the land. After clearly stating PROFEPA's breach of national and international law in denying the Cucapá people rights to fish, however, the commission also reinforces stereotypes of their inherent environmental sustainability.

> The cosmology of the Cucapá finds its roots in relation to the river where they have lived since ancestral times, since forever [*ya que desde siempre*] the ecosystems of the Hardy and Colorado Rivers have permitted the conservation of this culture. The Cucapá are considered children of the river, their origin myth identifies them as born of water. This group considers whale, deer and rattlesnake as symbols of their lineage and totemic entities, with dances and songs that evoke different elements of nature, as if searching for a reciprocal communication with it. (Waisman, Lichtinguer, and Arroyo 2002)

After making the notably infantilizing reference to the Cucapá people as "children of the river," which resonates with colonial stereotypes, the report goes on to specify that they still speak their native language, even though that is not actually the case (Spanish is dominant). By making use of such romanticized and exaggerated portrayals, the report reinforces the confusion between constitutionally guaranteed rights and rights bestowed on the basis of adequate conformity to indigenous stereotypes.

The trope of "authenticity" is pervasive in this dispute, underpinning the multiple and sometimes competing discourses of indigenous rights, environmentalism, and neoliberalism. Anthropologists have problematized the notion of "authenticity," tracing its origin as a colonial folk category that emerged out of contact imperialism in the late eighteenth and nineteenth centuries (Graham 2002). Others have explored the way this concept has become a repository of anxieties around the perceived homogenizing effects of the spread of capitalism (Clifford 2001; Gupta 1998).

Nonetheless, it is important to emphasize that ideas about what constitutes an authentic identity are not just imposed by nonindigenous actors but are often contested within indigenous communities as well. For example, as we will see in chapter 5, many Cucapá youth, who are monolingual in Spanish, criticize the notion that what makes them indigenous is speaking Cucapá; instead, they connect their sense of identity to shared conditions of subordination. Members of the cooperative express the belief that what makes them "Cucapá" is a long-standing residency in the delta and a history of fishing on the river. Of course, these signifiers involve strategic essentialisms as well, but it is important to recognize that they are not the same essentialisms invoked by human rights officials, NGO workers, and government officials.

Ambivalent Alliances: "They Seem to Care More about the Fish Than the People"

Current environmental discourses constrain not only indigenous subjects but also a set of social relationships in which new alliances between environmentalists and indigenous people have formed. The ecological damage to the delta has brought about a series of unexpected alliances whereby Mexican and US environmental organizations and NGOs have supported the Cucapá through numerous ecotourism and community projects as well as various reforestation efforts. These projects were often seen by local people with suspicion, however, because they were advanced as alternatives to fishing rather than as supplements to it. In fact, Don Madaleno, the Cucapá chief, would often comment that environmentalists and officials "seem to care more about the fish than the people."

Despite this perception, it was clear that many environmentalists in the area were genuinely committed to improving the conditions of life for the Cucapá people in the region. There were dozens of initiatives to find sustainable local economic alternatives.

Interestingly, many of these initiatives resolved the issue of the human presence in the delta by moving one step beyond the idea of the local people as stewards and, in fact, conflating the Cucapá people with nature at risk of disappearing. The Cucapá have a place in environmental discourses, but only insofar as they are represented as yet one more endangered species that needs to be defended. For example, Charles Bergman's *Red Delta: Fighting for Life at the End of the Colorado River* (2002), which was copublished with the US-based NGO Defenders of Wildlife, devotes each chapter to a different endangered species in the delta. A chapter is dedicated to the flat-tailed horned lizard; another focuses on the nearly extinct Yuma clapper tail. Toward the end of the book, Bergman also includes a chapter about the Cucapá people, awkwardly entitled "We Are Not Yet Dead Still." Conservation narratives therefore make this population visible, but only by being incorporated within the terms of a preservationist politics.

When NGO workers and environmentalists were confronted with the reality of Cucapá fishing practices, however, they often responded like government environmental officials and agencies: they turned away from representing the Cucapá as part of the nature at risk or as keys to the amelioration of the environmental degradation and instead toward seeing them as responsible for it. The NGO workers were particularly astounded by what they interpreted as a lack of foresight. As one of them commented: "Don't they realize that fishing these fish while they are with their eggs and using these nets will mean lower yields in the future?" Some saw the Cucapá community as the cause of environmental degradation: dumping garbage in the desert near the Hardy River, illegally fishing in the reserve, using unsustainable fishing practices (e.g., huge nets to catch the baby fish).

Local nonindigenous Mexicans in the area were also quick to point to Cucapá fishing practices as a central problem for river management. One resident of the delta was particularly concerned about the number of smaller fish caught in the tightly spun fishing nets some would stretch across the river. He took it upon himself to save the fish in the area and spent part of the 1980s removing nets to free the baby fish. Eventually, he went to prison for some months on account of thieving these nets. However, many local Mexicans shared his concerns and supported the lengths he went to in defense of local river trout and bass. At every meeting of the committee for the management of the Colorado and Hardy Rivers, government officials and nonindigenous locals would raise the issue of the Cucapá fishers' unsustainable practices as a central problem that needed to be addressed.

"We Fish by the Moon, Not by the Tides"

Cucapá fishermen and -women are not complacent about these accusations. Although few conceded that their fishing was the cause of the environmental problems in the delta, some of them expressed concern that their fishing practices could be contributing to an environmentally unstable future. Most of them, however, were quick to point out that the necessity of feeding their children outweighed these considerations. For example, Cruz, the man in whose house I stayed during my fieldwork, explained: "In the end, my priority is to put food on the table. It's not our responsibility to manage the environmental damage caused by so much greed and overuse in the US."

Many of the Cucapá fishers I interviewed also identified the fallacy in the argument that their fishing would make a substantial impact. Fishing 3 percent of the total corvina extracted in the zanjón would not be the cause of lower yields in the future, and their fishing practices were certainly not to blame for the parched and arid state of the delta. At the time, Cucapá fishing cooperatives had approximately forty boats that fished the zanjón, in contrast to approximately a thousand boats that frequented the area from surrounding fishing communities, such as Santa Clara and San Felipe. Since the building of the dams in the United States, the water that has reached Mexico has barely been sufficient to sustain the border economy in cities such as Tijuana and Mexicali, much less the riverine species in the lower delta.

I was often struck by the amount of information Cucapá fisherpeople had at their disposal about fishing politics in the area. The longer I stayed, I realized that this was true not just of the most politically and highly vocal fishers. Some of the shyest people were also armed with an array of facts that supported their arguments for rights and exposed the injustice of government policies. One night, after a funeral in the neighboring Kiliwa community, I sat around a fire with some of the other guests. It was almost three in the morning, and I asked a shy Cucapá fishing man named Víctor who was sitting by the fire if he was planning to drive back the three hours in order to make the high tide in the zanjón the next morning. He said he was. "We have to fish while we still can," he said, and proceeded to launch into a discussion about the plans to impose a *veda* (prohibition) in May that would make it possible for officials to implement even more severe penalties for fishing on the grounds. Although I had never heard Víctor speak a single word in a public arena, he now began rehearsing the figures and facts with the same expertise as Adriana or the cooperative's lawyer.

Some Cucapá fishers argued directly against charges of their "unsustainability" by describing how their practices incorporated means to ensure the sustainability of their fishing but explaining that they were no longer able to implement them because of government restrictions. In the past, fishing cycles were timed by the moon. "The moon is our guide," Don Madeleno explained. "The waters follow the moon and so we follow the moon too." He also told me that when the moon is waning and waxing, the fish have left their eggs and it is safe to fish.

On the first day of the 2006 fishing season, Cruz, the father in the family with whom I stayed, took a freshly caught corvina and beckoned me behind the house to show me how to clean the skin, cut it open, and remove the innards to ready the fish for cooking. He maneuvered the huge fish with impressive dexterity and expertise. As he sliced the side of the fish, large pockets of white gelatinous material slipped out of its side. Cruz held up some of this substance on his knife for me to see more closely. "Eggs," he proclaimed. He then explained that the Environment and Natural Resources (SEMARNAT) personnel do not take the rhythms of the moon into account when they make the rules about when people can fish. Instead, they go strictly by the tides:

> SEMARNAT makes the rules about when we can fish. Meanwhile, they don't know anything about this place, or fishing. They'll tell us not to fish, supposedly because the fish are with eggs. Then, they'll tell us to fish when they have eggs and we all know that if we fish them then we'll kill many of the fish to come before they are even born.

Cruz said that they have to fish by these rules anyway. There are so many fewer fish in the river and so many fewer months when the fishing can be done that Cucapá fishers have to fish when they can and take any opportunity. Indeed, some families rely on the corvina fishing season, now only four months long, to support them for the entire year. But Cruz emphasized that government management techniques fail while also creating circumstances in which the Cucapá fishers' own management techniques cannot be implemented. Cruz explained that, ultimately, the Cucapá people prioritize feeding their children and making a living over managing the environmental damage resulting from excess and mismanagement upstream, or by badly planned local government policies.

Therefore, in the Colorado delta, the alliances formed between some Cucapá people and environmental organizations are precarious and uneven. The discourses that have helped to foster these alliances rely on an essentializing argument that assumes that saving plants and animals will necessarily alleviate the social problems experienced by indigenous peoples. This imaginary has contemporary political appeal, as it allows for the assumption that native peoples' view of nature and ways of using natural resources are consistent with the goals of Western conservationists. However, as scholars have recently pointed out (Brosius 1999; Chapin 2004; Conklin and Graham 1995), and as the Cucapá people's situation confirms, indigenous peoples often seek self-determination and control over their own resources—a goal that does not necessarily align with the goals of conservation NGOs, whose primary objective is to promote the preservation of natural resources. It is precisely such a disjunction of interests that has created ambivalence among environmental officials about how to situate the Cucapá people in the environmental crisis in the delta.

The reduction of indigenous identity to a natural instinct for preservation also occludes other kinds of potential ecopolitical alliances. The links between indigenous people and otherwise marginalized, poor, and disempowered populations have been made irrelevant by this discourse, even though these populations often suffer similar forms of environmental discrimination. Therefore, while it is useful to look at the unexpected alliances that have formed and broken down between groups, it is equally important to examine what kinds of potential alliances are obscured in the process.

Shifting Political Boundaries

Hegemony is not the disappearance or destruction of difference.
It is the construction of a collective will through difference.
It is the articulation of differences which do not disappear.
—HALL 1991: 58

As the 2006 fishing season approached and preparations for the season got under way, the tenor of the Cucapá's fishing cooperative meetings changed dramatically: fishing cooperatives shifted their attention from the long-standing conflict with the biosphere reserve to a new set of monitoring

FIGURE 2.1. Government official documents fishermen. Photo by author.

techniques that were being introduced. Meanwhile, the village had become a hive of activity as people prepared for the season: boats were painted, nets were mended, and fishing crews were negotiated. Environmental officials cruised through the Cucapá settlement, documenting equipment and verifying receipts. Boats and equipment were registered to individuals who were photographed with their gear and crew. Officials emphasized that permits could not be transferred and that boats could not be lent to others. They also explained that these new measures, by making the fishers more identifiable, were meant to help prevent people from illegally renting their permits.

Adriana, the president of the fishing cooperative, held a meeting to explain and discuss the changes. There was a larger turnout than at previous meetings because the subject was not just the politics of the fishing conflict; it was also about getting practicalities in order, getting permits signed and equipment borrowed. We all filed into the school. The teacher took the children out to play so fishers could use the classroom. Sitting around uncomfortably in miniature desks, the crowd shuffled government forms as Adriana began her announcements. She explained that as a result of the more elaborate monitoring system, this year it was important to fish with as few "Mexicans" as possible.

Adriana emphasized that because of the ongoing conflict, how they represented themselves as a community was important. She then set out a series of rules: they should try to avoid taking non-Cucapá people onto the boats or hiring them in their crews; permits should not be rented to Mexicans; if people were sick they should pass their permits on to other Cucapá fishers. From the government's perspective the cooperative's permits were based on their status as fisherman (not indigenous fisherman); but Adriana's cautions emphasized that unless they fished with all-Cucapá crews, it would undermine their claims that the cooperative should receive special access to the nuclear zone.

When she made these announcements, the meeting room burst into discontented chatter. Some shouted out to Adriana over the din of disquiet, "What about my boyfriend? Do I have to marry him?" and "What about my sister-in-law? She has always fished with us!" Those people were referring to the fact that intermarriage across ethnic lines with nonindigenous Mexicans is very common in the area. Some muttered among themselves: "Who's going to clean the fish? We're not going to!" A man in the crowd began accusing Adriana of hypocrisy. "Nobody takes Mexicans out there like you!" Adriana responded, "This is not what I want. It's what the authorities want." She tried to pacify the disgruntled crowd by explaining, "We are in a fight. They are going to say, 'They are reclaiming their rights and then just renting out to Mexicans.' They are not going to support that."

The raucous discussion that ensued revealed that there is generally a great deal of cooperation between Cucapá fishers and nonindigenous locals ("Mexicans"). Cucapá fishers tend to fish with a wider network of people because their families extend into these networks. People wanted to fish with their in-laws, neighbors, and friends and depended on this social network. Like the majority of indigenous communities in Mexico, this Cucapá village is largely made up of a mestizo population (people of mixed indigenous and Spanish background).

The backlash to Adriana's new stipulations also revealed a complex set of relationships of exploitation and cooperation between the Cucapá and Mexican fisherpeople. Some people explained that the reason so many

Mexicans fished with the Cucapá cooperative was that the former would get greater yields with the Cucapá than on their own because they did not have permits to fish near the nuclear zone. Sometimes members of the Cucapá fishing cooperative with permits but no equipment would form crews with Mexicans who have boats and nets, and the Cucapá fishers would take a smaller cut of the profit. Other Cucapá fishers who already had equipment said that their incentive for fishing with Mexicans is that it is almost impossible to find helpers who were also Cucapá (with the exception of children). Cucapá people who wanted to fish would be better off getting their own permit than working for a crew cleaning fish.

Many scholars have drawn attention to a tendency in studies of environmental struggles to assume a monolithic "state" in opposition to an undifferentiated "community" (Garduño 2003; Moore 1998). Environmental struggles do not just pit given "groups" against each other; rather, these struggles themselves shape the political boundaries of "the state" by constituting how social boundaries are drawn. In the case of the Colorado River fishing conflict, the tendency to reify the Cucapá "community" is equally apparent (see also Li 2007). The conflict with the Mexican government has shaped the way boundaries between groups have been drawn and understandings of what community membership means. Membership has been defined by the state to exclude the network of mestizo families and obscure the heterogeneous composition of the community. The paradox is that in the case of current legal proceedings with the biosphere reserve, the Cucapá people themselves are also excluded from full membership in their own ethnic group as measures of authenticity are imposed on them that ultimately disqualify them as sufficiently indigenous.

Charles Hale (2005) argues that this is the ultimate achievement of the neoliberal incarnation of multiculturalism: it has restructured the political arena by driving a wedge between claiming cultural rights and claiming control over the resources necessary for those rights to be realized. Under the banner of environmental conservation, and through the discourse of the "ecologically noble savage," state policies constrain indigenous subjects and shape the boundaries of communities. We can see this principle in action in the Cucapá fishing conflict: by encouraging multicultural policies instead of class-based political organizing, for instance, and by controlling the final judgment over what constitutes ethnic difference, government policies make it radically difficult for indigenous groups (much less others) to gain control over the resources at stake.

The implementation of a particular construction of difference resonates with Stuart Hall's comments in the epigraph for this section. As opposed to the homogenizing projects often associated with state treatments of indigenous peoples (Kearney 1991; Jackson and Warren 2005; Stephen 2002), the Mexican state has put difference to work in regulating the distribution of resources to indigenous populations. Asad has made a similar point, recognizing that "dominant power has worked best through differentiating and classifying practices. . . . Its ability to select (or construct) differences that serve its purposes has depended on its exploiting the dangers and opportunities contained in ambiguous situations" (Asad 1993: 17).

Failed Articulations

In this chapter I have argued that multiculturalism is fundamental to the project of neoliberalism in Mexico. Hale's term "neoliberal multiculturalism" (2005) is intended to signal this profound linkage between the two political projects. In the case of the Cucapá fishing conflict, this coupling has provided a rationale for downloading the responsibility of environmental management and sustainability onto the Cucapá people, who are among the main victims of the environmental crisis. This further reinforces the preferred mode of neoliberal development in the border region: factory work, temporary work on farms, or ecotourism projects remain as the only legal economic options available to them.

Carmen Martinez Novo's (2006) work on indigenous migrant farmworkers in San Quintín, Baja California, provides an interesting parallel to the Cucapá case by showing how ethnic categories are mobilized under a neoliberal era. She describes how in San Quintín, certain state institutions such as the National Indigenous Institute, the Department of Public Education, and the Department of Popular Culture encouraged day laborers to organize under ethnic banners. She argues that these ethnic labels created a justification to offer indigenous migrant workers lower wages and worse working conditions than mestizos (2006: 34). Martinez Novo documents how these organizations argued that indigenous people are used to living in cramped quarters, perceive child labor as an indigenous tradition, and do not trust conventional medicine. Thus their poor working conditions and lack of access to services were said to replicate "traditional ways of life" (see also Briggs and Briggs 2003). Likewise, the case of the Cucapá fishing cooperative shows how the implementation of a particular construction of difference can prevent the distribution of resources. Here the Mexican state has put difference to work in regulating and limiting the distribution of resources to indigenous populations.

The conflict between the Cucapá fishing cooperative and the Mexican government is an example of how contested notions of indigeneity are unevenly aligned with local, national, and transnational discourses and policies. Therefore, this case study offers a productive comparison to recent work in anthropology examining how expressions of indigenous identity have been linked to broader social movements.

Li (2000) and Clifford (2001) have suggested that the concept of "articulation" provides a framework for understanding how a collective identity and set of interests are rendered explicit and expressible and also how that identity is connected to specific political subject positions. Specifically, an analytic attention to articulation avoids the predicament of undermining political movements by reducing them to historical contingencies or strategic essentialisms (Li 2000). The framework is also one way to avoid debates over authenticity by shifting focus to the articulation of indigeneity.

The notion of "articulation" has been particularly useful for explaining how certain subject positions are taken up in ways that resonate with wider political and ideological trends and become intelligible in relation to them. That is, the concept is powerful at explaining where these articulations of indigeneity are politically successful. However, scholars who have examined articulations have noted that they have inherent risks: the different interests at play in any articulation always threaten to lead to its unraveling (Li 2000: 169). As Stuart Hall (1983) cautioned, this is a process "without guarantees." As I have shown in this chapter, candidates for indigenous rights who do not conform to the global environmental standards expected from them are particularly vulnerable to accusations of not being sufficiently "authentic" (Ramos 1994). In other words, as the Cucapá case shows, global and local interests are not always so easily aligned to create a common agenda (Braun 2002; Conklin 1997; Conklin and Graham 1995; Jackson and Warren 2005; West 2006).

Although one advantage of a focus on the politics of articulation is precisely that it allows for contingency (in that no identification is inevitable), this perspective nonetheless shifts the focus toward instances in which claims to indigeneity are recognized and granted. In this chapter, I have argued that it is important to look at situations in which articulations of an identity fail or are not entirely successful—as with the Cucapá, who have not been able to take up the spots that are ostensibly made available for them by the state and NGOs in relation to their fishing rights. Therefore, the pairing of neoliberal policies and discourses of multiculturalism has created political conditions in which ethnic difference is brought to the foreground as a way of denying rights. By radically constraining the conditions under which articulations are possible, neoliberal multiculturalism can prevent the distribution of resources by thwarting these articulations.

The increasing use of ideas about multiculturalism in neoliberal programs has been interpreted as one of the ways that neoliberal forms of governmentality "co-opt" or "colonize" liberal discourses on social justice (Hale 2005; Inoue 2007; Povinelli 2002; Sieder 2002). With these analyses in mind, it is important to point out that while a particular Western liberal critique may be co-opted, it is not necessarily the same critique that would be made by Cucapá fisherpeople. Not all Cucapá people agreed that they should have different rights to fish the zanjón in the first place. Those who felt that they should not have different rights argued that the nonindigenous population in the area faced similar problems surviving in the decreased economic opportunities of the delta; they did not believe that the fact that they had been fishing in the area for so much longer was reason enough to deny fishing rights to their neighbors. This was a particularly common opinion among Cucapá people who had married non-indigenous Mexicans and saw for themselves the kind of hardships that their in-laws faced in making a living. Perhaps they also saw the difficulties they would have fishing on their own without their in-laws' help. Others seemed to hold this opinion based on purely egalitarian grounds. Cruz, for example, believed strongly that Cucapá people were equal citizens of Mexico. He explained, "What bothers me about the people here is that they are always talking about us as if we are *contra* the Mexicans. But we are Mexicans too." For Cruz, this meant that Cucapá people should be given the same opportunities as local Mexicans, should be both treated with the same respect and subject to the same environmental restrictions.

Cruz was in fact the founder of the cooperative that is now led by Adriana, and when he was its president he let anyone join the cooperative, regardless of their ethnic identity. At the time they were fishing in the Laguna Salada, not just for corvina but also for shrimp, bass, and catfish.

Cruz reminisced that not everyone was happy with his open policy. Don Madeleno said he should exclude Mexicans so that there would be more shrimp for the Cucapá fishers. But Cruz knew that the Laguna Salada would dry up, as the rest of the Colorado River had, which meant that everyone should try to get shrimp in the lagoon before it was too late. Sure enough, the Laguna Salada dried up a few years later, and all the shrimp that had not been caught were wasted in the desert.

These internal disagreements resonate with recent controversies over the indigenous movement in anthropology. In his 2003 article "The Return of the Native," Adam Kuper questions the initial assumption in the indigenous rights movement that the descendants of the original inhabitants of a country should have privileged rights, or even exclusive rights, to natural resources. He argues that this ideology exploits the racist, European right-wing political philosophy that true citizenship is a matter of ties of blood and soil (Kuper 2003: 395; see also Cameron 2007). Suzman (2003), in a reply to Kuper's article, further articulates this critique by pointing out that people best placed to claim the privileges due to indigeneity—often those most fluent in reified, Western constructions of indigeneity and perhaps already in positions of power—are not necessarily those most in need of assistance. James Holston (2008) argues, furthermore, that differential citizenship ultimately works to legitimate the rights of elites to special treatment by approving the compensation of inequalities.

At their best, differential rights based on cultural difference attempt to redress past wrongs as well as present inequalities. And the Cucapá fighting for these rights argue articulately that it is unjust to treat different groups in different positions of power as if they are equal. In fact, most Cucapá fishers argue that they are not even treated as equals but rather are explicitly discriminated against, often singled out by officials for breaking the same laws as many Mexican fisherpeople. In 2005 Cucapá fishers only owned forty of the approximately one thousand boats that illegally fished the area, yet they were issued half of the total fines for fishing on the reserve (Solis 2005). Solis (2005), a local journalist, explained these disproportionate fines by suggesting that the government has concentrated on controlling the fishing of the Cucapá people because they have systematically fought the restrictions, while local nonindigenous Mexicans have been less vocal. Adriana and the other fishing cooperative members pointed out that nonindigenous fishing groups have fought the restrictions, citing several violent confrontations between the government and Mexican fishing cooper-

The Making and Unmaking of Indigenous Authenticity   81

FIGURE 2.2. "Fish for Sale." Photo by author.

atives. But Adriana and others also believe that the government has often informed the other communities when they are coming in to raid the fishing areas, in order to further single out the Cucapá cooperatives.

Other Cucapá fishers cite more qualitative evidence for the ways they are discriminated against by officials. Ana Lucía, a twenty-six-year-old Cucapá fisherwoman, was detained on the river when she was five months pregnant and fishing for corvina. The officials told her and her crew to get off the water. When she refused, explaining that she was Cucapá and these were their ancestral fishing grounds, they pointed their rifles at her belly and led her out at gunpoint. She says this experience has not made her scared to fish, but she emphasized that officials would have never treated a nonindigenous person with such cruelty.

In this case, the focus on indigeneity in the Cucapá fishing cooperative's legal battles may well have reinforced the discrimination that disadvantaged them as a group in the first place. While Cucapá are often indistinguishable to officials by appearance alone, the permits that have allotted them slightly different fishing rights make them instantly identifiable on the river, and their claims to differential rights have deepened the racism and prejudice they experience while only minimally improving their access to fishing.

As the local incarnation of discourses and policies on multiculturalism have begun to unravel and lose their strategic potency, however, we have also seen the potential for new alliances, such as links between the Cucapá cooperative and other disenfranchised fishing cooperatives that suffer similar forms of discrimination. Because the region is poor and fishing is a central source of income for surrounding communities as well, local residents, including nonindigenous fishermen, have protested as the biosphere reserve has tried to enforce the bans. Yet these alliances are currently rendered irrelevant by mainstream environmental discourses.

Meanwhile, as fishing restrictions and low yields have made it increasingly difficult to make a living by fishing alone, people are seeking other economic alternatives. In the following chapter, I describe how some have responded to the criminalization of their fishing practices by seeking more lucrative illegal subsistence activities.

CHAPTER 3

"WHAT ELSE CAN I DO WITH A BOAT AND NO NETS?"

Ideologies of Work and the Alternatives at Home

IT WAS LATE AUGUST. Six of us worked by the side of the river cutting tamarisk in a work project for the local river users' association. It was only 7 AM but already 100 degrees—the sun had been up for two hours. We were covered from head to toe in clothing to protect us from the sun's rays, and we were soaked with sweat. Some of us had large clippers; the rest had machetes. The task was to take down the massive overgrowth of tamarisks on the east side of the Hardy River, the tributary of the Colorado that still reaches the village. The tamarisk, or *pino salado* (salt cedar), is the invasive, water-sucking species that plagues the banks of the Colorado from Wyoming to Mexico. It is a thick shrubby tree that was introduced to the southwestern United States from Eurasia near the turn of the twentieth century. It is now a dominant plant in the Colorado basin, and in addition to pushing out other species, it can absorb up to three hundred gallons of water a day.

We were cutting around the few mesquite trees in the midst of the tamarisks' growth. At 11 AM, with a pounding headache from the sun, I retreated to the meager shade beside the association's truck. I could do this because I was a volunteer. The rest would be paid 100 pesos (about ten US dollars)[1] for eight hours of work. So they continued on for another three hours in the blazing sun, ripping out roots, thrashing down the thick bracket, hauling the refuse into piles, and finally setting it all on fire.

In one break, as the others joined me to crouch in the shade to drink water, Andrés, a twenty-year-old Cucapá man, described how he made his living. He worked odd jobs such as this one when they presented themselves; sometimes he worked piling stones, sometimes building roads through the sierra, and in the fishing season he was a helper for those who have permissions to fish outside the nuclear zone of the reserve in the Gulf of California. For a while the conversation turned to rumors of the massive wages that can be made in the United States. But with the minimum wage on the border of Mexico set to forty pesos a day (about four dollars), the tamarisk cut is not a bad day's work. Nonetheless, people in the area agree that Mexican wages are not fair and that it is very hard to find enough work to cover the mere cost of living in the border region, which is higher than elsewhere in Mexico.[2]

Several months later, Andrés pulled up to our house in a pickup. He stepped out of the truck in beige alligator boots, a wide belt with a metal buckle, and a cowboy hat: a restrained version of the classic *chero* style associated in the region with the narco-trafficker.[3] He came to sell, or in this case lend, a gram of cocaine to my nineteen-year-old friend Leticia, who had texted him on his new phone. He showed up only a half hour later. I was not surprised to learn of Andrés's career change from poorly paid odd jobs to selling drugs. I had seen my share of people move in and out of trafficking or "burrowing" and also the relentless and frustrating lack of other forms of viable work.

This chapter examines how some local families have responded to the state's criminalization of fishing, the primary subsistence activity, by participating in the lower segments of the regional drug economy. Lack of work is a predominant anxiety in the region. Unemployment in the delta is a result of the economic transformations that have taken place over the last few decades, both through extreme environmental changes on the Colorado River and through the rapid industrialization of the border since NAFTA and the rise of the maquila industry (which have displaced many jobs to the border cities). In this chapter, I analyze how a complex web of global forces related to free trade agreements, drug trade networks, industrialization, and water scarcity have created the pull of the drug trade as an economic alternative.

The drug trade is an undeniable fact of life in the US-Mexico border region. Indeed, the traces of the narco-economy are everywhere in the border region: in the gang violence in the border cities, the drug addiction in rural enclaves and colonias, the vibrant folklore popularized in the *narco-corridos* of norteño music and the icons of Jesús Malverde, the patron saint of narcotraficantes, tucked beneath people's shirts.[4]

Throughout this book I have taken precautions to maintain the anonymity of many individuals about whom I have written. However, avoiding individual incrimination does not sidestep the larger problem of portraying people in a negative light by describing illicit activities in the first place. This type of portrayal, as it is manifest in local stereotypes, is already having an impact on its residents. Their perceived involvement in the narco-economy has weakened local and NGO support for the Cucapá people in their legal conflict over fishing rights in the zanjón. Some officials and local Mexicans have claimed that Cucapá fishing cooperatives are only an elaborate cover-up for their drug-trafficking operations. Officials argued that granting the Cucapá fishing rights would be equivalent to granting them permission to traffic drugs. These accusations are a way for NGOs in the area to justify their desire not to be involved. The idea that any money they might make from economic projects or ecotourism will only be misused to support drug addictions is a common sentiment in local water users' association meetings and other contexts.

Precisely such local exaggerations can be countered by a closer ethnographic examination. For the most part, people both in and outside the community tend to overstate the extent and character of the involvement of local people in the drug economy. There are rampant accusations that certain people are involved in the "Mexican mafia" at a very high level. But through my observations and interviews I confirmed that people only have low-level affiliations with trafficking groups. The role available to them is that of the *burrero* or *pollero* ("mules" or low-wage transporters), jobs for which they are significantly exploited. And it is worth pointing out that the drug economy has locally emerged, in part, as a supplement to fishing. In other words, fishing is not emerging as a "cover" for drug trafficking; rather, the latter has emerged among local people as an economic alternative due to the growing restrictions on their fishing practices.

Nonetheless, the effect of the drug economy was not a subject I initially intended to pursue. During 2006, when I carried out the bulk of my fieldwork, nine journalists who were reporting stories about the drug trade and related violence were killed in northern Mexico. The new dominance of Mexican cartels has caused a dramatic spike in violence along the two-thousand-mile US-Mexico border, where rival cartels have come into increasing conflict with Mexican and US authorities. It was clear that the drug trade was a dangerous topic to pursue. But in thinking I could avoid the subject, I was underestimating how deeply the narco-economy affected the lives of people in this region. In the end, I scarcely had to ask:

people came to me with these stories anyway. And the sheer pervasiveness of the narco-economy's effects on the lives of my informants is one of the reasons their stories need to be told.

Beyond the village where I did my fieldwork, the Colorado delta stretches out in salt and mud flats where, often, the only other human beings to be seen for miles are military patrols on guard for drug traffickers. Trucks full of soldiers and armed lookouts are a recurrent aspect of the landscape and a constant reminder of the narco presence and the resulting militarization of the region. These conditions also permeate daily life in the region. As Cruz explained, the narco-economy in this region "has touched everyone somehow at sometime."

While the US borderlands is a region in which all are embedded in the narco-economy in some way, the impact of the narco-world on this particular community both takes on specific meanings and brings particular economic opportunities. The Cucapá have become a target labor force for the Mexican mafia for the same reasons that other border indigenous groups have: they are poor enough to take risks trafficking and are strategically located geographically en route to necessary trafficking corridors. Some people also have permits to navigate stretches of the upper river and as a result are in a strategic position to traffic goods as well. Several people also explained that they are better as mules than nonindigenous locals because, as indigenous people, they know the territory and have better navigational skills for traveling through the desert. They also claim that the narco-bosses specifically recruited them because the "indios" knew the best routes and were more resilient to the harsh climate.

In other words, local participation in the drug trade capitalizes on what is perceived to be indigenous peoples' innate "knowledge of the land." This reveals yet another contradictory ideological tenant about what constitutes "indigenous identity," particularly in a region in which the same people recruited by the cartels because, as they themselves put it, "we know the land" are denied indigenous status by the state because of their lack of "traditional" ethnic markers such as "indigenous" fishing techniques as we saw in the last chapter, (or speaking an indigenous language as we shall see in chapter 5). Many local people, in this regard, take advantage of the "indigenous slot" (Li 2000) that is offered to them by the cartels partly because this positioning is denied to them by the Mexican government.

The collusion of local indigenous people in the narco-economy is multidirectional and has also involved attempts by state agencies to recruit them in antismuggling operations. Just as smugglers have enlisted the tracking skills of Native Americans, or forced them into cooperation, an article in the *International Herald Tribune* (Archibold 2007) chronicles the growing appreciation of US federal employees for the tracking skill among the Tohono O'odham in both the United States and Mexico. The Shadow Wolves, for example, are a US federal law enforcement unit of Native American officers that has operated since the early 1970s on the indigenous land straddling the Mexican border. One man I interviewed described his work as a military guide for the Mexican government. He tracked smugglers through the Sierra on Cucapá land and claimed that others had also worked in this capacity, though no one else volunteered similar stories.

This participation by local people in the different factions of the "war on drugs" opens a window onto why some people refuse, or are refused, work in the formal economy. Most people feel that work in maquila factories on the border and in tourist camps belies the powerful ideology of self-sufficiency and family management created by the experience of organizing fishing practices around the nuclear family. This organizational arrangement lends itself to more illicit and independent economic activities, such as drug trafficking and smuggling. Furthermore, involvement in the narco-trade is seen by some as a form of resistance to the forms of domination imposed on them by the US and Mexican governments, albeit a multidimensional resistance shaped by internal group politics. Those who have taken this alternative have retained a sense of pride and defiance drawn from the cultural salience of the northern Mexican persona of the narcotraficante.

A Crystalline Landscape: Drugs and Everyday Life

Esperanza drew slowly on her filterless Delicado (a popular brand of cigarettes in Mexico) and shook her head back and forth. "*Muy cochino*" (very filthy), she said, referring to the general state of things in the village. She was sitting out in front of the one-room museum, which is located at the edge of the village facing the road that runs north to Mexicali and south to the Gulf of California. The museum she guards features an array of photographs and beadwork, but it is almost impossible to make out these artifacts in the dark, windowless room, which has no electricity.

Nonetheless, Esperanza sat in front of the building every day on a bench beneath the mesquite tree, beading chakira and waiting—in case someone arrives. From this vantage point, she watched everyone and everything that comes in and out of the village.

Every few days, I sat with Esperanza for several hours, recording her eloquently performed stories, gossiping, and learning Cucapá. Our conversations were punctuated by every vehicle that came and went. She lifted her head from her beads, interrupting her own stories at every vehicle or body that passed. If she did not know who it was, she asked, "Who's that?" and then she guessed. If I had not sat down with her the day before, she catalogued the unidentified vehicles, sometimes enlisting my help: "Do you know who would have come through in a red truck with a missing hubcap?" But most of the time Esperanza had already interpreted the purpose of these unidentified vehicles. "Look who just stopped in there with Daniela," she would say. "They are going to buy drugs, you know. *Pura drogas, puro drogadictos, andando cristalino*" ("All drugs, all drug addicts going around high on crystal meth").

One day, Esperanza slowly extracted a faded newspaper clipping from her bag. She looked around to make sure no one was watching and passed it to me. It was a 1998 article from *La Voz de la Frontera*, a Mexicali newspaper, with the following headline: "Soldiers Confiscate 1,250 Kilos of Marijuana." The article described how the military confronted three boats on the Gulf of California and arrested several men, two of whom, names underlined, are from the village. She told me that she had many more such clippings back at her house and shook her head again: "Muy cochino."

Esperanza is several years older than her brother, Don Madeleno. Over the course of their lifetimes, they have seen dramatic changes, but they narrate these transformations in distinctly different manners. While Don Madeleno understands these changes in relation to the end of the river and the abuses of the Mexican government, for Esperanza the trauma of these changes is manifest in the terrifying effects of drug addiction and trafficking. Esperanza fixates on the internal symptoms of marginalization and feels that the most serious problems facing the community are illegal activities and drug addiction.

Methamphetamine, a psychostimulant popularly known as "crystal meth," is the drug that has had the most visible effect on the local population. This can be partly accounted for by the recent surge in the drug's availability in this area. Mexican methamphetamine production has been increasing dramatically in the past few years since the US government "cracked down" on domestic US production. In 2006 US authorities estimated that 80 percent of the methamphetamine on US streets was controlled by Mexican drug traffickers, with most of the supply smuggled in from Mexico. This was largely due to the introduction of domestic regulations in the United States in 2005 which restricted the availability of the chemicals necessary for production (UNODC 2010). During my fieldwork, methamphetamine seizures at the US-Mexico border had jumped 50 percent from 2003 levels, from 4,030 to 6,063 pounds, and several meth labs in Mexicali were exposed after erupting in flames (Marosi 2006).

According to the *American Psychiatric Manual* (1994) methamphetamine acts as a dopamine and adrenergic reuptake inhibitor that causes euphoria and excitement. Users often become obsessed with performing repetitive tasks such as cleaning, hand washing, or assembling and disassembling objects. Withdrawal is characterized by depressionlike symptoms and often accompanied by anxiety and drug craving. But in reality the drug affects different people differently. This variability was a source of fascination to Thalia, the sixteen-year-old girl who lived next door to the house where I stayed. She could imitate a handful of family, neighbors, and friends smoking cristal. One day she tried to explain how the drug worked: "It's a high that hits you fast so you can see it take its effect almost immediately. It doesn't affect them all in the same way." She mimicked the sharp inhalation with fingers poised in the downward pinch of the light. Then she enacted the concentrated hold of smoke in the lungs and its euphoric release. She followed this demonstration by describing the various aftereffects. "Rosalina just sits staring into the space around her, she laughs too late, talks too slow. Chicho talks and talks too fast, too much. When Cruz gets high, he goes all night in a frenzy of activity; he'll take the broom and sweep the sand in the front of the house until dawn." She stood up and imitated his frenzied hypnotic movements and the vacant look in his expression.

The expertise with which Thalia performed her inventory of effects, to the nervous laughter of myself and her mother, is only one of the many marks of the narco-economy in people's everyday lives. Substance abuse is a symptom of deeper dynamics of social marginalization and alienation. It is a response to poverty and segregation that is experienced by major sectors of any vulnerable population experiencing rapid structural change in the context of political and ideological oppression (cf. Bourgois 2002). Drug addiction and use, however, is not the principal focus of this chapter. I am more concerned about telling a story of how the narco-economy itself has emerged as an economic alternative to factory work and other income-earning strategies in the formal economy.

Alternatives to Fishing

Dozens of government and nongovernmental initiatives have been set out in the area to mitigate the effects of environmental degradation and economic displacement. These involve temporary work projects, cultural initiatives, environmental management programs, and other forms of support for integration into the border economy. Yet while some Cucapá people have taken up jobs in factories, tourist camps, and projects with NGOs, most have not.

Mario Rivas, a representative from the Commission for Indigenous Development (CDI), put the problem as follows: "There are so many NGOs proposing projects, or involved in some way or other in the development of this group of Cucapá people, that there are practically enough for every family to have its own NGO. So how is it possible that with all this funding and interest, these NGOs can't manage to do anything to improve the basic quality of life in this place?" The question of why the economic alternatives that are proposed by dozens of NGOs in the area are often unsuccessful is not something I can fully answer. However, while these projects and the organizations themselves are extremely heterogeneous, one project in particular is helpful in providing a sense of the dynamic at work here.

In 2005, the Colorado River and Hardy River Water Users' Association, a nonprofit organization encompassing a variety of actors from different local sectors, helped the CDI implement a work project for local people. It involved hiring people to clear the garbage from the pueblo and nearby roads and riverbanks. Because there is no local facility for garbage disposal, residents often burn or dump their garbage beside or behind their houses. Abandoned rusted-out bedsprings, crippled car parts, old tires, broken appliances, and burnt-out air conditioners are highly visible landmarks. Officials and NGO workers who visit the place often cringe to see children playing in rubble. Furthermore, the prevalence of such waste and the impact on air quality from the garbage fumes is a common concern in meetings of the local water users' association.

Halfway through the project to collect the trash in the village, however, the officials from both of the organizations involved noticed that the contracted workers were not completing their tasks quickly enough to fulfill the contracts. Elena, a representative from the water users' association, told me that at a meeting for the project in Adriana's house, she explained to the workers that because of these delays they would only be paid half of the promised wages then and the rest after the project was finished. The workers were outraged. They surrounded Adriana's house and would not let Elena, or the official from CDI, leave until they were paid what they were initially promised. Elena was shaken by this experience and has tried to avoid going into the village since.

From the perspective of government officials and NGO workers, this was the kind of behavior that was "typical" of Cucapá people. "They won't even clean up their own garbage if they're paid to do it!" commented one member of the water users' association. The frustrations around these projects on the part of many NGO workers center around what they see as a general local apathy and a deeply divided community. Most NGOs negotiate with a handful of local residents—either Esperanza and her daughter Manuela or Esperanza's brother Don Madeleno and his wife. Projects begin by consulting this small group of people to obtain permission and contacts, and there is often very little interaction with other locals. Jorge, the field officer from the water users' association, was from a ranch very close to the village and was already well known by community members from the time when he was a *vaquero* (cowboy) in the area. But he felt that he really did not know anyone there. "They are too hard to get to know. There is little interest and so much suspicion."

Participants in these projects had quite a different perspective on why NGO work programs tended to be unsuccessful. As Cruz described in chapter 2, there were dozens of initiatives in the region, but very few of them ever materialized. The NGO project organizers come in with promise of work and grand ideas, he said, but somehow the bulk of the money never reaches the Cucapá people. While NGO workers and representatives from government agencies often attributed failed projects to the divisions among the Cucapá people, or to lack of interest and participation, people in the village attributed these failures to corruption in the government and in the NGOs themselves.

Many Cucapá people I talked to tended to view NGO projects and workers as a homogenous entity, much like how they themselves are homogenized by some NGO workers. Don Madeleno, for instance, expressed confusion on more than one occasion in regard to the links between NGOs, government agencies, and the officials of the environmental reserve who were in charge of enforcing fishing restrictions. The blurring of boundaries between the intentions of NGOs and those of the government was exacerbated by the kinds of projects that were routinely introduced in the area. The overriding focus of every initiative was to find "alternative" sources of income as a way of replacing wages lost in fishing. Yet this goal blatantly contradicted the political project that most people in the village were committed to in some form or other: to win back their rights to fish in their traditional grounds and, if necessary, to continue to fish in protest of restrictions. They wanted to fish, not to make crafts out of tamarisk or build ecotourism camps for "gringos" on the river, as some of the projects proposed.

The fact that many of these work projects fail and that many Cucapá people are not interested in participating is often used as evidence of their "laziness" and as a sign of their complicity in reproducing the conditions of poverty in which they live. As their stories will show, however, another more lucrative and prestigious economic alternative has sometimes quite literally come knocking on local doors.

From Factories to Smuggling Routes: Navigating the Border Economy

Since the 1993 creation of the biosphere reserve, increasing restrictions on fishing have significantly eroded their principal form of subsistence. Alvaro, a thirty-four-year-old man who has fished since he was six, explained that as the fishing season has shrunk to three or four months a year some people have tried to make the money last for the rest of the year because there is very little supplementary income. But the money does not last.

According to data from the National Indigenous Institute from 2002, the volume of fish caught annually by the Comunal de Producción Pesquera Cucapá (the fishing cooperative) is 7.8 tons per boat. Since the cooperative operates thirty-two boats, the total catch is 250 tons in the season. In economic terms, 250 tons at six thousand pesos per ton represents 1.5 million pesos. Divided by twelve months and thirty-two boats, this is 3,906.25 pesos, or about four hundred dollars per month per boat (split unevenly by a crew of three or four people). This estimate does not calculate the high cost of overhead. Gas for one fishing trip alone costs fifty dollars. According to statistics gathered in 2005, the annual income of the average family in this village is less than twenty thousand pesos, or two thousand dollars (the data is based on a sample of thirty-five families; Pronatura 2005).

These monthly wages are not sufficient to support a family, for it costs approximately four hundred dollars a month for food for a family of five. On average, families spend close to forty dollars a month on drinking water and water for other domestic uses and approximately twenty dollars on electricity. Alvaro explained to me that people try to supplement their income by working in construction, selling scrap metal, participating in the government work projects mentioned above, and participating in the narco-economy.

The proliferation of maquiladora factories in the US-Mexico border region has often been the proposed labor alternative to local fishing communities. Maquilas have become the prevalent organization of labor in Mexico among transnational corporations and consist of administrative and technical operations located in the United States (or in another home country) and assembly sites located in Mexico due to its inexpensive labor (Dwyer 1994). These corporations import duty-free parts to be assembled in Mexico and the finished product is re-exported to the United States. The maquiladora sector was originally created with government support in 1965 to stimulate investment, encourage industrial development at the border, and create jobs for unemployed Mexicans affected by the termination of the Bracero (guest worker) program. With the implementation of NAFTA in 1994 the sector grew markedly, with a 40 percent growth in Mexicali alone.

Mexicali, the capital of Baja California, is the closest urban center (an hour and a half drive) and typifies the kinds of cities that line the Mexican side of the border. It is a major urban border center with a population of close to a million and is characterized by significant poverty in colonias or slums, juxtaposed by visible wealth due to the dominant presence of the maquila industries and the drug trade. During the 1990s, when the factories were starting to proliferate, there were campaigns to recruit workers from ejidos and colonias outside the city of Mexicali. At the time, dozens of people from the Cucapá village signed on to work in these factories, especially women, who were specifically targeted by recruiters (Tiano 1994). When I conducted my fieldwork almost ten years later, only two women were still working in the maquilas: Brianda and Lupe, both single mothers with several children. They worked from 4 PM to 1 AM four days a week in a factory that made medical masks. Brianda told me she did not think the pay was good but she thought that it was, realistically, the best work she would be able to find.

When I interviewed people about their work histories, they often emphasized how demoralizing working conditions in tourist camps, farms, and factories were. A handful of tourist camps in the area cater to Mexican and American hunters and fishers during the holidays and weekends, generally consisting of campground facilities. Several Cucapá people work at these camps, sometimes as guides on hunting expeditions, but work in the tourist industry has become increasingly difficult to find, particularly because the importance of fishing and hunting has decreased as wildlife has become less abundant.

Manuela and Ana had both worked in the factories in the 1980s. Manuela worked in a factory that made technological parts for televisions. An eight-hour shift paid about eight dollars, which at the time seemed like a good wage (twice the minimum wage). But she found the working conditions unbearable. She mentioned the fifteen-minute break to eat, and not being allowed to talk to her neighbor or chew gum. She also emphasized the constant surveillance of the factory floor to enforce these rules and said that working there made her feel like "the most humiliated dog in the world."

Manuela explained that the majority of people from the village had stopped working at the factories or were fired because they were unable to tolerate these working conditions. These were jobs where they had little personal responsibility and had to follow strict rules under hostile Mexican or American supervisors. These accounts complement the literature on factory life in the border zone, which has also highlighted its harsh working environments, which include low wages, forced overtime, and illegal working conditions for minors (Contreras Montellano 2000; Iglesias Prieto 1997; Kopinak 1998; Seligson and Williams 1981). Interestingly, many people I interviewed criticized conditions in the factories, but by highlighting subjective notions of dignity rather than the poor wages or unsafe working conditions. As a result, work in the Mexicali factories is currently not seen as a viable economic alternative. Nonetheless, lack of work at the local level is often identified as a major problem.

The Drug Trade in the US-Mexico Borderlands

During my principal period of fieldwork for this book during 2005–2007, the escalation of drug-related violence and corruption in Mexico frequently featured in local and international news noting the "Colombianization" of Mexico (O'Neil 2007; Roig-Franzia and Forero 2007; Walden 2007). As Campbell (2009) points out, now Mexico has become more synonymous with drug war activities than Colombia. The US Drug Enforcement Agency (DEA) estimates that 90 percent of all narcotics smuggled into the United States now enter from Mexico (UNODC 2010). While Colombian cartels still control the majority of the production of cocaine and heroin, which is also the more profitable part of the trade, transport to the United States and distribution there has come under the control of various Mexican cartels. Overall, Mexican cartels generate $38 billion annually according to US government estimates (Wyler 2011).

Given their proximity to the United States, the borderlands of northern Mexico are a center for narco-activity, run primarily by cartels located in the border cities of Tijuana, Ciudad Juárez, and Nogales (Campbell 2009). The indigenous groups in this area, in particular, have been negatively affected by the escalation of the trafficking of narcotics and its production. Perramond (2004) has documented how some Rarámuri (known as Tarahumara in English) who inhabit the Sierra Madre Occidental range that runs between the states of Sonora and Chihuahua are involved in small-scale marijuana production and are often forced into production ventures by traffickers. There is a similar incidence of involvement among the Papago (or Tohono O'odham in the United States), whose tribal land stretches seventy-six miles along the US-Mexican border. Most of the illicit goods that pass over this land go through dry river channels packed on domesticated livestock or carried by migrant couriers. Cucapá land is similarly located in narco-routes: it stretches across the desert corridor between San Felipe and Mexicali, the principal throughway from the Gulf of California to the border.

While marijuana and methamphetamine are produced locally, cocaine shipments are flown into this area from Colombia. Then they are shipped into the United States by foot, boat, or private vehicles or in commercial trucks. There is a permanent military checkpoint at the junction with Ensenada Road, just north of the Gulf of California, which makes it difficult to cross the desert corridor by land vehicle alone. Planes are the other option traffickers rely on. They land in the white expanse of the Sonoran Desert, and from there they disembark and risk the rest heading north on Route 5 above the checkpoint. The winding roads that connect the sparsely populated settlements through this part of the desert are gouged with diagonal ditches to prevent easy landings. Traffickers also take the goods on boats up the river to avoid the security checkpoint and disembark upstream.

For locals in this region, smuggling has become an economic alternative that pays relatively good wages and allows people to maintain some dignity by making them feel they are in charge of their own operation. Hence the narco-economy presents an apparent alternative to the social marginalization that many experience, especially because it allows people to reproduce economic family networks and also often utilizes the very same equipment as fishing (such as boats and outboard motors). The appeal of work in the drug trade has also been enhanced by the growing popularity of the cultural persona of the narcotraficante (Edberg 2004a, 2004b).

The social salience of the narcotraficante indexes a historical border character recognizable in revolutionary heroes such as Pancho Villa, a popular lower-class military leader of the Mexican Revolution, as well as legendary outlaws such as Joaquín Murrieta, a bandit in Baja California and Sonora. The narcotraficante, like these historical figures, is ideologically located in a particular structure of poverty and social stratification defined, as Edberg argues (2004a), around a central set of tensions: United States versus Mexico, elite versus nonelite, and periphery versus center. In recent years, these antagonisms have intensified as the United States has tightened border restrictions and increasingly militarized their enforcement (Negron 2007).

Schneider and Schneider (2005), in their work on the Sicilian mafia, argue that there is an all too common tendency to criminalize entire populations believed to be engaged in illegal activities. To counter such stereotypes, they trace the contrasting values and practices associated with the mafia and antimafia forms among the Sicilian population. With this caution in mind, in the following sections I examine how narco-trafficking is an extremely contested activity in order to outline the differentiated forms in which people engage with the narco-economy. This requires exploring how the various ideologies of work shape involvement in the narco-economy and the agency it comes to express.

Ideologies of Work

I began tracing local ideologies of work in November 2005, only several months into my fieldwork, after an incident that took place when the village hosted a festival attended by the other Cucapá communities and other indigenous groups in Baja California and Sonora. Several hundred people came to the event and spent a day and night of eating, singing, and dancing. There were also a handful of municipal officials, journalists, and other media personalities. A local and fairly well-known radio show host named Osvel Law tracked me down and asked me to do an interview about my experiences doing research there.

Most of Osvel's questions focused on the Cucapá people's experiences having lost both the Colorado River and their fishing rights. But Osvel concluded the interview by suggesting that perhaps the problem that the Cucapá people were facing was not racism or environmental marginalization. "People say," he indicated cautiously, "that the Cucapá are simply lazy and would prefer not to work rather than to work. What is your opinion on this?" In response, I provided a classic anthropological critique of "the culture of poverty" explanation, which blames people's poverty on their own culture, a view that I had become quite accustomed to from my interactions with Mexican officials and nonindigenous neighbors. I said that people who said such things were simply wrong and were blaming the victims for a problem that was much larger than anything that the Cucapá people could control on their own.

The day after the interview aired, a few people who had listened to the show told me that they were pleased that I had drawn attention to many of the local problems. But there was one thing that several people thought I was simply wrong about. "How could you say that the people here aren't lazy? Look at this place!" When I pressed them to elaborate, they explained that many of their neighbors are lazy because when the maquiladora buses come through to take people to work graveyard shifts in the factories in Mexicali only a handful go, preferring instead to suffer in their own poverty or join in illegal activities. I tried to counter this by suggesting that maybe terrible working conditions and negligible wages, instead of laziness, were the reasons people do not go to work in the factories, on the farms, or in the tourist camps. I added that I certainly would not go. Then several pointed out that I was fairly lazy myself, since, as the daughter in the family where I stayed put it, I mostly "just sit around writing in a notebook and recording things."

This experience introduced me to the primary and opposing views on the problem of widespread unemployment in the village. These local discourses align roughly with classic scholarly debates around structure and agency by alternating between explanations that emphasize individual responsibility and those that stress the social structural constraints around access to work. Officials and some Cucapá people themselves take on a series of racialized responses to the resistance or failure of some Cucapá people to integrate themselves into the legal economy, describing the failure to "adapt" and get jobs in the border industries through an idiom of ingrained poverty, deprivation, and inherent "laziness." The competing discourse shared by many other Cucapá people is that the interlocking structural forces compounded by ethnic, economic, and environmental marginalization severely limit their options.

My own nascent interpretation of the poverty experienced, expressed in my radio interview, insisted that local participation in the drug economy needs to be contextualized within a history of hostile ethnic relations and structural economic dislocation (cf. Bourgois 2002). Many people I talked to, however, continually reminded me that their own responsibility needed equal attention. By drawing attention to the interface between structural oppression and individual action, I started to track the way these tensions were lived out and described by the individuals who shared their stories with me.

Structures of Agency and Cultures of Poverty

The relationship between structure and agency is a central conceptual debate in anthropology. In its simplest expression, it poses the question of whether social structures determine an individual's behavior or whether human agency creates these structures. Most contemporary theorists attempt to strike a balance between the two positions, and the most notable attempts at reconciling these views are designed to resolve or dissolve that opposition. The concept of "structuration" (Giddens 1986) and various articulations of practice theory (Bourdieu 1977a; de Certeau 1988; Hanks 1990; Ortner 1984) are attempts to move beyond the duality inherent in the structure/agency dilemma. By these accounts, practice creates struc-

FIGURE 3.1. Soldiers stop in the village for water. Photo by author.

tures and these structures shape agency. Yet many of these perspectives have invariably met the critique that they fail to transcend this dichotomy (Connell 1987; McElhinny 2003; Smith 1999), Bourdieu's notion of habitus has been especially susceptible to this critique because of its structuralist overtones (King 2000; Schatzki 1997). Thus, the difficulty of navigating the dilemma in a way that reduces it to neither a structure nor a practice has persisted.

Neither of the two classic approaches is particularly helpful in sorting through the way in which versions of these discourses might actually get taken up by the people whom we study. The tension between these views of social action is part of the way people understand the conflicted position in which they are located. My view is that it is important to examine ethnographically how people on the ground relate to both aspects of the dichotomy. Some, as I have noted, would argue that their predicament was a direct result of various forms of discrimination, whereas others would claim that the incidence of drug trafficking and poverty more generally was a self-inflicted reproduction of poverty. But it is important to point out that those most involved in the narco-economy tend to highlight their own agency in direct reference to the structural constraints that shaped it. They draw on the tension between structure and agency to highlight their illicit practices as forms of resistance. I also found that people would argue with me and each other over the character of their agency, constantly negotiating the quality of their subjectivity: that is, whether they were victims, *huevones* (lazy asses), or revolutionaries.

Lived Antinomies: Victims, Huevones, and Revolutionaries

Octavio, a man in his forties, argued that the "excuses" people gave for why they were involved in drugs were generally off the mark. Quoting many others I had spoken to and with whom I was generally sympathetic, I suggested that the prominence of narco-related activities could be accounted for by the lack of jobs in the region. Octavio responded as follows:

> There are ways to work in the region, but the narco-economy is easier. It's fast because we are on the border. There's a lot of work here. They say there is none but, pardon the expression, they're huevones [lazy asses]. You can make fifteen hundred dollars in one night transporting drugs. The minimum wage in this region is less than five dollars a day.

Octavio gave an economic rationale for why individuals choose to work in trafficking. His understanding of the reasons some people were drawn into working as drug mules or burreros was by no means the dominant local interpretation, but it was similar to the stories people told about how residents were responsible for their involvement in the narco-economy because there are always other options for legitimate work.

Manuela had a particularly developed version of this opinion. She felt that economically things had changed for the better since the Colorado River had ceased to reach them. She argued that daily life was much more difficult when they depended on the river for their subsistence. In contrast to the romanticized and idyllic invocations of the past by some Cucapá people, who say that there were so many fish in the river they would jump right into your boat and that ducks clouded the sky, Manuela remembered her childhood as an impoverished time when the prospect of finding food on the table was precariously tied to the whims of the river. Sometimes there were simply no fish to catch and they would eat bean tortillas day after day. She described how she would rummage through garbage in the tourist camps for scraps with her siblings. Now Manuela receives a small but steady government stipend for her mother and herself to keep the museum open. She believes that she has adapted to the new circumstances in a way that is ultimately better. Manuela also pointed to her sister, who is a nurse, as another example of someone who has successfully adapted. Manuela claims that the problem exists only for those people who are still trying to survive off a river that has disappeared.

Some people resented Manuela's attitude, as well as the government stipend, which they claimed allowed her to make such an egregious generalization. This line of reasoning particularly frustrated nineteen-year-old Isabella. Her own narration of her experience being lured into smuggling helps throw into relief the sense of limited options available to those in situations like her own.

Isabella would often come to me when she was in trouble. She was a beautiful young woman, ambitious and full of enthusiasm. She did not like living in the village; she had never fit in there and had few friends. She spent most of her time trying to find a way out. This involved a series of strategies to secure her own finances. She worked in a glass factory in Mexicali for a month but was eventually let go. Occasionally she would clean houses. During my time there, Isabella also had a more informal array of strategies to supplement her income.

At one time, she had two men simultaneously convinced that she was pregnant, and she demanded money from both for doctors' appointments or cell credit (so that she could keep in touch). There were plenty of times when this particular income earning strategy seemed to be on the verge of collapse: an actual pregnancy scare, for instance, or the possibility that one alleged father might have a revealing conversation with the other. When I suggested that it might be easier to just get regular work, Isabella explained that it was simply too difficult to find steady work.

> ISABELLA: They don't give you work because you don't have this or that, you don't have primary or secondary school. So people go to what's easier. Partially, it's for lack of education that they don't give us work.
> SM: Is there discrimination?
> ISABELLA: Yes. A lot. People don't accept what we are.
> SM: What are you?

ISABELLA: Cucapá! They know where we live. We have to submit credentials. People say we're rats, drug addicts, drunks. There are people who talk like this. That's the way they are. That's the way they were born and the way they'll die. When we used to go to secondary school on the bus to Durango, they would say to me, "*Qué india ratera. Qué pinche puta india. Los indios no valen nada* [What a rat of an Indian, what a damn Indian whore, the Indians are worthless]."

Isabella explained that it was bad enough for the men to find work, but for women it was almost impossible. "There is not as much work. There are more opportunities for men than for women to work. Here, women can only work in the factories."

So when Isabella came to me one evening in a panic, explaining that she desperately needed to talk about something, I assumed that perhaps she was actually pregnant—a scare she had had only several weeks before. But she said it was worse than the last. She begged me not to get mad at her before explaining that she had "a package" she had to take to Mexicali. They would come after her if she did not deliver it that same night. She had had it for a while and had been so scared. She had changed her mind and did not want to go through with it anymore.

She explained that the friends who offered her the job said they would pay her two hundred dollars for a simple delivery. She thought it was a lot of money at first, but now she thought it was not worth it. She was too scared and did not want to go. But she knew that the reality was that not going through with it was more dangerous than making the delivery. They were calling her cell phone and threatening her. They would come to the house if she did not take the package to them.

It occurred to me at this point that Isabella had come to me hoping that I would either convince her not to go through with the delivery or offer her a ride. I was disturbed that she had assumed my willingness to clandestinely provide her with pregnancy tests might indicate a similar willingness to smuggle out drugs. I was also angry that she was putting me in such an impossible situation. I could not help her, but from that point on I knew I would be complicit in any harm that might befall her.

So she planned to go to Mexicali that night with the man who was there to buy fish from her mother. He would be taking the fish into the city to sell later that night. We were waiting for the fish outside her uncle's house;

he would bring them from the zanjón. The plan was to put the package in with her sanitary napkins and ask him to drive slowly, so that they would be less likely to be pulled over. She started to calm down, confident in her new plan. I went back to the house as they waited to make their fish deal. Hours later, when Isabella returned from Mexicali, she said it was over—she had completed her task.

The next day she was on to the next thing: she had given the money she had earned to her mother. I could not get her to tell me more about the episode from the previous night; it was no longer interesting to her. Her mother, who had figured out what was happening, did not want to talk about it either. But several weeks later, when I started talking about how I was planning to write a chapter on the narco-economy in my book, Isabella took me aside and told me she wanted to record her story for my chapter too.

> ISABELLA: I've worked cleaning houses, crossing drugs, a lot of things. I had to cross [*cruzar*] drugs out of necessity. There are moments when you can't find money and you become desperate because you want to find money to help your family. And this moment arrived for me. I had to find work. I had to do something because I thought I had to support my home. And when they wouldn't give me work where I wanted it, I had to put myself to work in what I could.
>
> SM: Why? Was your family having problems?
>
> ISABELLA: Yes, lots of problems.
>
> SM: What kind?
>
> ISABELLA: My parents were leaving. My brother left the house, came back, had a baby. My sister too. Then my brother spent two months in jail.
>
> SM: How did you get this work?
>
> ISABELLA: I asked for it. For this, you have to be really serious and not say anything to anyone.
>
> SM: What did you have to do?
>
> ISABELLA: Nothing, just take the stuff and deliver it secretly and not be nervous. That's the first thing that you have to do, not get nervous.
>
> SM: When did you realize that it was dangerous?
>
> ISABELLA: For a child like me, not knowing what problems I was

getting into, at first it seemed easy to do, but when the days and months were passing, when you can't always get it in [to Mexicali], I started to feel scared.

SM: Why did you have it so long?

ISABELLA: You are left thinking, with whom can I go? Who will do me the favor? And you start thinking, Why am I doing this? Is it too dangerous? I could lose someone. I could lose my family.

Isabella's experiences underscore the tremendous pressure she was put under by her employers. At nineteen, she was vulnerable and particularly susceptible to their efforts to bring her on board, a point she emphasizes by referring to herself as "a child" (an emphasis she also made to justify her behavior).

Isabella explained that she accepted the risks and incentives of working as a burrera through an idiom of necessity and family obligation. Her awareness of her vulnerability placed her actions firmly within structures of gender and ethnic discrimination. Lack of education, discrimination, and an economy that provided few opportunities, especially for women, were the structural forces through which Isabella understood how "the moment arrived" for her when becoming a burrera was her only option.

It is important to note that in explaining her decision to work as a burrera she emphasized a series of circumstances which, while vaguely articulated, made it clear that she was not in control. These are structural constraints that ultimately led to her decision to "put herself to work." This seemed to suggest that it was actually *in spite of* the structural constraints that she took this work, not simply *as a result of* them.

In her study of women and the drug trade, Del Olmo (1990) finds that women's work tends to be marginalized even within the production and trade of illegal drugs. She also argues that women tend to be at greater risk of exposure because their work often takes place within the home, where the police are most likely to search. In this village, the gender division of labor that Del Olmo describes is less pronounced (which, as I explain in chapter 4, is arguably true for the division of labor more generally). Nonetheless, the figure of the narcotraficante often represents a form of male gendered power. Edburg points out that female narco-traffickers, who are increasingly featured in the northern Mexican folklore, fit into the formula of power achieved "outside the rules" as a form of rebellion against "traditional values" (2004a: 270; see also Campbell 2008; Mondaca Cota 2004). While this is true to a certain extent in this context, the cachet of the narcotraficante is still more accessible to men because of the machismo inherent to representations of violence in the region. Nonetheless, Isabella's narrative displays some of the triumphalism that is associated with the macho power of the narcotraficante.

This element of triumphalism is a noteworthy aspect of narco-trafficking's local appeal. For many of those involved, the drug trade represents an alternative to the exploitation and alienation they experienced in the legal market. While the economic rationale is, at least on appearance, an understandable draw, the risk, instability, and danger involved in this practice seem to far outweigh the benefits. Many people I interviewed were also extremely aware of these risks and underscored the vulnerability and instability generated by their position in the drug trade.

For example, after voicing his criticisms of people choosing to work in the narco-economy, Octavio qualified that he "was not a saint" and went on to describe his own involvement and eventual disenchantment working for the mafia after he was ripped off on one of his runs.

> I was supposed to make five thousand dollars on one day, but the bosses took most of it. The bosses don't do anything. They send an assistant [*ayudante*] who sends an assistant who sends an assistant. You never even meet the boss or see him, so he never gets caught. Only the assistants get caught. So I earned fifteen hundred dollars instead of making five thousand dollars. They told me five thousand dollars, then gave fifteen hundred. I had to cross and make the delivery to LA.

Octavio's frustration over the risk he took for ultimately insufficient compensation highlights the routine exploitation that the lower-level participants in the drug trade are subjected to. The opacity of the mafia's upper echelons to which Octavio also refers further limits their accountability.

Ana also relayed the incredible anxieties she experienced when her son was working with the mafia. She recalled the horror and misery she felt when Javier was in jail serving a sentence for trafficking up the river on his boat. She felt that the bosses had betrayed Javier by not only letting him take the fall for the operation but also failing to take care of him while he carried out his sentence.

Perramond (2004) has pointed out that trafficking in Mexico involves a large amount of specialization and separation of sectors. The largest and most powerful operators vertically integrate so that the wave of violence resulting from the current "war on drugs" hits the bottom of the industry. Thus the drug trade victimizes those people who are involved as much as the factory or the fishing restrictions victimize them.

The exploitation that characterizes this involvement in Mexico's drug trade complicates both Octavio's explanation based on "lazy" economic opportunism, as well as the "resistance" to structural oppression that Isabella describes. Neither of these explanations taken on their own fully accounts for the draw of the narco-economy. Javier's experiences trying to survive his prison sentence, Octavio's accounts of exploitation by his bosses, Isabella's terror at the threats from her suppliers, and Ana's agony in knowing her son was suffering in jail were only some of the experiences endured from filling the most vulnerable role in the narco-economy. In this light, participation in the narco-trafficking as mules is not an escape from subordination at all; rather, it is a particularly dangerous instantiation of broader relations of subordination.

Nonetheless, the narco-world is valorized despite the violence with which it is associated. The celebration of the drug trade is more understandable when contextualized within a larger cultural tradition and a history of antagonism on the border (Akers Chacón and Davis 2006; Bacon 2004; Dunn 1996; Heyman 1999; Pagán 2004). Work in the narco-economy is for many local people a resource for resisting oppressions by the Mexican and American governments in the border zone. This symbolic resource is best characterized by the persona of the narcotraficante.

"When I Wore My Alligator Boots": Dignity and Banditry in the Borderlands

America is the boss of Mexico in everything, except for drugs.
—ALVARO

The relationship between the role of the narcotraficante and the history of antagonism on the border is articulated in the *narco-corrido*, a genre of folk song extremely popular in northern Mexico and in the village where I did my fieldwork. These songs tell the history of men and women working in the drug business on the border. They narrate the adventures of clever smugglers, wealthy druglords, and clumsy border guards. Decades of profitable commerce and official protection, as well as the expansion of the drug market and the number of traffickers, are the background that inspired some *corrido norteño* composers to record the modern history of drug trafficking (Astorga 2005; Valenzuela Arce 2002).

The songs are popular among the large rural working-class populations on the border, although their popularity has extended to other parts of Latin America and the United States. Scholars of Mexican folklore trace the origins of the narco-corrido to the romance ballads brought over by Spanish soldiers during conquest. Paredes and Bauman (1993) have argued that the genre of early corridos developed in response to an emerging and racist body of Texas folklore portraying Mexicans as cruel, thieving, and racially degenerate. He argues that a large part of the narco-corrido audience is made up of rural people who are associated with poverty and "Indianness." Edberg (2004a, 2004b) adds that the narco-corrido portrays outlaw heroes in a stance against US power, represented by the predominantly US-owned and -operated maquiladora sector and increasingly by the presence of the American Immigration and Naturalization Service (INS), border patrols, and DEA agents along the border.

Corridos arose from a common and generally favorable disposition toward individuals who disregarded the imposed legalities of state power on the border. In this respect, smugglers, illegal immigrants, and outlaws have been represented by these popular images as an outgrowth of a shared social situation. Ramírez describes the relationship between the hero and the world around him or her as the "confrontation between the hero and hostile Anglo-American forces" (1990: 72). These are the social connotations from which much of the prestige of being a narco-trafficker emanates.

It was Javier's experience adjusting to life as a *former* narcotraficante that first drew my attention to the prestige and cultural capital associated with this role. Once out of jail, Javier began fishing for shrimp at a meager wage with his *cuñado* (brother-in-law) in San Felipe. This was a demoralizing transition for him because he felt it as a loss of prestige. Despite his return to the life of fisherman, Javier still had his alligator-skin boots. At various times, when he would wear them for a special occasion, he reiterated the importance of the alligator-skin boots for legitimating his past working with the mafia. He said that while you may see people dressed as cheros (from *ranchero*, with cowboy hats and wide metal belt buckles), the alligator-skin boots are how you know if they are really narcotraficantes. His boots cost more than two hundred dollars—and people in the area cannot purchase such things unless they are narcotraficantes. The dress, which references the classic rancher look, is one of the ways this persona indexes a rural past.

The chero dress reflects some of the dynamics in northern rural Mexico by portraying a tough survivor of the sierra. The association between ranchero dress and narco-trafficking was particularly strong during the time of my most intensive fieldwork (2005–2006); more recently it has faded out as narco-culture has become increasingly commercialized (see Muehlmann forthcoming). But it is important to note that historically the link between the narco-economy and the ranchero lifestyle in northern Mexico was more than stylistic. Bowden and Aguilar (1998) trace the links between narco-trafficking and its rural roots, arguing that NAFTA put many Mexican farmers out of business and that many turned to drug cultivation and trade as an alternative.

The associations of narcotraficantes with displaced rancheros, or the rural poor, in northern Mexico draw attention to some of the ways that drug trafficking intersects with a history of US domination on the border. Because the majority of the drugs consumed in the United States are smuggled through Mexico, this region is the main battleground of the US "war on drugs." In the illicit drug industry, most of the value of those drugs is added after they enter the United States, by some estimates up to 97 percent (Gaviria and Mejía 2011). The irony in this fact—that it is the US prohibition of drugs, rather than the Mexican supply of drugs, that creates economic opportunities for drug traffickers—is part of what makes the role of the narcotraficante a paradoxical and subversive site for confrontation with US dominance. Cruz, who had worked with the police force for several years in the 1980s, was particularly eloquent about the responsibility of the United States for the success of Mexico's drug economy.

> One day, I was talking to an American about how Clinton was pressuring Mexico to control the drugs—speaking badly of the Mexican police. I said to the American: "All the drugs that come from these places, from Colombia and Mexico, where are they going? Who is the biggest consumer of drugs? America. The drugs that these countries are producing aren't for their personal use. They're for the biggest consumer in the world: the United States." The voice of Clinton was throwing dirt at Mexico, saying that it's Mexico's fault that there are so many drugs in the US. I said to the American, he was "*echando caca* [talking shit] about Mexico, and who consumes these drugs? Your people."

Cruz went on to point out the irony in the fact that while Mexicans and Mexican businesses are otherwise unwelcome in the United States, the drug economy defies trade restrictions and immigration laws. "It's the number one economy for Mexico with the US. There are no other businesses. You can't sell fruit or sell other things across the border. You can't even cross the border. So they are going to sell drugs."

As Cruz's anecdote and Alvaro's comment at the beginning of this section indicate, the narco-economy is sometimes portrayed as an explicit, even nationalistic response to US power over Mexico. The history of US-Mexican relations has produced a marked antipathy toward the United States on the part of Mexicans. Paredes (2003) argues that this antipathy emerged with the annexation of two-fifths of the Mexican nation to the United States in 1848 and the repeated US economic and military incursions into Mexico since then, which undercut proclamations of respect for Mexican national sovereignty. The recent and escalating tensions on the border as a result of heightened security protocols by the US drug wars and economic displacements since NAFTA have only heightened the antagonism on the border (Andreas 2000; Juffer 2006; Payan 2006).

This local discourse against US power adds a particular complexity to local narratives of resistance through the narco-economy. The repressive forces that people experience on a daily level are linked to the Mexican state (fishing regulations, military outposts, and blockades). The most ubiquitous signs of state force in the region, however, are the US border patrol and DEA, and the most obvious association with exploitation and worker displacement are the US-owned maquiladoras. It is in this dimension, therefore, that the view of drug trafficking as a form of resistance to US domination blends with the view that this practice also challenges attempts by the Mexican government to regulate their lives.

The narcotraficante's heroic character and association with the rural poor is further indexed by the fact that Mexico's narco-world has a patron saint: Jesús Malverde. The legend of his adventures takes place at the beginning of the twentieth century in the state of Sinaloa. Malverde's adventures involved stealing from the rich and giving to the poor before he was finally put to death in 1909. In the capital of Sinaloa, Culiacan, there is now a chapel dedicated to Malverde, which also features a bust of the virgin of Guadalupe. Malverde has gained a huge following in the north, where he is thought to have powers to protect and bless workers growing marijuana and smuggling cocaine. He has since gained a considerable following in the United States and Colombia for similar reasons.

Significantly, Jesús Malverde is more than just a "narco-saint." He is recognized by many across Mexico and the United States as a protector of the poor, as "The Generous One" or "The Angel of the Poor." Indeed, Malverde's legend arose during the reign of Mexico's longest-running dictator, Porfirio Díaz (who ruled from 1876 to 1880 and from 1884 to 1911). This period, known as the Porfiriato, was characterized by the influx of foreigners, a time of advancement for the wealthy classes but of increased poverty and hardship for the lowest classes. It is not uncommon to see youth in the village where I did my fieldwork wearing pendants of Jesús Malverde, whom they claim protects them.

Edberg points out that in many respects the narcotraficante, as represented in narco-corridos, follows the pattern of "social banditry" described by Hobsbawm (1969). Hobsbawm argues that social bandits "are peasant outlaws whom the lord and the state regard as criminals, but who remain with, and are considered by their people as heroes, as champions, avengers, fighters for justice" (1969: 17). Like Hobsbawm's social bandit or "noble robber," the narco-trafficker starts from a personal experience of injustice that leads him or her to outlawry and the righting of wrongs.[5]

This trajectory from an experience of injustice is often traced in people's descriptions of how they entered the drug economy. In her interview above, Isabella was quite clear that it was because she was unfairly denied work in the legal economy that she found her own work. Alvaro was even more explicit in tracing his beginnings as a narco-trafficker to an experience of injustice. He explained that he began trafficking the year that officials from PROFEPA confiscated the equivalent of a thousand dollars' worth of nets when he was trying to fish for corvina. Alvaro recounted the exchange he had with officials that day in the zanjón. He said to them: "Who is going to support my family if you take away my nets? Are *you* going to support my family?" In this case, the turn to narco-trafficking was a response to the outrage of being denied the right to work, the capacity to feed one's family. "What else was I supposed to do with a boat and no nets?" he said. The suggestion that he could get a job in a factory or washing dishes in a tourist camp was equally infuriating for him. He explained that the wages would barely support his family. But there was more to it than that. These legal alternatives were what the government had been telling his family to do instead of fishing for years. This meant that, for him, a job in a tourist camp or a factory would be the ultimate surrender.

While Hobsbawm's social bandit helps highlight how the narcotraficante represents an oppositional resistance, this analytic lens also reduces this agency to a nascent politics conceptualized as a potential revolutionary impulse. By this view, Alvaro's and Isabella's agency is displaced onto the persona of the narcotraficante, which indexes the revolutionary heroes and critiques the encroachment of industrial capitalism. The problem with applying Hobsbawm's social bandit to the kind of resistance described by Alvaro, Isabella, and others is that it simplifies the structures of domination and subordination they experience as well as the kinds of resistance they give rise to.

In particular, this explanation fails to account for where this alleged revolutionary impulse falls short and for the contradictory way that forms of self-identified resistance come to reproduce, rather than subvert, systems of power. The romanticized role of the narcotraficante is more similar to cultural representations by marginalized people in other parts of the world, through which illegal practices are idealized in response to experiences of alienation: for instance, how youth gang leaders are mythologized in Kansas City (Fleisher 1998), how a young man's use of drugs in Philadelphia is seen as a redress of the humiliation experienced in the mainstream world (Anderson 1992), how selling crack and gaining respect are linked in Harlem (Bourgois 2002), or how in a Brazilian favela gangs offer a place of belonging and a sense of identity that low-paying jobs do not provide (Goldstein 2003).

The contribution of cultural performance theorists to debates over poverty, structure, and agency has been to show how through practices of opposition individuals sometimes augment the hegemonic structures that marginalize them in the first place (Bourgois 2002; Foley 1994; Willis 1981). Willis (1981) shows how working-class kids followed the shop-floor culture of their fathers, which glorified manual labor and proudly resisted the urban schools' ideals of bourgeois mentality. This counter–school culture simultaneously relegated "the lads" to school failure and ultimately to working-class jobs. Foley (1994) shows how Mexicano high school students in North Town, Texas, reproduce hierarchies of class and race by resisting the dominant Anglo-American rituals of capitalist consumption and communicative performance. Similarly, Bourgois (2002: 17) shows how street culture's resistance to social marginalization is the "contradictory key to its destructive impetus."

What these authors point out is that forms of resistance in these cases are ironically self-destructive because they ultimately reproduce the forms of hegemony that they purportedly challenge. In much the same way, those that end up trafficking drugs, while resisting the border industry, wind up just as exploited by working conditions in the drug economy. Yet this emphasis on "self-destructive" attitudes obscures the obvious fact that we began with: that forms of compliance to dominant systems of power also reproduce hegemonic structures. Thus the idea that the forms of resistance described in this body of scholarship are "self-destructive" implicitly assumes that forms of compliance are not and that upward mobility is a viable alternative. Arguing that resistance is the paradoxical mechanism that reproduces marginalization and rationalizes "self-destruction" implies that those who suffer from the economic marginalization and exploitation of the legal economy are somehow better off than those exploited by the illegal economy.

The suggestion that economic activities are "self"-destructive when subversive, as opposed to when compliant, also assumes that working in the legal economy does not involve expressions of agency and resistance. What is interesting about the narratives I have described here is that whether people worked in the legal or illegal economy, they tended to highlight their own agency. Manuela explained that her sister and herself had "adapted" to the new economic situations by not trying to continue living by the river that could no longer sustain them. Manuela, like Octavio, was critical of people's involvement in the narco-economy. They attributed involvement in trafficking to laziness, which is also a way of highlighting individual responsibility for involvement in illegal activities. As I have argued, the destruction, vulnerability, and exploitation that people experience is similar when they fish to when they work in factories or on farms. People's participation in both the legal and illegal border economies involves expressions of agency and resistance as well as modes of compliance.

The forms of resistance found among the narco-traffickers whom we have met in this chapter are more dynamic and multidimensional than they appear at first glance. Alvaro and Isabella, in their choices to become involved the narco-economy, are doing something more nuanced than opposing domination. As Ortner (1995: 177) argues in her review of ethnographies of resistance, we need to recognize that resistors are more than simply producing a *re*-action. Rather, "they have their own politics." Indeed, for some, work with the narcos appears to take its shape not just in relation to the oppressive American or Mexican presence but also in relation to the internal dynamics of the group.

This became clear on the day before the fishing season began in 2006, when officials came to implement a new set of monitoring techniques. As I described in chapter 2, the officials were clear that their intention with these regulations was to monitor who was fishing when and to dissuade the illegal renting of permits. Adriana, the president of the fishing cooperative and daughter of the traditional chief Don Madeleno, was equally clear in her meeting with the fishing cooperative that the official's intentions were actually to make it even more difficult for them to fish in general. Her approach was to have things run as smoothly as possible on the day that officials came to register the boats. Adriana, along with the more active members of the cooperative, had already decided that they would fish anyway, regardless of the measures put in place. She urged her cooperative to have their boats painted and their receipts ready to hand over.

Alvaro, on the other hand, understood the increased restrictions on fishing to be about controlling drug trafficking rather than about restricting the illegal renting of permits or the use of boats beyond fishing seasons and times. He explained that what these restrictions were *really* about was tightening their grip around the illegal drug trafficking in the zanjón. For him, the registering of equipment, numbering of boats, and inspections were all measures to control and undermine these activities.[6]

Alvaro and his brother Rafael, both longtime fishermen who had in the last several years started making illegal shipments with their boats, were clearly irritated by Adriana's approach. Rafael proceeded to paint on his boat not just his number, but also a lewd caricature of someone bending over and revealing his buttocks. At first I assumed their irreverence was directed at the officials, whose strict and thorough inspections were creating a palpable tension as they made their rounds from house to house. As Adriana closed in on the boat making her way from one busy crew to the next, however, it became clear that it was her reaction they were anticipating. When she ordered them to hide the painted figure behind a pile of fishing nets, they sheepishly obeyed.

In part, I think Alvaro and Rafael's insubordination to Adriana had to do with their sense that she was complicit with the officials. Despite the tremendous work Adriana did for the fishing cooperative, people outside her closest circle often voiced the opinion that she was using the system for her own recognition and personal well-being or to support her immediate

FIGURE 3.2. Preparing boat for registration. Photo by author.

family alone. Some said she did not really care about the rest of the village. There was a sense in which her literacy with forms of negotiation with the government, as well as the perceived benefits that followed, had the effect of distancing her from the rest of the group.

In fact, the resentment that people expressed toward Adriana was not unlike that expressed toward Manuela, the legal director of the museum (tended by her mother Esperanza), who had commented on how living conditions had improved since the river stopped reaching them. Some people pointed out that Manuela was critical of local involvement in the narco-economy because, with her government stipend, she could literally afford to be disapproving. It is noteworthy that those people who were most critical of the narco-economy were also most fully integrated in the legal economy (with the exception of Octavio, who also admitted to crossing drugs at one point in his youth).

Manuela, like Adriana, was well versed in methods of interaction with the government. She knew how to write a grant proposal to procure funds for art projects or to go to indigenous gatherings; she was a liaison with

NGOs who worked in the region and knew how to make a formal complaint to the Human Rights Commission. These characteristics were one of the ways that internal differentiation was manifest in the village. While this differentiation is not always visible to outsiders, it can reveal the social configurations within which people are acting and the different perspectives from which they understand their social and economic situation as a group.

What was most interesting about the differing perspectives on the fishing inspections was that each version seemed to identify what the *real* threat to the government was. Adriana and her followers insisted that their form of protest was always to fish anyway, to fish forever. Alvaro and Isabella, by contrast, took a more ironic stance. For instance, when Alvaro said, "What else can I do with a boat and no nets?" he was not making a literal statement about his powerlessness; rather, he was describing his own refusal to comply. Similarly, Isabella emphasized that her foray into smuggling was how she ultimately *put herself* to work. Both seem to slyly point to the complicity that either their employers or the government officials had in the illegal activities with which they involved themselves. Furthermore, what Alvaro seemed to be arguing, in a statement that could be read as a threat, was that if they were not allowed to fish they would do the one thing that the government considered even worse than fishing—indeed, what both the Mexican and US governments had declared war against: drug trafficking.

On the surface, it appears that the people who participated in the illegal economy were the ones who highlighted the structural aspects of their entrance to the narco-economy. Isabella talked about the racism that indigenous people experience when trying to get legal work and about the lack of opportunities for women. Alvaro linked his entrance into the narco-economy with the crackdown on fishing restrictions. But on closer examination it is evident that they did not highlight structural determinants in order to obscure their own responsibility as individuals or to absolve themselves of the illegality of their acts. To the contrary, both Alvaro and Isabella described the wider economic changes and history of racism to underscore their own agency despite these wider forces. Thus it is precisely the tension between discourses focusing on the structural determinants of the rise of the narco-economy and those focusing on the agency of individuals that allows for Alvaro, Isabella, and others to articulate their own resistance to the cycles of subordination and marginaliza-

FIGURE 3.3. Discarded sign in front of the museum. Photo by author.

tion through which they navigate, on a daily basis, in order to survive in the changing economic and ecological conditions of the Colorado delta.

In contrast to the previous chapter, which explored the local meanings and transnational contestations around fishing rights, this chapter provides a useful comparison in regard to how identities are constituted through struggles over natural resources. As we have seen, some Cucapá people have specifically rejected the activist mode of identification that views fishing as constitutive of their culture and have instead become more integrated in the lower echelons of the regional narco-trafficking networks.

Therefore, while the Cucapá claims as "an indigenous fishing people" were not taken up by the state, many local people have been able to connect and "articulate" their identities with the narco-economy. On the one hand, this articulation mobilizes a specifically indigenous position, as they have been able to take up the spots made available to them by the cartels as "Indians who know the land." This "indigenous slot" is very different from the ones that scholars have so far chronicled and that was made available in the context of the local cooperative's claims for indigenous fishing rights. Specifically, their role in the drug trade does not rely on a romantic assumption that indigenous knowledge about the land invariably translates into knowledge that is more sustainable or into "kinder and gentler ways of behaving towards the natural world" (Krech 2005: 82).

While the Cucapá's fishing activities have been restricted (and, indeed, criminalized) in their own territory by state actors, the narco-economy has recognized the boundaries of the Cucapá territory as well as the specific skills that a long-term occupation of this territory has fostered. But as I have argued, the significance that narco-involvement has for local actors is not just shaped by the traces of colonial encounter. Beyond expressing a particular connection to the land, work in the narco-economy also engenders a position against US domination of the region that fuses with a specific form of Mexican nationalism, one that is extremely poignant in the social landscape of the US-Mexico border. Furthermore, I have argued that the narco-world creates possibilities of articulation that are not simply a conjunction between local and state and transnational actors. It is also shaped by the internal dynamics of the group and by more intimate contestations over what it means to be Cucapá. In the next chapter I will continue to explore how more local contestations over the expression of a specific Cucapá identity play out on another categorical expression of difference by analyzing how ideologies of gender connect with water scarcity, the fishing conflict, and the struggle for subsistence in the delta.

CHAPTER 4

MEXICAN MACHISMO
AND A WOMAN'S WORTH

"ARE WE MEXICANS?" Cruz asked. "No, we're Indians," Ana said firmly. "We're Cucapá." It was at this point in the conversation that I started listening from the sleeping area late one night. Ana and Cruz, the mother and father in the house where I was staying, had just returned from Mexicali, where they had been visiting Cruz's mother in the hospital.

At first I thought Cruz was joking with his question about whether they were Mexicans,[1] or that he was really drunk or high and that was why he was not making sense. But as I listened to the conversation through the plywood wall separating us, I slowly began to understand what was happening. "This is your son," Ana said, referring to Javier, who was asleep on the couch. "And you have two daughters and twelve brothers and sisters." The conversation continued in this unusual manner, with Ana explaining to Cruz what should be obvious to him. It seemed that Cruz could not remember anything. Ana and Cruz talked late into the night, and eventually I drifted back to sleep.

I was hesitant to leave the sleeping area the next morning. I could hear that Cruz's sister had just arrived, and he was apologetically explaining that he did not recognize her. Her two-year-old son was pushing the door open to the room where I was sleeping, so I could not hide any longer. I came out of the room slowly, careful to focus on Cruz's nephew because I wanted to delay meeting Cruz's eyes. A *gringa* suddenly emerging from his own home could only confuse him more. I could immediately tell when I looked at him and said "Buenos días, Cruz," as I always did, that he did not recognize me. Ana motioned me to the table and mechanically passed me a cup of hot water. I distracted myself by carefully stirring instant coffee into the water, concentrating on the crystals dissolving into a dark swirl. Meanwhile, Ana explained what was going on: after leaving the hospital the night before, Cruz had broken down crying, and after he recovered his composure he could not remember anything: his name, who Ana was, or where they were going. Nothing. Cruz interjected that he had found my contact card in his wallet and Ana had explained that I was staying with them. Several minutes later, Berenice, Cruz and Ana's daughter, emerged from the sleeping room as well: another round of introductions.

In chapter 2, I explored the way that a particular notion of indigeneity is often imposed on local people by the state, NGOs, and international organizations. However, these categories are also authenticated, contested, and imposed at a much more local level in complex ways. In addition to negotiating the terms of authenticity imposed on them, locals also engage in contentious debate over what constitutes Cucapá identity. This chapter explores how these more "internal" struggles over Cucapá identity are established and contested, especially in connection to gender relations.

In this chapter, I focus on a particular Cucapá view of gender that is often articulated in opposition to Mexican machismo. My analysis begins with an ethnographic account of Cruz's illness that developed after his wife, Ana, left him for a local nonindigenous man, "a Mexican," leaving a wake of gossip, ultimately about gender and family, in her path. I argue that the narratives that emerged around Cruz's episode illustrate how gender roles are locally produced and contested.

As the indigenous rights movement has gained more ground in Mexico, especially since the Zapatista uprising in 1994, a tension has emerged in the perceived incompatibility of indigenous autonomy and women's rights among indigenous people. In many cases such rights for women were contrary to the traditional male-centered practices of indigenous communities. This tension often made demands for indigenous self-government and for recognition of indigenous women's rights mutually exclusive.

Cucapá women's leadership is a particularly striking counterexample to the stereotype of the subjugated indigenous woman in Mexico. In contrast to other indigenous groups in Mexico, some of which have been accused of making claims for the political autonomy of a people whose culture doesn't recognize "women's rights" (Hernández Castillo 1998), the Cucapá's claims to indigenous autonomy in the fishing conflict are primarily voiced by women and underwritten by a powerful discourse on women's contemporary and traditional superiority to men according to Cucapá custom. For example, women play the predominant leadership roles on almost every level of political organization. Women hold the majority of fishing permits, are more politically active, and are far more vocal in meetings. In fact, it was not unusual to find men standing along walls holding children and babies as their wives participated in public debate. Among many people I talked to, these characteristics and others we shall explore are construed as evidence of women's power and value. As Don Madaleno explained to me, "In this culture women are more intelligent than men. They are more valuable."

Therefore, gender is an important ideological terrain on which Cucapá identity is negotiated. The local expression of a specific Cucapá identity around gender is framed in opposition, not just to gender stereotypes of indigenous women in Mexico, but specifically to gender stereotypes of Mexican identities, which are famously evoked by the figure of the macho male. Local gender ideologies are nonetheless rife with contradictions. As a result, making sense of how gender roles were articulated in relation to Cucapá identities, the fishing conflict, and subsistence practices was one of the most challenging aspects of social life I analyzed. Unlike the kinds of inconsistencies that arise with people's sense of their indigeneity, people often talk about gender dynamics in ways that explicitly contradict each other. It is tempting to avoid analyzing ethnographic material that presents inconsistencies, or alternatively to try to smooth out incoherence and contradiction by finding an analytic narrative that is encompassing. As I will argue here, however, the contradictions that emerge in relation to local gender ideologies reflect social change and the tensions created by lived experience in this region.

In the following pages, I explore this gender dynamic by tracing two interlocking contradictions that emerged during my fieldwork. Starting with an analysis of Cruz's adamant insistence that he had lost his memory, against his family and neighbors' own interpretations about his condition, I follow the conflicting historical narratives on the establishment of women's primacy in the social and political sphere. I explore the dynamic of Cucapá women's political roles and the way the ideology of gender that emerges from these processes forms the basis for a wider cultural identification and symbolic resource.

Cruz Forgets? One Man's Amnesia as a Case of "Mexicanization"

Cruz kept flipping through the photo album I gave the family for Christmas. He did not recognize his pregnant daughter, Ruby, in the pictures.

She had gone to Mexicali with them the night before and stayed to take care of her sick mother-in-law. I had taken photos of her displaying her seven-month-large belly for the camera. He also did not recognize his friends, the house, the baby photos. He just kept flipping through the pages over and over again.

The news of Cruz's condition slowly reached other parts of the village. I walked with Berenice, who was in shock, to the homes of his brothers and sisters to ask them to come to the house. One by one they filed into the house. Cruz kept asking, "Who are you?" and Ana kept explaining. His sister sat outside the house crying for a long time. He did not remember her. Meanwhile, Ana, who was living with her new partner, Juan, in a nearby settlement, was paralyzed by Cruz's episode. She had gone with Cruz to visit his mother in the hospital the day before and had yet to return to Juan's house since then. She said she was afraid to leave him again in such a strange psychological state. She had never seen him like this before.

I drove Cruz to the doctor later that day. Ana and Javier came as well. We were all quiet, except for Cruz. "It's so beautiful here!" he repeated as we drove past the Sierra Cucapá and through the ranches and desert on the way to Ejido Durango. Later on the drive, he pointed to my wrist. "That's a nice bracelet," he said. "Thanks," I said. "You gave it to me for Christmas." He did not remember. Ana defused the awkward moment that followed by correcting my Spanish (I used the verb *dar* for "to give" instead of *regalar*, "to give a gift"). As we drove along this road, the only road that leads from the village, people driving by honked at us as they always did. Cruz waved back, confused, but happy to discover he had so many friends.

When we arrived at the doctor's office and explained the situation, the receptionist took out an empty chart and started asking questions. "What's your full name? How old are you?" She kept directing these questions to Cruz after we had just explained that he did not remember anything. "I don't know," he kept saying. Finally we sat down and let Ana answer the rest of the questions.

A week after Cruz fell ill, I ran into his *comadre*,[2] Gina, at a gas station on the way into Mexicali. Gina lived there and, along with her husband, had been friends with Ana and Cruz for twenty years. "You're so naive, Shaylih," Gina laughed, after I presented my account of Cruz's amnesia and the events that had transpired since her last visit. "He's just playing with you. It's not real. He's manipulating everyone." Her reaction fell in line with what I had been hearing from other people. After several days of utter confusion, friends and neighbors had settled into agreement about what was going on with Cruz. His condition was a mental block; he was so overwhelmed by the shame of his wife's recent betrayal and her abandonment of him, in addition to the myriad other problems in his life, that he did not *want* to remember who he was—or who anyone else was, for that matter. While his illness displayed all the symptoms of what would be diagnosed as general amnesia in a biomedical model, his family and neighbors understood it as an inability to come to terms with his wife's independence: her freedom to forge her own destiny and choose whether to stay with her husband or leave him for a new life. His illness was interpreted as a sign of Mexicanization: a lapse into machismo.

In much the way I had been trying to defend his account over the previous few days, I insisted to Gina that Cruz was not feigning his condition. I explained that I had taken a course in cognitive psychology in school and that Cruz was displaying the exact symptoms of general amnesia. The doctor in Durango had even explained that the recent stress in his life as a result of the divorce, coupled with the sudden illness of his mother, had created the classic conditions that could produce a case of amnesia. Furthermore, in the days that followed his selective memory loss followed a textbook pattern. He remembered general information but had forgotten most of his personal history. In fact, he kept remarking at how strange it was that he was able to speak Cucapá, Spanish, and some English; that he knew that GMC stood for "General Motors Company"; that he knew the words of the songs on the radio but could not recognize his own children.

Gina continued unswayed by my interpretation, "Listen, Shaylih, you have your books and everything you've learned in school, but I have my experience, and I know Cruz. This is not a medical issue. It's like a tradition, it's a different culture. Men are different here, they're not like men in Canada. They're *machistas*." By calling Cruz a "machista" (commonly translated to "macho man"), Gina was invoking one of the most widely known cultural types associated with Mexico. Gutmann (1997a), in his portrait of the working-class men in Mexico City, traces the stereotype of the macho man and how it has become ubiquitously linked to a "typically Mexican" macho. He argues that the Mexican man in this stereotype is represented as the undifferentiated category of the lower-class hard-drinking sexist (see also Limón 1994).

Gina's invocation of "machismo" reminded me of Cruz's response when Ana first left the house and moved in with Juan over a month before the onset of his "illness." Cruz spent days vacillating between states of anger and drunkenness, and then more days scarcely present in the daily household routine (when the family assumed that he was off high on cristal). When he finally calmed down, he came back to the house and went through a period in which he seemed to be performing just how *cool* he was with the situation. He sat at the table with his sombrero tipped over his sunglasses, languidly dangling unlit cigarettes from his mouth. He changed his outfits often, testing different-colored sombreros against his headband of traditional chakira beadwork and long black trench coat. I took pictures, surely only fueling his elaborately self-absorbed displays.

Nonetheless, Cruz's attitude seemed to improve quickly. "I'm not angry at anyone. It's not anyone's fault," he said when supportive friends and neighbors would drop chastising comments about Ana's departure. Then he would launch into a speech, directed at me, about how Mexican men are machos. "They run around on their women, but when a woman does the same to them, they can't handle it. They snap." This idea had become a standard in Cruz's repertoire. "Cucapá men are not like that. I'm not like that. I don't blame Ana. I want her to be happy, but I'm not convinced that Juan will take care of her."

His self-reflection on the situation negotiated a tension between portraying himself as a man who respected his partner's freedom and independence (the way a Cucapá man *should*) and a more paternalistic attitude that seemed to question Ana's ability to use her freedom to choose a path for herself wisely. Over and over again, Cruz emphasized both her right to do as she pleased and her incapacity to know what the right decision for herself would be.

Cruz's separation from Ana became a springboard for a general reflection on their twenty-four-year relationship. Sometimes he would delve into elaborate, romanticized accounts of how he and Ana first became a couple, how she fell in love with him despite the disapproval of her family. He reminisced about how he built her a house that was the envy of all the neighbors because it was one of the first with cement rather than dirt floors. At other times, he would turn to more negative portrayals of their time together and emphasize that she dominated him and that he suffered physical abuse at her hands. "There is a reason you won't find any baseball bats in this house." This was the line he would use to open the story of the night Ana beat him with a bat and left him lying naked on the front stoop overnight. "I never hit Ana," he would repeat, to highlight the contrast between himself and Ana's violent character. "I'm not like a Mexican man. She doesn't know how men are. All she knows is me."

It was as if Cruz's narrations of the differences between the way a Cucapá and Mexican man would behave in his situation foreshadowed his friends' and family's future interpretation of the way he was, in fact, behaving. In effect, the local interpretation was that Cruz's illness was an expression of the structural maladjustment of being a macho man in a culture where a woman could do as she wished.

"We Believe That Women Are Worth More Than Men"

The extent to which Cucapá women engage in activities that elsewhere in Mexico are more conventionally considered to be men's is often overlooked by NGOs attempting to incorporate local people into their projects. This became particularly evident in a meeting with the local Water Users' Association in February 2006 to discuss a problem that had developed with the tamarisk removal project, which aimed to remove the overgrowth of tamarisk (*pino salado*), a water-sucking plant, from the Hardy River in order to foster habitat for other species of plants. The project depended on the labor of Cucapá men, but because the fishing season was now in full swing no one from the village could be convinced to participate, for this would involve taking a significantly lower wage.

After this shortfall in labor had been described in detail, a woman from the United States working as a volunteer stood up and suggested that if the men were off fishing, the Water Users' Association should instead hire Cucapá women and children to work on the project. The volunteer went on to say it was ridiculous to assume that only men would be interested or capable of working on the project. She described a similar project she worked on with a native reservation in Canada where the female population was ignored as a potential workforce. Those attending the meeting quickly became convinced of her suggestion as a potential solution as well as a socially progressive direction to move the project. At this point Ana, the only Cucapá attending the meeting, awkwardly explained that this was not, in fact, a viable solution because women were also out fishing. Since Cucapá women are often the heads of their crews, they would be even less likely to forfeit a tide to the tamarisk project.

The majority of people I talked to expressed the view that Cucapá women, unlike Mexican women, do everything that men do and more. They also emphasized that men take on many of the responsibilities that are often women's in Mexican society. Men were especially quick to point out that they could make tortillas, could bead chakira with the same expertise that women could, and shared in the child-rearing duties.

When I asked about leadership roles and why the chief, Don Madeleno, was a man rather than a woman, several people responded that he was voted in by popular opinion because of his wisdom and charisma but that a woman could easily be in his place. Indeed, the comisario or ejidal leader who was appointed by a council of Cucapá was a woman, as were the leaders of the fishing cooperatives.

Local assumptions about women's autonomy became more accessible to me, as an outsider, in the period that followed Ana and Cruz's separation because Ana's behavior often became an explicit topic of conversation among her friends and family. One day after driving into Carranza, a colonia forty minutes away, with Don Madeleno and Doña Berta Martínez, Ana's parents, the three of us stopped at a small Chinese restaurant owned by members of a Mexican family who were old friends of the Martínez family. I had met the owners with Ana only a week before. When Ana and I visited, she decided not to tell Lupita, one of the owners who came to greet us, that she and Cruz had split up and that she was now with someone else. She answered Lupita's routine questions as if everything was the same as usual, steering the conversation toward her children. When we left, Ana guiltily confided that she had avoided the subject of her recent divorce because she just could not bear to face any more scorn for her decision to leave Cruz.[3]

Doña Berta, in contrast, had taken her daughter's recent divorce as her favorite subject of conversation. She had never approved of Cruz and was eager to spread the news that Ana's opinion of him had finally come in line with her own. One of the first things Doña Berta said to Lupita after they made their initial small talk was that Ana and Cruz were no longer together. Lupita was offended that Ana had not said anything and kept bringing the conversation back to her omission. "Why didn't she say anything?" I suggested that she was embarrassed. Doña Berta nodded in agreement and launched into a description of everything that had happened, painting a very negative portrayal of Cruz, his drug addiction, his violent behavior. She went on to extol the virtues of Juan, Ana's new partner.

When Lupita disappeared into the kitchen, I took the opportunity to follow up on my questions about women's roles. I asked, "Is it hard for a Cucapá woman to change her life the way Ana did?" Doña Berta began a long account of how she too had left her first husband in her late teens, for he was an alcoholic who had treated her very badly. When she gathered the courage, she "escaped" to the United States to live with relatives, recover from his abuse, and hide from him. Doña Berta emphasized that although this was difficult, especially with her young children, things were nonetheless better for Cucapá women then and it was easier for her to make this change than it had been for Ana. In the "old days," a woman could always leave a situation that made her suffer. She talked about Cruz's drug use and the suffering he put Ana through. But people were judgmental and unaccepting of Ana's decision to leave him. She said that the difference was that nowadays many people in the village are becoming *mestizada*: mixing with Mexicans and their culture.

I was interested in the way Doña Berta's account of Cucapá gender roles was explicitly opposed to stereotypes of Mexican men and women. This was underscored by her interpretation of deviations from Cucapá gender roles as evidence of Mexicanization. She explained that Ana's choices were not accepted by other people because there had been a shift away from traditional Cucapá attitudes and toward "Mexican" gender expectations. She also described Cruz's episode, and his possessiveness of Ana, as another example of this shift. In Doña Berta's account of her daughter's divorce, the distribution of these gendered/ethnic qualities was particularly complex since Cruz, whom she portrayed as being domineering and abusive, was Cucapá and Juan, whom Doña Berta approved of overall, was Mexican. I tried to interrogate this tension by asking Doña Berta whether she worried about Ana being with a Mexican man. She responded that Juan actually had indigenous blood, for he had distant relatives of Yaqui descent and was therefore more respectful of Ana's individuality than a full-blooded Mexican would be.[4]

In Doña Berta's account, Cruz, who was Cucapá, displayed the classic features of a "Mexican macho" as a result of a partial cultural assimilation. Juan, on the other hand, despite being a Mexican, was not seen as a macho because of his partial indigenous ancestry. Doña Berta's resolution of a potential contradiction in her preference in son-in-laws, however, deviated from standard accounts of gender on one important point.

Usually, when people elaborate on gender roles, they make a distinction between "Cucapá" and "Mexican" views of women rather than between "indigenous" and "Mexican" views. Most of the people I talked to were clear that their different views of gender roles were a characteristic not simply of their indigeneity but, more specifically, of their Cucapá identity. In short, they did not see gender roles as something they had in common with other indigenous groups. Therefore, while the powerful role of women was often articulated against Mexican stereotypes, as we have seen above, most people thought that this was a view of gender that was particular to "the Cucapá culture."

The complex ways in which expressions of gendered and indigenous identities are mutually informing has received some attention in anthropology (Canessa 2005; Montoya, Frazier, and Hurtig 2002; Tsing 1993; Weismantel 2001). More specifically, scholars have argued that colonialism did not affect the gender dynamics of indigenous groups in the same ways and that in some cases—as, for example, with Trobriand women (Weiner 1976, 1988)—the status of women was not undermined by colonial rule. But authors have also shown that in many other cases—among the Baule in western Africa or the Montagnais-Naskapi of the Labrador Peninsula in eastern Canada, for instance—the impact of colonization and capitalist power resulted in the sharpening of gender oppression of women by local men (see Etienne 1980; Leacock 1977, 1980).

Likewise, in this Cucapá village most people argue that because of their immersion in mainstream Mexican society, and particularly in the last several decades of regular interactions with nonindigenous Mexicans, gender inequality has deepened the oppression of women. Doña Berta was particularly explicit that Cucapá women were better off before the "mixing" with Mexican culture began. Cucapá women often see Mexican women as restricted in terms of what is appropriate for them to do, especially on their own. I began interviewing nonindigenous local women in colonias nearby to get a sense of whether they shared this perspective.

Ana's comadre, a nonindigenous woman named Gina, was particularly vocal about what it meant to be a woman in Mexico. She said, "Men here are used to having a woman who takes care of the children, raises them, does everything. The man is free. He can go all over the place, and when he arrives at the house he needs his clothes clean, the food ready, the children cared for. Women in Mexico have to do everything at the same time. The Mexican woman suffers a lot."

I asked, "Is it the same with Cucapá men and women?" Gina replied,

"In some ways Cucapá men are worse.[5] But Ana never had to ask permission to go someplace. I did. And if he says, 'Don't go,' I don't go." Ana was listening and intervened: "Juan is not my boss and I'm not his boss. Tomorrow I'm going with you [referring to me] to the fishing meeting. I'm not going to ask for permission." Gina added, "You want to know something? My comadre is more courageous than myself."

The capacity to control one's mobility, to go where and when one wanted without having to ask permission from one's husband, was a topic that arose again and again in my conversations about Cucapá gender roles. Above anything else, mobility was what seemed to mark Cucapá women's independence and power. The restraints that a "typical Mexican man" was seen to put on women's mobility were made very clear in Ana's characterization of her new partner, Juan. Contradicting her own mother's opinion of him, Ana saw him as a classic example of a Mexican macho. In private, she laughed off her mother's idea that this machismo would be attenuated because of Juan's distant Yaqui connections. The ultimate expression of Juan's machismo, in Ana's view, came one day when we took an impromptu trip into the city to buy propane for the stove. Juan was working at the time and was not aware of our departure. When we came back, he was upset that Ana had not left a note saying where she went, for he had worried about her. Juan's gentle reprimand made Ana absolutely furious. For weeks after the incident, she would bring it up as evidence of how controlling, domineering, and macho he was. She argued that he would never be able to accept her independence as "a Cucapá woman," and she was equally adamant that she would never compromise her independence on his account.

The challenge that this mobility wages against hierarchical gender roles also imbues Cucapá women's independence with a set of negative connotations among nonindigenous people who live close to the village. Gina, again discussing her own feeling of immobility, made a comment indicative of how being out alone was morally judged by others:

> I want to be like you, and go out and meet people. You don't care what people say or think about you! It's not the case with me. I have my spouse and my children. I would like to learn more about the people, talk more to people. I'm not afraid to talk to people.

Gina made it clear that it is not her fear of talking to people that prevents her from going out.[6] Instead, what keeps her at home is the fear of how her actions, and those of her family, will be perceived. Gina's emphasis on "not being afraid" is worth noting, for Cucapá people often explain the lack of independence experienced by nonindigenous women in terms of the "fear" they feel. María Sevilla, a local middle-class woman and wife of a Mexican who owned a construction company, was often mentioned as an example. People in the village claimed that they knew María could drive. Sometimes you would see her driving with her husband and children in the car. However, she would not go anywhere by herself because, like a "typical Mexican woman," she was afraid to do so. I asked María herself about this, and she elaborated a different rationale for why traveling alone as a woman was not a good idea. She had a particularly strong and negative view of the mobility of Cucapá women. "Cucapá women are always running around all over the place, but it's not about independence. I'm a feminist, but Cucapá women take feminism too far.[7] It shows a lack of respect for your husband."

The idea that it is morally compromising for a woman to be out by herself without the supervision of a male took on a particularly negative connotation through the association between being alone and prostituting oneself. Eventually María's criticism of Cucapá women digressed into a series of accusations about particular women going to Mazatlán, a bar on the highway that is synonymous with prostitution (*anda en Mazatlán*).

The trope of female mobility provides an interesting contrast to Anna Tsing's (1993) analysis of Meratus women's stories of travel in her book *In the Realm of the Diamond Queen*. Among the Meratus, a group of shifting cultivators in Indonesia, subsistence practices require that they move frequently to establish new garden plots. Men also travel quite often to maintain political contact with other Meratus groups. Tsing explains that because travel and regional experience are important in constituting authoritative Meratus subjects, a Meratus woman must turn gender assumptions about travel around in order to present herself as a subject of knowledge and experience (1993: 225). Set against a backdrop where women are endangered by travel because of potential male sexual aggression, many women spoke of being "not brave enough" to travel. Therefore, in the stories that Meratus women tell, the courage to travel outside the community becomes the courage to question local standards of male privilege. Tsing argues that these stories therefore disrupt local conventions of women's fear and silence and usurp men's exclusionary rights to bravery (227).

Cucapá women's mobility can be seen to disrupt similar local conventions of men's exclusive rights to independent travel through an assertion of a fearless attitude that is seen as missing in nonindigenous women. However, unlike the narrative travels of Meratus women, María's and Gina's comments indicate that nonindigenous local women see the mobility of Cucapá women through the lens of concerns over sexuality and, in particular, fidelity. Instead of seeing Cucapá women as risking the advances of aggressive males by traveling alone, they view them as deliberately involving themselves in promiscuous behavior.

Conflicting Gender Hierarchies

When you interview my mother, ask her if she doesn't
feel shame for abandoning her daughter at seven
months pregnant like a damn dog.
—RUBY

Despite claims that men are as capable as women are of carrying out domestic duties, they are not considered equally responsible for domestic work. While Cucapá men may bead, cook, and take care of the children, they are very rarely the primary person to do so in a household. This unevenness was readily apparent in the day-to-day activities of Cucapá households. In other words, despite the impression that Cucapá women "take feminism too far," as María put it, and the fact that they have strong leadership roles, the traces of gender inequality on the social landscape are very clear.

While it is true that different gender roles may not necessarily indicate inequality (Scott 1988), the local expectations around Cucapá women's domestic duties are reflected in a number of contexts in which women are negatively evaluated, in a way that men are not, for *not* taking primary responsibility for this work. The scorn Ana experienced after leaving Cruz, for instance, was partially articulated through accusations of negligent parenting. Even though her children were grown up and had partners of their own, her eighteen-year-old daughter, Ruby, was pregnant. And grandmothers have significant parenting obligations when their daughters have young children. Ruby was furious that Ana left and was vocal about feeling abandoned by her. Ruby and her friends and family did not expect Cruz to be of any help, both because it was not considered his role and because he was a drug addict.

In a parallel expression of women's role as primary caregiver, women who use drugs are subjected to a very strong stigma that is not equally projected onto male drug users. Ileana, a twenty-six-year-old woman who was married and had one eight-year-old daughter, was a clear example of this double standard. Both Ileana and her husband were known to be regular users of cristal, but it was Ileana who experienced the social sanctions of their shared addiction. Many people, both men and women, deliberately ostracized her, often citing her addiction while having a child as the rationale. Her husband was never subject to these same criticisms.

One manifestation of the tensions between how women are portrayed in public and their lived experience surfaces in domestic violence. Especially in the fishing season, when cash is more abundant and so are alcohol and drugs, I observed a distinct rise in violence among residents, both domestic and otherwise. On several occasions, Cruz's cousin came to stay in our house with her children after her husband had attacked her in a fit of jealousy. Other sporadic and temporary relocations after such incidents marked the path of similar violent outbursts.

The relatively high levels of violence in the village, mostly in the form of fistfights or brawls involving three or more people, are often naturalized. Because I would often be left visibly unsettled after a fight or domestic dispute involving violence, this topic came up several times naturally in conversations. Those closest to me commented on several occasions that it seemed I was "not used to" seeing these kinds of outbursts but that for them this violence was "normal." Fistfights were considered an inevitable part of conflict resolution. Disciplining children by hitting them was also fairly routine. Manuela made this case to me most bluntly: "My mother beat me all the time when I was a kid." She proceeded to describe how she also hit her daughter when she was young, justifying it by saying she was a terror of a toddler and young child. Manuela suggested that it was my privileged middle-class upbringing that left me unprepared to assimilate the regular displays of violence I witnessed there.

The kinds of public violence that took place in the village were not limited to domestic incidents or to the abuse of women. People pointed out that sometimes women would beat their husbands as well. By emphasizing this point and claiming that the violence was actually distributed evenly across genders, they resolved the tension between beliefs about the society's value of women and the domestic violence they experience. It was true that on several occasions I noticed Pablo away from the house a night or two, only to learn later that a violent outburst from his partner, Ruby, was the cause. Yet in social contexts where men are more clearly dominant, violence against women takes on an entirely different quality because it is intensified by their subordinate position in relation to men (Alcalde 2007: 20; McClusky 2001). In short, where women are more vulnerable and more economically dependent on men, male violence against women is more oppressive than violence against men by women, especially in contexts where there has been a long historical legacy of gender oppression (Levinson 1989).

In this context, where women's dependence and vulnerability is at least ostensibly "inverted" (that is, most women and men here would not argue that women are more dependent or vulnerable but rather the opposite), the issue of domestic violence raises questions about how to interpret spousal abuse against conflicting gender hierarchies. When people pointed out that women beat men too it was a way of both reaffirming local narratives of women's power and pointing out that domestic violence takes on different meanings where gender-power dynamics are culturally specific. They were also suggesting that violence against women was more visible to me than violence against men by women because of my own cultural biases.

In tension with the self-conscious portrayals of women's equality I gathered during my fieldwork, most of the early ethnographic accounts of the Cucapá describe the division of labor as gendered in a very rigid manner (Gifford 1933; Gómez Estrada 2000; Kelly 1977; Sánchez 2000). Kelly (1977), whose fieldwork was completed in the 1940s, and Gifford (1933) portrayed men as hunters and fishermen and women as foragers and domestic caretakers. Women are also documented to have been more involved in chakira beadwork (Gómez Estrada 2000; Sánchez 2000). Sánchez (2000) records Esperanza's narratives on the early days of fishing with her daughter in the 1970s as the first women to do so in the Laguna Salada.

These descriptions of traditional divisions of labor directly contradicted what the majority of people I spoke to claimed to be true, both currently and historically. For example, Don Madeleno claimed that both women and men traditionally fished and hunted. When I asked him why ethnographic books on the Cucapá did not mention women's fishing and hunting, he gave two possible explanations. First, he suggested that none of these scholars spent any significant time doing research in the village, so they may well simply not have noticed the extent of women's involvement in these practices. He also pointed out that most of these accounts were written by male ethnographers, implying that their gender bias may have been responsible for this omission.[8]

There were several indications that current views of gender highlighting the power of women may well have developed relatively recently as a form of boundary-marking against "Mexican culture." While most people I talked to agreed that Cucapá women had always fished, Manuela and Esperanza adamantly claimed to have been, in the 1970s, the first Cucapá women to fish the Laguna Salada. They were aware that this claim would be controversial: "You'll see," said Manuela, "you ask anyone around here and they'll tell you I'm lying, that women have always fished, but my mother was the first woman to fish, and she took me with her." Indeed, many others did explicitly contradict Manuela and Esperanza's claims, drawing on the dominant narrative that Cucapá women had "always" fished. They said that Esperanza and Manuela were just trying to take credit for the group's progressive views on women's roles. Esperanza and Manuela claimed, by contrast, that others were trying to deny them the recognition they were owed.

Felix Coto, a Cocopah elder from Somerton, Arizona, recalled the trajectory of shifting gender roles among his Cucapá relatives in Mexico in much the same way as Doña Esperanza and Manuela. When I talked to him on the reserve in Arizona, he said that what I had read in the history books was true: in the past, Cucapá women did not fish. He remembers when Manuela and Esperanza began fishing in the 1970s because he heard about it in Somerton. It was a scandal that Cucapá women in Mexico were fishing. Felix described how in Somerton there was also a shift in power from men to women as a result of the rise of the "women's movement" in the United States. Women started running things, and to this day the men resent it. Felix explained that the Cocopah women in Somerton still have far less "power" than Cucapá women in Mexico and have always had very subordinate roles in the family. What he had always heard growing up was that wives are supposed to walk one pace behind their husbands. This was meant both metaphorically and literally: women in Arizona really did walk one pace behind their husbands, and many still do to this day.

Felix emphasized that something happened among the Cucapá people in Mexico to make this shift in power more profound there than in Somerton. He argued that the Cucapá in Mexico had a "gender revolution" in the 1960s and 1970s. As fishing in the river resulted in decreasing yields and the Laguna Salada completely dried up as a result of the damming upstream, they were left without any form of livelihood. According to Felix, women at this time began taking on more public roles than men. They began making more decisions in regard to leadership and also began taking charge of fishing crews. Men, on the other hand, retreated from these roles. Felix's account resonates with the work in social science on the so-called crisis of masculinity in Latin America (Gutmann 1997b; Valdéz and Ovarría 1997; Viveros 2001, 1997). These accounts have emphasized the impacts of economic and social restructuring in Mexico on the lives of its men (Escobar Latapí 1998). For instance, Gutmann (1993) shows how, in one colonia in Mexico City, women's increased involvement in paid labor and the growing participation of men in realms such as housework resulted in an erosion of male ideologies associated with machismo (see also de Barbieri 1990).

Felix underscored his interpretation by pointing out that now there were very few male figures taking on political roles in the village, besides the chief, Don Madeleno, who at seventy-four had become frail with age.[9] Felix then listed, in contrast, the women who run the fishing cooperatives and the museum: Virginia, Adriana, Esperanza, and Manuela. On a later occasion when Felix made a trip to Mexico, I went with him to visit Doña Esperanza in the museum. When we arrived, Doña Esperanza greeted him, and in their opening exchange she pointed at him with her finger. Felix turned to me and exclaimed: "See, she just pointed at me! Women don't point like that at men traditionally. That's totally new!" Doña Esperanza laughed and winked at me playfully as we settled down to talk under the mesquite tree in front of the museum.

The Weight of Water

"Is this one of those things where it looks like the women are in charge, but really they're representing the interests of their husbands?" I was standing on a dirt road talking to a newly hired NGO worker when he made this comment. He was going to be working on several projects in the village and was there introducing himself to some of the residents. He arrived in the middle of frenzied preparations for the fishing season. He made the above remark as we stood in front of the house of a fishing meeting, watching as it came to a close. We were in front of a table of women organizing forms for the next meeting. His comment was a typical response to the political prominence of women in the village, for many are quick to assume that they are simply acting on behalf of their husbands.

Cucapá women's leadership, especially in relation to conflicts over the Colorado River, makes this case unique in terms of the way women's roles have been documented and analyzed in three related literatures: that of women's movements and leadership in Latin America, women's roles in the "water crisis" more globally, and, finally, indigenous women's rights in Mexico specifically.

Outsiders have often remarked on the leadership of Cucapá women, particularly in the context of the internal disputes within the "Cucapá community." For instance, in 2001 an observer for the National Human Rights Commission remarked that

> in general terms, it's possible to see a general apathy among the Cucapá who have difficulty uniting in a common front to resolve their problems. In reality there are few families interested in the solution of the problems they have, and the women are the driving force that has prevented further community disintegration. (Alarcón-Cháires 2001)

Many scholars of Latin America have argued that when women enter the political arena they do so as an extension of their roles in the household (Brana-Shute 1980; de Barbieri and de Oliveira 1986; Mota 1980; Martin 1990; Schmink 1981). They enter through their roles as wives and mothers, legitimizing their struggle by expressing their political activity as an outgrowth of a woman's love for her family. According to this body of scholarship, women's place in Mexican politics is reserved for moments of historical crisis, economic change, and government repression (Martin 1990). Political repression, in particular, contributed to the formation of many women's political movements in other parts of Latin America in the 1970s, such as Las Madres de Plaza de Mayo in Argentina and similar groups in El Salvador and Guatemala. These groups came onto the political stage at moments when traditional male politics had proven inadequate (de Barbieri and de Oliveira 1986).

Women's leadership in the Cucapá case is not interpreted locally as an extension of domestic responsibility in the way women's political activity is described by this body of literature. Rather, Cucapá women are seen in the village as inherently better suited for political involvement because of gender-specific attributes such as intelligence and skill in verbal contestation. However, this literature does resonate with Felix Coto's description of

FIGURE 4.1. Women at a fishing meeting. Photo by author.

how an environmental and economic crisis precipitated a shift in gender-power relations.

Regardless of whether the fishing crisis in the delta in the 1970s was the political impetus for the current shape of gendered politics or whether women's leadership has deeper historical roots, the current gender balance places women in a position that is quite unique compared to other cases in Mexico and around the world where water scarcity is an issue. Cruz-Torres (2001) has pointed to the need to incorporate gender into political and ecological studies because environmental degradation often has very different gendered effects. Cucapá men and women have experienced the effects of water scarcity in very different ways, not just in relation to each other but in relation to the way water scarcity has manifested itself in other ethnographic contexts (see also Sundberg 2004).

The literature on the mounting world water crisis has emphasized that women bear the "weight" of water scarcity (Bakker 2007; Bennett, Dávila-Poblete, and Rico 2005; Coles and Wallace 2005; Obando 2003). This is meant figuratively: in many cultural contexts it is the work of women that is most immediately affected by water scarcity because much domestic work—washing, bathing, cooking, and cleaning—requires water. It is also meant literally, as it is often women who are responsible for carrying water from great distances. It is commonly cited that in rural areas of the "Third World," women and young girls must walk an average of six miles every day to get enough water for their families.[10]

Cucapá women experience this "weight" under very different circumstances. In addition to being responsible for providing water for domestic purposes, Cucapá women bear the political burden of negotiating for their water rights and access to their traditional fishing grounds. When I asked why there were more women than men at fishing cooperative meetings, Ana initially suggested that it was because women held the fishing permits. She explained that women would therefore be the ones to negotiate better rights for these permits. The fact that women had more permits than men was puzzling in itself, however. It was not that these women's husbands were "Mexican" and not qualified to have their own permits. Ana went on to clarify that women had been more active in petitioning the government for permits with the formation of fishing cooperatives in the 1970s.[11] She therefore seemed to suggest that it was women's assertiveness that led to the uneven distribution of permits along gender lines.

Others explained the prominence of women in fishing politics through local gender stereotypes. Cruz suggested that women were more active because they were better suited for arguing and were, quite simply, smarter than men.[12] He had given the same rationale for why only women ever worked in the factories. He gave the example of the factory where Manuela worked during the 1980s assembling parts for television sets. Cruz said that she had to work with really complicated electronic equipment, making all the colored dots add up for the color pictures on the screen. In his opinion, that work was just too detailed and intellectually demanding for a man.

The issue of what kind of autonomy is carved out by and for Cucapá women also raises questions within larger debates over the meaning of women's rights in the context of class oppression and the oppression of indigenous people (Hernández Castillo 1998, 2002; Mohanty et al. 1991; Streicker 1995). In Mexico, there has been a tendency to see women's rights and indigenous rights as opposed to each other, for colonial and postcolonial accounts have usually emphasized male dominance over women among indigenous groups, as a way of rationalizing state interventions in these groups as benevolent and progressive. Hernández Castillo (2002) argues that women's rights have been used by both feminist and nonfeminist intellectuals and politicians as a way of opposing indigenous peoples' demands for autonomy.

Hernández Castillo (2002) argues against the supposed opposition between indigenous and women's rights by chronicling how in the past several decades the women's movement in Mexico has gradually strengthened and gained force in indigenous communities.[13] The Cucapá case is a particularly striking example that undermines the stereotype behind claims that the struggle for indigenous rights would necessarily impact negatively on the rights of indigenous women. The Cucapá people's claims to indigenous autonomy in the fishing conflict, in fact, are primarily voiced by women and underwritten by a powerful discourse on women's superiority. Therefore, there is nothing intrinsic to indigenous autonomies that necessarily opposes them to women's rights.

"Mejor Sola"

When you interview Ruby, ask her if she will ever speak to her mother again. Ask her if she still loves her mother.
—ANA

The story of Ana's separation is helpful for understanding the contradictory ways that Cucapá women's autonomy is actually lived out on a day-to-day basis. In many social contexts with pronounced gender inequalities, the idiom of romantic love enables women to assert their individual needs while at the same time conforming to the principles of a male-dominated household. Bourgois (2002), for instance, argues that in traditional Puerto Rican households gender confrontations expressed themselves in romantic scenarios where elopement was an acceptable strategy a woman could use to make an assertive life-cycle change, replacing the authority of her father with that of her husband. While Ana's life change may have looked like just such a strategy on the surface, she emphasized that she was not in love with Juan. To the contrary, she saw him as a temporary safe haven and a stepping-stone to a position of economic self-reliance that would allow her to better support her children independently.

Nonetheless, Ana settled in with her new partner in his house a few miles from the village. During the drama that surrounded her separation from Cruz, she often expressed ambivalence about Juan. Ana's financial planning was revealing of the way she negotiated her relationships with Juan and the other men in her life. She was constantly planning to increase her independence by saving enough money to be self-sufficient. She believed that control over her own money was the best way of assuring that her husband and son-in-law could not control her or her children.

Throughout the year, by working as a cook in a nearby tourist camp Ana made barely enough money to support her family. Her real financial planning began in the fishing season, when, on a good tide, she could come away with several hundred dollars. Because Ana did not have her own boat or motor, she depended on Francisco, her *nuero* (son-in-law, Berenice's husband), to provide his equipment, and for the past five years he had been working as the head of her fishing crew. He did this in exchange for access to Ana's fishing permit, which allowed better access to the area close to the nuclear zone, where there were better yields. Ana also depended on Juan, her new husband, to help on her crew because he offered to work for her at an *ayudante*'s (assistant's) wage.

Ana's dependence on her partner and son-in-law was a constant source of anxiety for her, not only because it compromised her independence but also because she deeply mistrusted both of them when it came to her finances. For example, she started suspecting that Francisco was finding ways of underreporting how much corvina was caught by her crew and selling the rest on his own. She reasoned that there were all sorts of ways he could potentially do this while she was on the boat and he in the truck, or vice versa. When Berenice and Francisco fought with each other, she would express her other suspicions: for example, that Francisco was only with Berenice to use her for her mother's fishing permit. Soon Ana had her own son, Javier, working on the crew, trusting him to watch over Francisco. Because Ana worked as a cook on weekends, when the tides fell she had to send her crew out on their own. At these times, her suspicions shifted to Juan. She was agitated by the idea that he would know exactly how much money she was making when Francisco apportioned the cut to send to her at the end of the day. She quickly made arrangements for Francisco to give her the money directly, without going through Juan.

Ana's ultimate goal was to buy her own motor and boat so that she would not have to depend on Juan or Francisco. But soon her plans were redirected at putting a down payment on her aunt's house on the side of the road, where she could start a *tienda* (store). We spent countless hours discussing the details of the arrangement: how she would get the initial money to invest, how she would go about stocking and running the store. She was principally concerned about finding a mode of employment for her daughter, Ruby, and for Ruby's husband, Pablo, whom she imagined could live and work in the store. At the time she was supporting them all through her own work. She insisted that she could not tell Juan about the store until it was almost finished. It was not that she was worried that he would prevent her from going through with her plans. To the contrary, she said she could not tell Juan about the store because then he would want to help her. "Better to do it alone, right? It's for my children; it's not for Juan." Ana felt that she could use Juan as a support only to a certain point before it compromised her independence.

There has been significant discussion in anthropology about what constitutes powerful roles for women in cross-cultural perspective, taking account of the fact that power manifests itself differently in different social contexts (Cervone 2002; Lancaster 1992; Medicine 1987; Sanday 1981). Ana, like other women in the village I spoke to, defined her rights as a woman around standards of individual freedom rather than group solidarity. While in many respects this resembles classic liberal feminism based on a notion of individual rights (symbolized in this case by economic independence as well as mobility), it nonetheless has important differences from classic liberal notions of women's rights. Men in particular stressed not that women were equal to them but that they are "smarter," "more capable," and "more valuable" than men—a biocultural inequality that underwrites their superiority. This view did not seem to translate into the idea that men and women have different "rights," but it did result in a situation where men and women were seen to have different responsibilities. And women's responsibilities "naturally" far outnumbered those of men. This imbalance in the amount of work women take on is one of the contradictory outcomes of the way women's roles are defined.

An Ethnographic Reversal

I was both disturbed and deeply fascinated by Cruz's condition. He was one of my primary hosts and one of my most articulate educators. He was an exception among those I met because he made an effort to explain things to me explicitly, and he had a rare capacity to make generalizations about what it meant to live in the delta and be Cucapá. He took on this role quite consciously, at times criticizing others for not participating in my education as actively as he did. He once told me: "You know what I don't like about the people here? You are here to learn about our culture. But they all come to the house and want to tell you gossip—*chismes*! They don't tell you, as I do, about our customs, our words, our *conocimientos* [knowledge]. They just want to talk gossip." Cruz also made a point of directly introducing me to people he thought would be able to help me. Generally, the way I met people during my fieldwork was by sitting on porches, drinking coffee, and attending events at which I was informally introduced to more people. With Cruz, however, if someone he thought was important whom I had not met came up in a conversation, he would lead me right over to his or her house and introduce me on the spot.

I was reflecting on all this while sitting with Cruz in front of the house several days after the incident when he first lost his memory. We both watched as a man he had introduced me to only weeks before approached the house. I quickly filled Cruz in on the details: "This man is your sister's ex-husband. His name is Felix. He's a good friend of yours and he fished with you on your crew for years in the '80s." There were countless moments in the days that followed Cruz's amnesia where I found myself describing to him the very people whose lives and personalities he had narrated to me just weeks before. This was the ethnographic reversal in which I found myself. Sometimes, I heard myself describing word for word to him what his own take on an issue was, not feeling compelled to spell out how people disagreed with him. A few months later, Cruz seemed to be back to normal, although there were still incidents around his amnesia that he did not remember well.

Anthropologists have critiqued psychological models of memory as exclusively individual. Antze and Lambek (1996: xxi) argue that any invocation of memory is part of an identity discourse that is closely linked to what people, as social actors, "think about memory, what they remember and what they claim to remember." They emphasize that memory is intersubjective, dialogical, and better understood as ongoing engagement rather than a passive process of absorption and playback (Fentress and Wickham 1992; Gordillo 2004). Forgetting is as much an active process as remembering is (Hanks 1999a; Terdiman 1993; Young 1996, 2005). Identity is not constituted by a fixed set of memories but resides in the "dialectical, ceaseless activity of remembering and forgetting, assimilating and discarding" (Antze and Lambek 1996: xxix).

Of course, Cruz is by no means a "typical" Cucapá man, nor are the events that transpired after Ana left him in any sense representative of everyday experience. What I have argued here, rather, is that Cruz's very atypical experience activated a series of discourses about local expectations of gender norms. Through Cruz's own narrations of both his memories and his forgettings, he negotiated with his friends and family over the complex subject positions available to him as a Cucapá man. His friends and family refused to locate his illness in a biomedical model. Instead, they understood his memory loss within a sociopolitical model, identifying gender-power maladjustment as the cause. In the process of this re-identification, they draw attention to a set of contradictory gender relationships. The complicated process whereby women and men are carving out a space for themselves is also a process whereby they are carving out a space for distinct expressions of Cucapá identity.

This process, whereby particular gender roles have crystallized as representative of Cucapá identity, has mirrored in important ways the history of how Mexican masculinity has become fundamental to defining the Mexican nation. Some Mexican authors trace the origin of "machismo" through Freudian narratives explaining that its origins lie in Spanish conquest (Paz 1961; Ramos 1962; Ramírez 1959). When Hernán Cortés and his conquistadors arrived in Mexico, they raped many indigenous women, and this act of violence is seen as giving birth to the Mexican people (Fuentes 1972). These authors have argued that these real and symbolic "illegitimate births" marked Mexican society with the exaggerated and arbitrary associations of masculine domination that became emblematic of Spanish colonial societies more generally (Palma 1990; Montechino 1991; Viveros 2001).

Fuller (1996) argues that while these authors rightfully place the dynamics of gender relationships in the Spanish colonies in the context of their historical specificity, their accounts obscure the particularities brought on by the processes of modernization that these societies are currently experiencing. This is precisely the type of corrective that Américo Paredes (2003) provides in his tracing of the concept of the macho to more recent historical origins, drawing connections between nationalism, racism, and international relations and the advent of the notion of machismo. Paredes shows, through an examination of Mexican folklore, that prior to the revolution the words "macho" and "machismo" were rarely used. It was not until the Mexican Revolution that a particular version of the macho man came to prominence. He links the inception of machismo to the rise of Mexican nationalism, accompanied by sentiments of distrust and inferiority toward the United States (see also Irwin 2003). It was in this context that, Paredes argues, the Mexican male became associated with courage and linked to the machismo that became a nationalist symbol of Mexico.

Gutmann (1996) argues that in the United States the term "macho" has an explicit racist history, associated with negative character traits projected not onto men in general but specifically onto Mexican, Mexican American, and Latin American men (see also Stern 1995; Gilmore 1990). It is interesting to note that a similar stereotyping and similar racial hierarchies has occurred in this case around Cucapá gender and ethnic stereotypes. Fueled by feelings of distrust toward the Mexican state and dominant Mexican culture that has marginalized them, many Cucapá people have forged a distinct gendered ethnic identity explicitly contrasted to machismo. As Stuart Hall writes, referring to the way in which negative contrasts create collective identities, "When you know what everybody else is, then you are what they are not. Identity is always in that sense, structured representation which only achieves its positives through the narrow eye of the negative" (1991: 21).

The gendered identities expressed here are oppositional in much the way that Hall describes. Cucapá women and men are *not* what Mexican men and women are. And the extent to which Cucapá men and women are evaluated as authentic in their gendered identities is gauged in relation to their degree of dissimilarity to Mexican stereotypes of the independent macho man and the immobile submissive wife.

However, the eye of the negative in this case is not as narrow as Hall's description seems to imply. The nature of these gender roles, the historical trajectory of gender-power relations, and the influence of mixing with "Mexican culture" all complicate these local interpretations. Esperanza's family traced a different historical trajectory than Don Madeleno's, Doña Berta outlined a generational diffusion of women's independence, and Cruz adamantly declared himself an authentic Cucapá man despite almost everyone else's assessment to the contrary.

The idea of a seamless "native point of view" has been with anthropology since its inception (see Malinowski 1922). The poststructuralist critique of monovalence and the rise in popularity of multivocal ethnographic techniques served to undermine the concept of the singular native voice on a theoretical level (Bakhtin 1994; Behar and Gordon 1995; Clifford and Marcus 1986; Marcus and Fischer 1986). But engaging with this literature did not sufficiently prepare me for the extent of discordance and contradiction I often encountered in the field. As in any other place, people contradicted each other constantly in mundane ways and often contradicted themselves as well. But from the day that Cruz "lost his memory," the degree of disagreement I encountered began to intensify, both in the account of what was happening to him and in the issues that this incident came to express. It was as if Cruz's illness came to embody the contradictory processes through which gender-power relationships are being defined and redefined.

It is possible that Manuela and Esperanza's claims about being the first women who fished in the 1970s are not contradictory with the ethnographic record. Earlier women could have fished, they could have stopped at some point (because of colonial and state interventions or economic development), and then they could have resumed these roles at a later moment. An elaboration such as this is tempting because it encompasses local contradictions in a larger context that seems to absolve them. But such an interpretation would obscure the significant fact that people themselves explicitly presented these narratives as controversial.

In general, when most people I talked to told me the story of a long history of fishing by both men and women, it was clear that this story provided them with a resource for underwriting current beliefs about the prominence and superiority of women. However, those who subscribed to this version of history would also point out that it was a contested narrative. Esperanza's family and allies emphasized an account involving recent changes in gender relations, knowing that it undermined the collective narrative of long-standing female dominance. And by underscoring that others would say that they were "lying" about being the first female fishers, they also drew attention to their marginalization and feelings of alienation.

Therefore, what is at stake here is not a simple reconstruction of the empirical historical past. And it is not my intention to resolve local contradictions by tracing a new account of how gender-power shifts may relate to a history of fishing in the area. Instead, what emerges from the conflicting historical discourses is that gender has become the terrain on which difference and identity are worked out, but they are being worked out in a way that is still rife with the contradictions of changing gender-power dynamics.

While locals continue to negotiate how gender roles signify their identity, state officials and policies increasingly judge their identity through an entirely different idiom, which highlights and isolates indigenous language capacity as a major criterion for recognizing indigenous rights. In the following chapter I examine how people, particularly youth, respond to this imposition.

CHAPTER 5

"SPREAD YOUR ASS CHEEKS"
And Other Things That Shouldn't Get Said in Indigenous Languages

AMONG THE CUCAPÁ PEOPLE who live in Mexico, only a handful of elders still speak the Cucapá language; everyone else has shifted to speaking Spanish. Doña Esperanza often reasoned that it is important for the children to learn Cucapá because "it's good to be able to talk a language that outsiders don't understand." The notion that one of the strategic values of their indigenous language is specifically related to its incomprehensibility to outsiders is one of the themes I explore in this chapter. In particular, I analyze the use of indigenous-language swearwords by the younger Cucapá generation as a critique of, and a challenge to, the increasingly formalized imposition by the state of indigenous-language capacity as a measure of authenticity and as both a formal and an informal criterion for the recognition of indigenous rights. I argue that this ethnographic case can also be read as a critique of the notion of language as a cultural repository popularized in recent linguistic anthropological literature on language endangerment. The Cucapá case also provides a counterpoint to the work on articulation with which I have engaged thus far.

Hall's recognition of the "nice double meaning" of the term "articulation" included the sense of "language-ing" and expressing: "to utter, to speak forth to be articulate" (Hall 1996: 53). However, the quality of "being articulate," and all that is bound up with that characterization, is much less explored in this literature than the process of articulating an identity. This is because the moment where identity becomes political, at least on the level Hall is interested in, is only when the second sense of the word comes into effect (when an articulation as an expression of identity is connected to and taken up in a specific political context). The "unity that matters" for Hall (1996: 53) is not so much the one that coheres elements of a discourse together but, rather, the joining together of this discourse to a set of historical circumstances that make it intelligible.

However, there is a long tradition in linguistic anthropology that has explored the political and ideological dimensions of precisely the social processes that deem some discourses and, indeed some groups of people, "articulate" in the sense of "language-ing" that Hall and those who have drawn on his work circumscribe. This literature has argued that even the most commonsense evaluations about what constitutes "standard language," for example, have much less to do with the characteristics of language varieties themselves and more to do with social evaluations of the groups that speak those varieties (Hill 2008; Labov 1966, 1972; Lippi-Green 1997).

In the case of indigenous-language politics, the very intelligibility and recognizability of a group as "indigenous" in the first place has been linked to their capacity to speak an indigenous language. The notion of language that emerges in this political climate is familiar to anthropologists. Indigenous-language competence is elevated to a primary criterion for defining cultural difference through the assumption that there is a necessary relationship between language and culture. In the last few decades, work in anthropology has questioned such encompassing models of culture as a coherent, bounded system (Clifford 1988; Comaroff and Comaroff 1999; Ortner 2000, 2006; Roseberry 1989). Parallel critiques in linguistic anthropology have problematized understandings of language as closed systems that correspond to cultural groups and territories (Armstrong-Fumero 2009b; Duchêne and Heller 2007; Gal 1993; Hill 2002; R. E. Moore 2006; Muehlmann and Duchêne 2007).

Nonetheless, many linguistic anthropologists have continued to support claims that language and culture are inextricably related (Harrison 2007; Hill 2003; Nettle and Romaine 2000; Woodbury 1993). This language ideology has been reinvigorated in the scholarly and activist literature on language endangerment in the last several decades as indigenous languages have increasingly competed with, and been replaced by, more dominant languages all over the world. Campaigns to "save" endangered languages have been connected to efforts to rescue cultural heritage, knowledge, and practices (Crystal 2000; Maffi 2001; Nettle and Romaine 2000; Skutnabb-Kangas 2000). Indeed, variations of the proposition "when a language dies, a culture dies" have served as rallying cries for these efforts.

Below I describe how Cucapá youth themselves critically engage with the assumption that their identity is located in their fluency in the Cucapá language by analyzing two sets of linguistic practices in which Cucapá swearwords are central. The first set involves boundary-marking that distinguishes an insider group from outsiders. The second prompts a reexamination of the first by showing that boundary-marking practices can also function to appropriate and parody authority and thereby subvert it. I describe how this latter set of linguistic practices emerges in a historical and political context in which the purported authenticity of indigenous people is often judged under definitions imposed by the state. Cucapá swearwords function both to disavow the assertion that the Cucapá's identity is located in their indigenous language and to critique linguistic competence as a condition of the group's access to resources.

Until the 1980s and 1990s, public discourses in many parts of Latin America discouraged politicized indigenous identification and were directed at assimilation (Alonso 2004; Gordillo and Hirsch 2003). As we saw in chapter 2, this was also the case in Mexico until the 1980s and 1990s, when the government began implementing neoliberal, multicultural policies and encouraging "cultural recovery" (Hale 2005; Sieder 2002). These policy changes also radically transformed the way state actors interacted with indigenous communities around language issues, introducing in those communities a host of government programs that now celebrate indigenous languages (see Gustafson 2009 for a discussion of similar language-policy changes in Bolivia). Among the Cucapá, these changes have in some cases transpired within the span of a single lifetime and have been experienced as a profound contradiction. The very characteristics that in the past formed the basis of the Cucapá's subordination—a lack of fluency in Spanish, "backward" customs, and isolation from modern conveniences—have now become the very characteristics that the state requires to recognize their rights.

One night at dusk, sitting on the flatbed of a truck smoking cigarettes with Cruz, I tried to engage him on these contradictions, particularly the fact that after centuries of discrimination based on their cultural and linguistic differences, which led to high levels of cultural and linguistic assimilation, the government now expected them to speak the Cucapá language to grant them certain rights. As a boy, for instance, Cruz had feared punishment if he spoke his indigenous language in school. I told Cruz that I saw this as the ultimate betrayal by the Mexican government, which now dared to require from the Cucapá the same practices it had discouraged for generations. Cruz responded blandly to my rant as he exhaled a cloud of smoke: "Yeah, well," he said. "That's the great contradiction. Now the government *wants* us to act like Indians."

The Cucapá Language

As we have seen in previous chapters, the loss of the capacity to farm and fish in the delta has forced a rapid integration into the economic systems of the border region. Cucapá people went to work in factories, on farms, in construction, trucking, building roads, selling scrap metal, and, most recently, in narco-trafficking. This process has brought about a gradual process of cultural assimilation into Mexican society. As today's elders were entering the regional workforce, they encountered a strong disincentive to speak their own language because of discrimination against "the Indians." The Cucapá and many outside observers perceive that their cultural traditions, including their language, are at risk of disappearing. In this sense, their sociolinguistic situation mirrors that of the many people around the world who are shifting to the economically and culturally dominant languages (Gal 1979; Grounds, Tinker, and Wilkins 2003; Hill 1983; Hinton and Hale 2001; Kulick 1992; Mufwene 2001; Mühlhäusler 1996).

During my fieldwork, only ten of the three hundred people that lived in the village were identified by the community as active speakers, and they were between sixty and eighty years old (Gordon 2005). According to people I interviewed, there is a similar age-based distribution of language speakers in the other settlements where Cucapá people live (in the state of Sonora and the reservation in Somerton, Arizona). In the generation made up of the children of these fluent speakers, their linguistic competence is much harder to assess because they almost never speak Cucapá. Some of these people claim they do not know any Cucapá; others claim they can understand but cannot speak or are embarrassed to speak. This variation results from the particular sociolinguistic situation in which each individual was raised: whether Cucapá was spoken in their houses as children, whether their parents married nonindigenous Mexicans, and whether their parents continued to make an effort to speak Cucapá as Spanish became the dominant language.

There are exceptions to this general sociolinguistic pattern. For example, Doña Bertha and Don Madaleno often speak Cucapá when they are together, and their children seem to have a higher level of receptive competence than others of their same generation. Doña Bertha and Don Madaleno have also made a great effort to teach the language to their nine-year-old grandchild, who can recite a list of phrases and words. But for the most part, they follow the norm of speaking to their children and grandchildren in Spanish. Cruz has a higher degree of linguistic competence because he was raised by his grandparents, but I never observed a situation where he had a conversation in Cucapá that involved more than basic salutations.

These days Cucapá is spoken only when primarily elders are present, which for the most part takes place when relatives visit from Arizona or Sonora. It is rare, however, for elders to come together in company that does not include the younger generation. As one woman in her midsixties, Doña Katiana, explains, she does not get a chance to speak Cucapá because she has no one to speak to. This isolation is due not only to the high levels of assimilation but also to the deep divisions within the community, which have polarized two of the major families, resulting in a situation where it is rare for these community members to interact all together in any setting, let alone in Cucapá.

People offer a range of explanations for why their indigenous language is obsolescing. Some gave economic explanations. For example, Felix, a fisherman in his late thirties, explained that people do not teach their children Cucapá because "they see more benefits speaking Spanish or English than speaking Cucapá." He explained that to get hired working on the farms or in tourist camps you do not need Cucapá. He did not see any benefit in teaching a language to his children that will not help them "advance" in the world.[1]

In general, most elders also linked the lack of linguistic reproduction to the political and economic situation in which parents were "too busy" struggling to subsist or too involved in the conflict with the government to teach their children. Adriana, Don Madaleno's daughter, who has devoted the last thirteen years of her life as an activist on behalf of Cucapá fishing rights, often expressed a similar view. One afternoon, for instance, while Adriana waited in a court in Mexicali to receive a fishing permission, she commented to several journalists: "We should be at home teaching our language and traditions to our children. Instead, we're here yet another year arguing with lawyers about the right to feed them." Don Madaleno made a similar argument: "With all these fights, the fight for the land, for the water, and to fish, we don't have time to focus on teaching the children how to speak Cucapá."

Historically, the Cucapá's lack of fluency in Spanish significantly disadvantaged them in conflicts over resources and rights. Yolanda Sánchez (2000), a local historian of Mexicali, argues that the Cucapá lost a significant portion of their land claims during the revolution because negotiations were conducted entirely in Spanish, and at the time they were almost entirely monolingual in Cucapá. Sánchez attributes their lack of success in pursuing their claims to their inability to represent themselves legally or even fully understand the processes that were taking place.[2]

Whereas not speaking Spanish may have impeded their legal negotiations in the past, the Cucapá are now finding that a lack of fluency in their indigenous language is increasingly delegitimizing their current legal claims. In their battles for fishing rights and access to work programs and in appeals for general access to resources and support from the government, their claims are continually undermined on the basis of their purported lack of indigenous authenticity. Yet many of the youth have found ways to use the few Cucapá words they know to challenge this claim.

What Is and Is Not Said in Cucapá

Inspired by the literature on the loss of ecological knowledge that often coincides with language death and, in particular, by Jane H. Hill's (2003) work on the ecological vocabulary of the nearby Tohono O'odham community, I originally hoped to do a miniature survey assessing which plants and animals were still known by their Cucapá names. I was curious to know which words people still used, imagining that some ecological vocabulary had survived as a result of the persistence of activities in which this vocabulary was indispensable (perhaps, I thought, in fishing or in local medicinal practices). When people told me that they spoke only a few words of Cucapá, I often tried to elicit what those words were. This effort almost always met with little or no response. Put on the spot, people could not remember their vocabulary or felt embarrassed pronouncing the words. They would often say either "the basics" ("hello," "how are you") or *groserías* (swearwords), but they would always refuse to tell me what bad words they knew.

Instead of persisting with this line of questioning, which was not proving very productive, I began listing words and asking whether my interviewees recognized them and knew what they meant. This was a much more effective way of determining the vocabulary people still knew, and it was the only way of determining whether they knew groserías, and, if so, which ones. Through this line of questioning, I confirmed that swearwords were indeed the Cucapá vocabulary that most people knew. In fact, the smaller the Cucapá vocabulary of any particular person, the more likely it consisted of groserías. I also found an age-based correlation, for the younger generation, males and females between fourteen and thirty, was particularly familiar with this particular vocabulary.

Cucapá swearwords form an exclusive vocabulary, one that nonindigenous people are not supposed to know. This was indicated in several ways during the course of my stay. Sometimes my teachers would explicitly say, "Don't tell anyone this." At other times, it became clear in more expository ways that the vocabulary was not information that should be easily shared and that, indeed, like all practices of solidarity, the use of Cucapá groserías negotiates a boundary that depends on its exclusivity.

Discovering that an important linguistic practice involves a vocabulary that is not supposed to be shared with people who are not group members presents specific ethical problems for presenting it in an academic context. Some of the stories I relay in the following discussion and the vocabulary I describe were taught to me after I had been given formal consent to include them in my research. It was clear from the way the vocabulary functioned socially, however, that publishing these words for an anonymous audience would betray a social contract. Accordingly, I provide English translations, instead of Cucapá words, to represent the way the words function in specific contexts. Because I intend not a lexical analysis but, rather, an ethnography of a particular vocabulary in use, these translations do not significantly compromise the story I tell.

Learning Cucapá groserías myself and discovering how they are used was a complicated project. I formally began one day as I sat with a sixteen-year-old neighbor, Thalia, in her house working through her Cucapá word list. Her grandmother, Doña Esperanza, arrived and started correcting our pronunciation and helping us add new words. After practicing colors, kinship terms, and some practical phrases, Thalia wanted to practice and expand her list of groserías.[3] At first Doña Esperanza was slightly embarrassed or uncomfortable that I was hearing these words. Soon she began to find some amusement in my enthusiastic attempts to pronounce "dick" and "asshole" in Cucapá. I recalled, in Doña Esperanza's shift from embarrassment to stifled laughter, that this was not my first lesson with her involving words not listed in Crawford's (1989) *Cocopa Dictionary*. Weeks earlier, I had recorded Doña Esperanza's story about a witch, whose name derived from a phrase that translates "to spread your ass cheeks." She translated the name after her performance of the story, under her breath and with a mischievous look, then quickly told me not to tell anyone. Doña Esperanza had the same air of mischief and secrecy on the afternoon that Thalia and I exchanged swearwords. The next morning, I found the words "la gringa is a whore" (written in Spanish but with the Cucapá word for "whore") affectionately etched into the layer of dust on my car's back window.

Several weeks and many rehearsals of my new vocabulary later, Doña Esperanza and her daughter Manuela invited me to a meeting of estranged members of the community, relatives of theirs who identified with their own political faction. The group was aligned with the leader, or comisario, of the Cucapá's ejido rather than with Don Madaleno, the traditional leader. I was interested in attending because I had not met the comisario, nor had I met the members of Doña Esperanza's family who lived in nearby villages. This section of the community felt marginalized for political reasons and by their spatial isolation from the larger Cucapá settlement.

As soon as the eleven women attending the meeting sat down, they launched into the litany of accusations and complaints against Don Madaleno that I had come to recognize as typical among Doña Esperanza's circle. After several fairly biting comments about the other family, a woman named Gabriela paused to scrutinize me. Manuela had already introduced me as "a student," there to learn about "Cucapá culture." Nonetheless, Gabriela asked Manuela to confirm that I could be trusted not to take anything back "to the other side." She explained that on one occasion a journalist had published, word for word, what she had said about the other family, identifying her as the source. Manuela assured them that I was her friend and that they need not worry. But Gabriela still looked wary. After an uncomfortable pause that indicated Gabriela's sustained distrust, Manuela resumed her assurances, explaining that I was her neighbor (thankfully, she did not mention that I was living with Don Madaleno's daughter), that sometimes I slept in her house, and that we spent time together every day. Finally, she leaned over and prodded me to tell the group what she had taught me thus far. She nudged me and asked me to say "whore" in

Cucapá. To my surprise, no one reacted to her request. No one responded until I timidly produced the word, at which point everyone laughed uproariously. Then Manuela, looking proud, ordered me to say "dick," "tits," "ass," and, finally, "wet vagina" in Cucapá. All present laughed with surprise as I produced this vocabulary, and Manuela, also laughing, explained that she had had to teach me the words in Spanish as well. After this embarrassing demonstration of my solidarity, the women resumed their discussion in a much easier manner and did not question my presence again.

In several ways, the role of swearwords in this encounter resonates with sociolinguistic work on slang and expletives. In this body of literature, swearing has often been analyzed as a practice of solidarity. For example, Nicola Daly and colleagues (2004) analyze the sociopragmatic functions of "fuck" and its role as an indicator of membership in a specific community of practice. In the context they examine, swearing, which is associated with a working-class dialect, is a powerful in-group marker and represents a form of "covert prestige" (Labov 1972; Trudgill 1972). In such contexts, the negative affect and strength associated with swearwords in standard settings are converted into positive attributes when the words are used between members of a community of practice. However, such an analysis is not entirely applicable to the above example, in which my performance of swearwords gained my entrance to the meeting. Although my knowledge of the Cucapá words identified me as an insider, my recital of these words also functioned to mark me as an outsider, to warn me that gaining the trust of the group required a public performance.

I was not the first outsider to be initiated into the exclusive world of Cucapá groserías. A story circulates among the area's NGO crowd about a conservation workshop held by a local environmental NGO. During the workshop, one of the conservationists asked Osvaldo, the twenty-nine-year-old son of the chief, to teach them some basic Cucapá phrases. They wanted to know such expressions as "Hello," "How are you?" and "See you later" and assumed, as many do, that Osvaldo would know how to say these things in Cucapá. Reportedly, Osvaldo went along with the request and carefully spelled out the correct pronunciation for each phrase, painstakingly going over his lesson with the eager and grateful conservationists. Later that day, when the chief arrived, the conservationists had the opportunity to test out their new phrases, only to discover by the chief's shocked expression that Osvaldo had taught them swearwords instead of friendly greetings and small talk.

Sitting on Doña Katiana's porch one evening, Cruz proudly told a similar story. One day, a pair of Jehovah's Witnesses came knocking on doors, "teaching the word of God." When they arrived at Cruz's house, only his twin daughters, who were sixteen at the time, were there to receive them. The Jehovah's Witnesses asked if the girls would teach them how to say something in Cucapá. They wanted to know how to ask for water. Instead, the girls taught them a phrase that literally means "ass and vagina" but more figuratively translates into "tits and ass" in English (that is, it is a phrase used to objectify sexuality by referring to pertinent body parts). The Jehovah's Witnesses thanked them and moved onto the next house, which was Manuela's (this was a poignant turn in the story, as Cruz told it, because Manuela is well known for her temper). Cruz continued:

> Then they arrived with Manuela. [He begins imitating their high-pitched voices] "Hello ma'am, how are you? We'd like to talk to you, but we also speak Cucapá. Yeah? Yeah. We want to ask you for something. Let's see... Tits and ass" [in Cucapá]. [We all laugh as Cruz trails off imitating Manuela's response as she shooed them from her doorstep.] "Go to hell, you! You're asking for my ass!" [more laughter]

These two anecdotes, like my experience at the meeting, suggest that Cucapá groserías perform a boundary-marking role, marking off a group of insiders from outsiders. The role of the swearwords in the two anecdotes about the conservation workshop and the Jehovah's Witnesses is to force the outsiders to recognize themselves as such. When the conservationists realize they have been duped or when the Jehovah's Witnesses are chased off Manuela's porch, they are sent a distinct message that they are outsiders.

The anecdotes themselves, or the retelling of the way swearwords were used and the circulation of these stories, perform the inverse function: they mark off a group of insiders. A dozen similar stories circulate among locals. When they are told, the groserías are always said in Cucapá and never translated into Spanish. When those present erupt in laughter, they indicate that they understand the words and, in the process, identify themselves as insiders.[4]

The three examples I have discussed—my own "initiation" at the meeting and the stories of the Jehovah's Witnesses and of the conservationists—have important differences. The audience is constituted in different ways. In the first example, my initiation, the audience was present when the utterances occurred; in the second two, the audiences are re-created as the incidents are retold as narratives (of course, the story about my initiation may well be circulating by now, too). Swearwords also perform slightly different functions in the three examples. In the case of my initiation at the meeting, my performance gained my access to the meeting, as I was eventually permitted to stay. In the other two cases, the performances ultimately restricted access: the Witnesses were chased out of the yard, and the conservationists offended the chief.

However, all three of these examples share a common element: a staged performance that subjects the outsider to the scrutiny of the group. This points to an important dimension of these interactions that cannot be accounted for as functioning at the level of boundary marking alone. Indeed, the symbolic work that swearwords accomplish needs to be understood as negotiating a more complex power dynamic than simply marking an in- from an out-group. To understand this dynamic it is necessary to examine another set of linguistic practices in which it is the Cucapá, rather than reluctant or unknowing outsiders, who perform the swearwords.

As it became more clear to me that the persistence of swearwords was a social fact, rather than simply a product of the crowd I had fallen in with, I started approaching my friends and returning to my former interviewees to ask what they thought about this—why they thought these were the only words learned by the younger people. Sometimes people would respond, "It's because the young people *are* groseros (rude)."

These comments bear a surface resemblance to the discourse of nostalgia that Hill (1998b) found among older speakers of Mexicano (Nahuatl) in central Mexico. She describes how people express nostalgia about days gone by and about a time when they spoke *puro mexicano* (pure Mexicano). Today, by contrast, the young people speak Spanish, and children come out of school "groseros." Unlike in Hill's case, however, the elders were hesitant to argue that speaking Cucapá was a pure cultural form. A discourse of nostalgia around the past did exist, in that elders said the old days were "better," but it involved reminiscing about a time when fishing was good and locals could support their own families; it did not elaborate a linguistic ideology that grafted cultural purity onto linguistic form.

Furthermore, although elders would sometimes be dismissive of these kinds of linguistic interactions, calling the youth "groseros," when I questioned them pointedly they would tell me more stories about similar encounters between youth and outsiders. Seventy-six-year-old Inez told me a story that proved particularly helpful in explaining how these practices are understood.

> Sometimes you go out in the sierra or in the desert and the soldiers are there and they won't let you pass. They stop you, pointing their guns at you on your own land, and they ask you your business. At times like this the *chamacos* [kids] simply say, "Soy Indio" in Spanish and then in Cucapá they say, "Go fuck yourself!" to which the soldiers say "Oh, *pásale* [Go ahead].

The form of this interaction initially places the Cucapá chamacos in the same position of vulnerability as the conservationists, the Jehovah's Witnesses, and the anthropologist in the previous set of examples. When the Indian meets the soldier (presumably on the lookout for drug smugglers in this heavily militarized border region of the Sonoran Desert), he is asked to prove himself to the soldier, to justify his presence. As in the previous set of examples, cursing the authenticator is the substance of this performance.

Doña Inez's anecdote supplied a more general context for these utterances. It is a context in which indigenous people are continually called on to prove their authenticity. They are asked to perform their indigeneity, at great stakes, in a myriad of different contexts by different kinds of authenticators. What does it mean when telling an authenticator to "go fuck yourself" passes as evidence? To understand this we need to look more closely at how language has come to represent indigeneity specifically through its nondenotational content, authenticating speakers on the level of form alone.

"Do You Speak Your Language?"

The Cucapá's indigenous-language capacity is one of a cluster of characteristics used for or against the group in different constitutional claims to land and fishing rights. As we saw in chapter 2, a primary assumption about what constitutes authentic indigenous identity is that indigenous people are natural conservationists (Bamford 2002; Chapin 2004). The discourse of the ecologically noble savage assumes that the preservation of nature necessarily preserves indigenous cultures, and vice versa, because indigenous people are seen to have an essential relation to nature, just as they are assumed to have an essential relation to language (Muehlmann

2007). In chapter 2, I explored how the Cucapá strategically engaged with the environmental movement by manipulating these assumptions (see also Conklin and Graham 1995). We also saw how environmental officials used the Cucapá's failure to live up to specific characteristics of the "ecological Indian" to impede their access to fishing rights.

A set of authenticating measures determining who is and is not indigenous endures, despite indigenous groups' constant resignifying of indigenousness. Ethnographic work on indigenous movements in Latin America has shown over and over again that the binary between indigenous and nonindigenous is never unproblematic. In describing the complexity of indigenous identification in regard to language, Jean E. Jackson and Kay B. Warren point out that "cases exist where pueblos do not speak their traditional language, others where non-indigenous populations do speak a traditional language and still other cases where people speaking a language feign total ignorance of it" (2005: 558). Alcida Ramos (1995: 268) even documents a case of one indigenous group, the Pataxó of northeastern Brazil, who no longer speak their language but, recognizing the importance of such signs of indigeneity for dominant society, have acquired the language of another indigenous group and strategically adopted it as their own.

The powerful assumption that the authenticity of indigenous identity is closely linked to the knowledge of one's indigenous language has resulted in some states requiring a person who has moved out of a community to either still speak its language or be classified as formerly indigenous (Jackson and Warren 2005). Although actual linguistic practices are far too complex for such policies to be entirely enforceable, indigenous-language competence continues to be a primary criterion by which institutional authorities define indigeneity. In this case, language competence has been imposed as a criterion of authenticity in a variety of formal and informal ways, primarily in restricting access to constitutional rights and to cultural projects and resources. The Cucapá youths' participation in a culture and conservation project vividly illustrated such authenticating practices at work.

As more attention has gone to finding alternative sources of income to fishing, NGOs have proposed ecotourism projects, language revitalization projects, and cultural restoration projects. Participation in these projects requires a certain level of "cultural knowledge" and reflexivity. Language competency is often used as the indicator for such qualities. This became particularly evident during the preparations for a mapmaking project.

Things That Shouldn't Get Said in Indigenous Languages 159

Santiago, the director of a program titled "People, Conservation, and Nature" at a binational NGO, initiated a mapmaking project in the three main Cucapá communities: in Sonora; in Baja California; and in Somerton, Arizona. I volunteered to help with the preparations by attending meetings, taking notes, and consulting on various aspects of the planning. The project involved training a small team of youth, forming an advisory team of elders and carrying out interviews, and then producing maps with the support of trained cartographers. In a preliminary meeting, Santiago told me that the first criterion in the selection of youth participants should be fluency in Cucapá. I was surprised, for he had been working in the village for more than ten years, and I imagined he had a better sense of the local sociolinguistic dynamic. I explained that the fluency requirement would be unfair, as none of the youth were fluent speakers of Cucapá.

Nonetheless, at the next meeting of the three communities in May 2006, Santiago announced that he would select people based on their fluency in Cucapá. It was a disgruntled meeting, as the youth in the group had been unaware that there would be a selection process in the first place, much less one that would effectively exclude them all. One young man, who had been a part of all the preparations, stormed out of the meeting before it was over.

Later that night, long after Santiago had left, several young women gathered around the front of our house, gossiping about the meeting, about Santiago's brand-new car, and about the injustice of the selection criteria. Thalia thought that it would be "almost impossible to find a young person here who speaks Cucapá." As the conversation progressed, the group became more incensed about the whole issue. Here are some of the comments I recorded from that night:

> EVA: It's embarrassing not to be able to speak Cucapá because everyone who comes here says, "Tell me how to say this in Cucapá" or "Tell me how to say that." They think that we *have* to speak Cucapá because we are Indians. [She goes on to tell the same story Cruz told about the Jehovah's Witnesses' Cucapá lesson.] It's not fair—we should be able to work, the young people, even if we don't speak Cucapá. Santiago is a crazy damn *pelón* [bald guy].
>
> LUCIA: Because we don't speak Cucapá we shouldn't get opportunities?

EVA: [directed at me] Why does he want us to speak Cucapá? Does *he* speak Cucapá?

SHAYLIH: He thinks it would be better for the project, give a better sense of the land.

EVA: Well, then, instead of buying new cars he should buy us someone to teach us Cucapá!

LUCIA: It doesn't take out my Cucapáness, if I don't speak it. I have Cucapá blood.

SHAYLIH: You think you're still Cucapá, even if you don't speak Cucapá?

LUCIA: 100 percent.

In the end, Eva decided not to participate in the mapmaking project (she fell back on her previous plan to find a job in the factory where a handful of women she knew worked and to entrust her newborn baby to the care of a neighbor during the day). She did not attend the following meeting in June 2006 that was held exclusively for the potential youth participants. Lucia, Victor, Osvaldo, Raul, Ivan, Thalia, and I went. Over beers and burritos at the tourist camp down the road, Santiago quizzed the group about why they wanted to be involved in the project (specifying, "besides the compensation").

Osvaldo was the most vocal at the meeting. After several previous meetings, he seemed to have learned the style of rhetoric that Santiago was looking for. He started off hesitantly, saying that he thought it would be a good idea for outsiders to learn about all of the places in the area. Santiago encouraged him to continue, asking what benefit the project would have for the community. Osvaldo said it would probably be good for some of the Cucapá to learn about the places, too. Finally, after more cajoling from Santiago, Osvaldo said, "Oh, yeah, and our children's children . . ." as if remembering something that Santiago had said in the past about preserving Cucapá culture for future generations. Santiago replied, "You're learning, Osvaldo!" No one else seemed comfortable talking through the course of the meeting, but Osvaldo's performance seemed to carry the group.[5]

Finally, the moment came when Santiago asked the group to describe their language competence. "Do you speak Cucapá?" he asked, addressing the whole group. Osvaldo continued in his role of leader and answered this question without hesitation. "We know the basics," he said. "You know, 'Hello,' 'How are you,'" and then he proceeded to say "Go fuck yourself" in Cucapá as if that were a Cucapá greeting. After several other giddy exchanges of swearwords among members of the group, Santiago seemed to have heard enough. "Okay, I don't know what you're talking about," he said. Seeming to be satisfied precisely by his lack of comprehension, he moved on to make the final arrangements to begin the project.

In this interaction, as in the anecdote about the youth meeting the soldiers in the desert, the Cucapá youth are asked to perform their indigeneity. The two interactions contrast with the first set of examples I discussed because, in these instances, the Cucapá are subjected to the scrutiny and evaluation of outsiders. When proof of their authenticity is requested, Cucapá swearwords simultaneously fulfill the request from the perspective of the authenticators and function as a refusal on the part of the Cucapá people who utter them.

By contrast, attempting to join the Cucapá in some manner, the conservationists, the Jehovah's Witnesses, and the anthropologist were asked to perform these very words. In those instances, the Cucapá youth took on the role of the authenticators, not just for themselves in those moments but also for the audiences who will continue to hear the stories as they are repeated. In this set of examples the outsiders are subjected to the scrutinizing gaze of the Cucapá in a way that marks off social boundaries.

At the meeting for the mapmaking project, I felt that I was being paraded out in front of an audience dressed up in an uncomfortable costume of words. I knew these words' meanings, but they still felt foreign and awkward. In retrospect, I wonder if the Cucapá youth I observed feel any differently when they are called on to perform their indigeneity. For them, the condition for their authenticity is that they speak words that, at some level, are foreign to them. In mimicking the forms of the subordination they experience by subjecting outsiders to just such a performance, they challenge the criteria used to authenticate them as "Indians." This combination of appropriation and parody, or "mimesis" (Pemberton 1994; Siegel 1986; Taussig 1993), is, therefore, a gesture of resistance to the criteria by which they are able to access resources and lay claims to the state.

Therefore, more than simply drawing a line between outsiders and insiders, the use of Cucapá swearwords in the second set of interactions complicates the assumed hierarchies that these groups presuppose; it creates what James Scott has called a "hidden transcript": a "critique of power spoken behind the backs of the dominant" (Scott 1992: xii). By reversing roles, subverting their authenticators, and subjecting the outsiders to the very methods of evaluation so often used against them, these youth also express an irony fundamental to their experience of what it means to be indigenous (see Gal 1995).

In short, the Cucapá youths' use of swearwords in the case of the mapmaking project was a critique of the assertion that their lack of fluency in Cucapá should deny them opportunities to work on projects about their own culture. It was a recognition of the injustice of the criterion and a defiant claim on the resources at stake.

What Should and Shouldn't Get Said in Indigenous Languages

Groserías figure centrally in these linguistic practices as more than a means to draw social boundaries, for they are also fully intended in their most literal interpretation: as insults. That Cucapá swearwords, as opposed to Spanish ones, are featured in these practices is also more than incidental: they derive much of their potency from manipulating expectations of what an indigenous language should express and by overturning expectations about the kind of knowledge indigenous people should have.

Hugh Brody (2000), an internationally recognized anthropologist, land claims researcher, and policy adviser, claims that indigenous languages generally have no swearwords because in indigenous communities anger is considered "childish" behavior and, as such, is scrupulously suppressed.[6] Although this assumption is certainly not one that most linguists would subscribe to, the linguistic anthropology literature on indigenous languages implicitly encourages it, if only by emphasizing the more "elevated" aspects of such languages. Partly in reaction to legacies of assimilatory policy and the undervaluing of nondominant languages, linguistic anthropologists have focused on the positive knowledge that is "encoded" in indigenous languages (but see Garrett 2005 and Kulick 1995, 1998, for exceptions). Accordingly, the ecological, medical, and spiritual vocabularies found in indigenous languages have been celebrated and enthusiastically recorded (Harrison 2007; Hill 2003; Maffi 2001, 2005; Nettle and Romaine 2000; Skutnabb-Kangas, Maffi, and Harmon 2003).

Alcida Ramos (1994: 78–80) has pointed out that these stereotypical assumptions about indigenous knowledge conceal an intolerance and paternalism that comes to the fore when indigenous people betray these expectations. For this reason, reporting on the Cucapá's linguistic practices is also politically precarious. If one describes how these words function in actual circumstances, some people may read the account through a negative lens. In much of the media and academic literature on language death, it is conceptualized as a tragic, irrevocable loss of precious knowledge that could benefit all of humanity. Therefore, I hesitate to add my list of Cucapá swearwords (like "fuck your mother" and "spread your ass cheeks") to the more idyllic archives of indigenous languages, such as the Hopi vocabulary, which can still imagine time in sophisticated ways (Whorf 1964), or the O'odham words for the plants and animals integral to their cultural traditions (Hill 2003).

Similar discomfort at exacerbating negative stereotypes is evident in the burgeoning literature on the use of English swearwords by Aboriginal youth in Australia. This work has examined the overrepresentation of Aboriginal people among those charged with "offensive behavior" or "offensive language." David Brown and colleagues (2001) show that indigenous people account for fifteen times as many "language offences" as would be expected given their proportion in the community (see also Heilpern 1999).

Marcia Langton (1988) argues that this correlation can only be accounted for within the historical perspective of ongoing conflicts between the police and indigenous people (Brown et al. 2001; Cunneen 2001). She argues that swearing is a way for Aboriginal youth to exercise their own "legal method" by portraying the police and their legal culture as grotesque (Langton 1988). Although this literature has argued that swearing is designed precisely to challenge systems that are perceived as illegitimate and oppressive, it also contains a strongly paternalistic stream arguing that Aboriginal youth do not realize they are using culturally offensive linguistic forms. For example, Rob White (2002) contends that indigenous cultures' perceptions of civility are so radically different from those of Western cultures that children are not penalized for their use of swearwords, which are so routinely used in everyday communication that, indeed, they are not even experienced as offensive. Thus these culturally confused youngsters perceive themselves as being penalized for a "normal" communicational pattern that "in their cultural universe is . . . not experienced by them as 'swearing'" (White 2002: 31).

These two tendencies, to deny that swearwords exist in indigenous languages or to argue that indigenous swearing in English is so naturalized that it is unidentifiable as swearing, reflect a deeper ambivalence about indigenous people. The ambivalence indexes a dual stereotype of "the

Indian" similar to the one we saw in chapter 2: on the one hand, as the noble savage inherently fluent in ecological wisdom; and, on the other hand, as a violent and obscene substance abuser. These arguments undermine the strategic savvy of these speakers by disarming their linguistic practices of their powerful discursive effects. Evaluations of indigenous peoples' swearing are filtered through expectations about what these people should and should not be saying. And these expectations, in turn, are constructed through a set of stereotypes about how indigenous people should behave more generally.

Don Kulick (1995) identifies a parallel tendency in the portrayal of women as silent or speaking submissively, with reference to rules of politeness (Lakoff 1975). Kulick (1998) critiques this tendency by exploring women's speech in Taiap, a Papuan language, in obscene public displays called *kroses*, which are sites of gender negotiations ideologically opposed to the politeness of speech in men's political oratories, which downplay tension and disagreement. The sociolinguistic literature on gender and swearing is useful for my analysis because it highlights how women's swearing functions in a range of ways that, against the backdrop of prevailing sociocultural norms and expectations, can provide a powerful identity resource for female speakers (de Klerk 1992, 1997; M. Gordon 1993; Keenan 1974; Sutton 1995).[7] This work has shown that swearing functions not only to mark identity but also to negotiate and actively constitute that identity (Sutton 1995). In the interactions I observed among the Cucapá, swearing functions not simply to transgress dominant censorships and the authority that enforces them but also to creatively respond to and subvert that authority (Woolard 1985). Yet it is important to note that the swearing I examine here is distinct from everyday forms of obscenity. When obscenity features in displays of anger, as insults, or in playful vulgarity among youth, it is always expressed in Spanish, the "native" language of the majority of Cucapá people in this region.

For the youth, the use of Cucapá swearwords is less about engaging in the sociality of the obscene than about negotiating claims to indigeneity. In all of the ethnographic instances in which I heard Cucapá swearwords used, the words were uttered in situations in which outsiders were present; they were employed in response to a challenge to Cucapá authenticity or, as in the first set of examples I described, in a boundary-marking mode.

Nonetheless, the use of Cucapá swearwords in these limited contexts may well index both a sociality of the profane that is currently practiced in

Spanish and one that may have been practiced when people were fluent and interacting in Cucapá. Although this chapter is concerned with what Cucapá swearwords do as opposed to what they mean, during my interviews and informal conversations with elders, cross-cultural comparison of the meanings of swearwords was a running theme.

The central Cucapá phrase that I have analyzed in this discussion is one that I have translated into English as "fuck you." In Spanish, the semantic equivalent of "fuck you" translates as "fuck your mother" (*chinga tu madre*), reflecting the powerful role of the mother figure in Mexican culture. However, elders translated the literal meaning of the Cucapá expression as "fuck your mother, your grandmother, and your grandfather." In interviews, the elders agreed that the literal meaning of the insult reflected the powerful institution of the extended family in Cucapá culture. This meaning was opposed to the individualism of US culture (in which the insult is to the individual) and to the Mexican preoccupation with the role of the mother. The original meanings that the elders emphasized hint at the ways these swearwords may have formed a system of obscenity that predated the shift to Spanish.

Whereas elders explained that the literal meanings of the words were different than in Spanish, the youth, significantly, translated these insults into their Spanish equivalents, glossing the words as local Mexican swearwords. Indeed, the youth were unaware of the literal meanings in Cucapá. That the youth and elders translate the verb for sexual violation in Cucapá into *chingar* in Spanish is also significant because of the prevalence and flexibility of this word in Mexican Spanish and in daily practices of obscenity.

The extensive use of the word *chingar* in Mexico is famously explored by Octavio Paz in *The Labyrinth of Solitude* (1961). Paz argues that the prevalence of the Spanish word *chingar* indicates that the "essential act of the macho—power—almost always reveals itself as a capacity for wounding, humiliating, annihilating" (1961: 82). Paz and others (S. Ramos 1962; Spielberg 1974) have argued that the principal theme of Mexican swearing involving the verb *chingar* is humiliation. However, José Limón (1994), unsettled by the delegitimizing effect this literature has on the Mexican working class, notes that the verb *chingar* also expresses an element of social violation. He describes it as a word often used when speaking of political and economic hardships.

That the Cucapá youth translated the swearwords they used into the

Mexican verb *chingar* may indicate that, as it does for Limon's working-class Mexicans, this linguistic practice represents an "oppositional break" (Limón 1994: 134) in the alienating socioeconomic conditions they have found themselves in. When the Cucapá curse their authenticators, they simultaneously claim membership in a group that has a specific historical relation to the nation-state. Swearwords act as a disavowal of the assertion that the Cucapá's identity is located in their indigenous language and as a refusal to accept fluency in Cucapá as a condition for access to resources.

Unlearning Cucapá: Last Words

Some people thought it was strange that I did not already know how to swear in Spanish when I arrived in Mexico. They said that swearwords are usually the first kinds of words that foreigners learn when they come to the delta. I wondered about this generalization. Can it be true that, statistically, swearwords are the first words one learns in a foreign language (perhaps after "hello" and "thank you")? Most people I talked to about this certainly seemed to think this is the case. I was interested in the assertion because it seemed that, in the case of the Cucapá language, swearwords were the last to be unlearned. The long-term implications of this trend struck me as particularly daunting. Twenty years from now, when the ten or so Cucapá speakers have passed away, swearwords will be the only words spoken in Cucapá.

Paul B. Garrett (2005) argues that swearwords in bilingual settings can sometimes form a code-specific genre. He examines how young children in St. Lucia are socialized to "curse" in a creole language that under most circumstances they are discouraged from using. However, apart from Garrett's (2005) case and Hill's (1983) observation that cursing outsiders is one of the limited contexts in which the Nahuatl language is now used, little evidence suggests that swearwords are consistently the final words of dying languages. Interestingly, Kulick (1995) hints that the opposite process may be taking place in Melanesia, where one of the many effects of missionization has been the eradication of obscene language in village life.

Although the Cucapá youth are still learning swearwords, I am not arguing that the last vestiges of their indigeneity reside in profanity. To the contrary, their strategic use of swearwords criticizes the very idea that their indigeneity resides in the Cucapá language. Like the elders, the youth believe that what makes them Cucapá is a connection to the land, the river, and a history of tension with the Mexican government.

For the youth, groserías may well seem the only words they need to know in Cucapá, since whatever vocabulary they possess will not be understood by outsiders. This puts Doña Esperanza's comment, quoted at the beginning of this chapter, into perspective. It is good to learn Cucapá because it is a language "outsiders don't understand." The outsiders who frequent the village seem to agree. The soldier who meets the Indian in the desert does not care that he does not know what the Indian says to him; those incomprehensible words prove to the soldier that the Indian *is* an Indian. In the mapmaking meeting, Santiago did not need to know what the youth were saying in Cucapá for him to be convinced of their linguistic competence. It was as if his *not* knowing what they were saying was evidence enough of their cultural alterity. To the soldier, the lawyer, the government official, the conservationist, it is not the meaning of the words that matters but their very incomprehensibility.

I have argued that it is within this context of repeated appeals for proof of indigenous authenticity that one can understand the use of Cucapá swearwords. These swearwords gesture to the irony of these appeals in the context of the long history of injustice the Cucapá people have experienced. Ironically, the Mexican constitution currently requires self-identification for a group to be recognized as indigenous. Cucapá swearwords declare just such a self-recognition, even if through channels that erode dominant assumptions about the cultural force of indigenous languages.

However, the Cucapá go one step further. When they offer "go fuck yourself" as evidence of their authenticity, they draw attention to the authenticators' lack of access to the knowledge they would need to determine the fulfillment of their own criteria. This move draws attention to the limits of the project of "legibility" in which indigenous identification is embedded. According to James C. Scott, the modern state attempts to make the populations it administers more "legible" in order "to create a terrain and a population with precisely those standardized characteristics which will be easiest to monitor, count, assess, and manage" (1998: 81). As the Cucapá youth's swearing points out, however, the use of language as a standard characteristic may render indigenous populations more visible to the state, but it simultaneously perpetuates colonial imaginaries of the Indian as impenetrable and exotic.

Graham (2002) points out that the symbolic value attached to indigenous languages as emblems of authenticity gives them a special status among signifiers because, in addition to communicating through content, they signal ethnicity at the level of form in the same way as nonlinguistic forms such as bodily ornamentation or traditional dress. In this case, from the point of view of outsiders, the referential content (i.e., the meaning intended) does not matter: the form alone (i.e., "sounding indigenous") serves to authenticate the speakers. However, from the point of view of the in-group, for which these interactions are also performed, the propositional content is extremely important. The linguistic interactions examined here are a particularly sophisticated use of this dual nature of indigenous language as a semiotic medium because swearwords play off the nondenotational significance of indigenous language (that is, how the words sound) to outsiders while simultaneously drawing on the referential aspect (what the words mean) for the insiders. Whereas the acoustic form of the Cucapá swearwords signifies the youths' authenticity to the outsiders, the content, which defies indigenous stereotypes, would actually undermine their authenticity if these same audiences understood it.

To curse the unknowing outsider also expresses the Cucapá's acknowledgment that they do not have control over the conditions of their own recognition. This awareness forces us to ask questions about our role as anthropologists in ratifying those very conditions. Although some will argue that the essentialisms perpetuated by the ideology of language as the primary conduit for culture are strategic, we have to ask ourselves how strategic this conception of language is when it does not align with the views and realities of the local people we hope to advocate for. Many linguistic anthropologists insist that language is the "vehicle" of culture and, indeed, that "when a language dies, a culture dies." What are the political implications of this idea when entire populations of indigenous people are learning dominant languages? Indeed, linguistic anthropologists themselves predict that in the next century half of minority languages will be lost (Krauss 1992; Maffi 2005). What will the ramifications of the insistence on the language-culture link be a century from now, when the majority of indigenous people will not speak indigenous languages?

The use of Cucapá swearwords also indicates how academic and state appeals arguing for the "recovery" of cultural wealth may sound to the indigenous people who are supposed to benefit from it. These appeals argue that cultures are important to "save," not just for the good of a specific community but also for the benefit of national patrimonies and, indeed, for all of humanity. From this perspective, it does not matter whether "saving the Cucapá language," for example, is a priority or even an interest among Cucapá people. Nor is it relevant that people no longer speak Cucapá because of centuries of racism and marginalization.

Turning back to "the great contradiction" to which Cruz referred so casually: How do the Cucapá make sense of the fact that, after centuries of repression and discrimination on the basis of their cultural difference, they are now being told that they should act like Indians? How do they respond to claims that their speaking Cucapá is not only what makes them who they are but is also inherently valuable to all of humanity? I think by now one can guess how they might respond.

CONCLUSIONS

AS I DROVE OUT of the Colorado delta, following the river up from Mexico through California, Arizona, and Colorado, the contrast upstream was striking. Just three hours north of the village, in Palm Desert, California, luxury hotels have misting devices to keep their guests comfortable while they sit by the pool. The Marriot Hotel lobby's indoor lake and waterfalls take more than fifty million gallons to fill. This is where the water diverted from the Colorado River goes: golf courses, ranches, swimming pools, and thirsty cities such as Los Angeles and Las Vegas. The United States–Mexico border, like the Colorado River itself, bisects a region of dramatic inequalities.

As the conflict continues in the delta over whether Cucapá people should fish on the grounds of the reserve and how to protect the local flora and fauna from further depletion, water continues to be siphoned off by more than a dozen dams upstream. Mexican environmental officials continue to haggle with the Cucapá over the few dozen boats that fish the nuclear zone each year. Instead of focusing on increasing the river's flow through negotiations with the United States, Mexican government policies construe "overfishing" as a principal cause of environmental degradation in the area.

By drawing on current environmental discourses local state actors as well as NGOs have framed the debate in the delta in terms that have shaped the boundaries of the groups in conflict, as well as aligning them with and against each other in specific ways. They have done so by drawing on essentialist notions of indigeneity and the environment, popularized by the transnational environmental movement and other international actors. As a result, controversy over the sustainability of the Cucapá's environmental practices has developed around assessments of their indigenous authenticity. In the process, the degradation of the Colorado River delta has been largely represented as a "local" ecological crisis.

This environmental crisis, however, like most ecosystem abuses, is just the local expression of a process generated by powerful state and capitalist actors in both the United States and Mexico. The Cucapá people have experienced the brunt of the environmental damage done to the delta, while simultaneously being targeted as objects of intervention because of their alleged responsibility in the crisis. As is always the case in narratives that blame the victim, this focus exonerates the more powerful political actors and institutions that have prevented the Colorado River from reaching the Sea of Cortéz.[1] This ethnographic case, therefore, exemplifies how environmental conflicts are never just about "the environment." Sometimes, they become the terrain on which other ideological conflicts play out. In the case of the Cucapá fishing dispute, debates about the conservation of the river have become a battleground for struggles over how cultural difference should be recognized and what constitutes that difference in the first place.

This conceptual focus, on how the fishing conflict became the terrain for other struggles, resulted less from the questions that I brought to this research than it did from my interactions with people in the Colorado delta. As I described in the introduction, when I first began talking to locals in Mexico about the effects of water scarcity in the region they tended to shift the discussion away from the specter of environmental crisis and toward the local lack of work. Instead of situating the fishing conflict within the terms of "environmental crisis," they emphasized the conditions of poverty and injustice that made day-to-day survival so difficult in the region. It was this refocusing of attention that led me to the approach I have taken to exploring these issues here.

Starting from the particular confrontations and encounters engendered by the fishing conflict, this book has explored some of the ways that the inequalities experienced by the Cucapá people are organized through specific modes of social differentiation. I have analyzed the way that idioms of ethnicity, class, gender, and language have shaped how people have negotiated the dramatic structural, ecological, and discursive transformations that have characterized their lives over the last few decades.

As we have seen, the fishing conflict revolved around whether Cucapá people were sufficiently indigenous to receive differential fishing rights. In this case, the controversy over fishing in the protected zone ultimately had less to do with environmental impact and more to do with the maintenance of social categories. Furthermore, ideologies of work, significantly shaped by notions of poverty and class, influenced the way that local people negotiated alternative forms of livelihood available to them, both in the factories and in the narco-economy. We saw how highly pejorative experiences of class and poverty contributed to the cultural appeal of the narco-world, which provided a complex resource for resisting perceptions of both local and state forms of oppression related to fishing regulations.

I have also explored how gendered dimensions of leadership have shaped the contours of the fishing dispute as well as the changing dynamics of gender and power in the community more generally. We saw how Cucapá women have taken up the primary political roles in relation to both the local organization of fishing crews as well as the more formal negotiations with the government over fishing rights. Furthermore, my analysis reveals how women's prominent role in this crisis, and in social life more generally, is a focal point for the way that many Cucapá people understand the specificity of their ethnic identity in relation to the state and nonindigenous neighbors. Finally, this book has also analyzed the way that language ideologies further underwrite conceptions of indigenous authenticity and function as a means by which to control the distribution of resources through government and NGO work programs. I argue that the linguistic practices used by Cucapá youth in response to such language ideologies ultimately work to subvert and critique them as measures of authenticity.

In each case, it was evident that these social categories are not experienced as discreet and autonomous but rather overlap and reinforce each other in ways that constrain and facilitate how local people have navigated environmental and political change. The effects of these changes and the way that local people have responded to them are intimately linked to the experience of being gendered, indigenous, and poor in contemporary Mexico.

More important still, I have argued that it is crucial to recognize that the social categories that are foregrounded by this ethnographic case, particularly indigeneity, gender, class, and language, do not simply shape the contours of environmental conflict. What we have seen is that it is precisely through conflict that local subjectivities are articulated and produced. What it means to be a Cucapá woman or fisherman, for example, is intimately bound up with contemporary struggles over claims to resources and the right to a certain mode of livelihood. Furthermore, these expressions of identity are forged through several levels of political and historical constraint that go beyond the immediate fishing conflict. Local subjectivities are shaped by longstanding conflicts and compromises with the

Mexican and, in some cases, the US government. They are also articulated in the context of both complicit and conflictual interactions with NGOs, water users associations, and the narco-trafficking networks of the region. Local identities and subjectivities also emerge in tension with other members of the community.

In order to better understand these dynamic processes of identity formation, I drew on Stuart Hall's concept of "articulation" as well as on the work of critical ethnographers who have developed it as a way of understanding processes of identification (Clifford 2001; García 2005; Li 2000; Nelson 1999; Yeh 2007). The concept has been useful because "articulation" refers to the formation of a collective "voice," but always in a constructed and contingent sense (Clifford 2001: 478). That is, articulations are positively asserted but are also limited and prefigured by fields of power and their historical embedding (Li 2000: 152). This concept has also been useful for analyzing the Cucapá case because it describes how individuals are summoned into certain positions but also how they identify with these positions, negotiate their terms, criticize them, and transform them. Dove has pointed out that this perspective allows us to avoid debates over authenticity by shifting focus to the articulation of indigeneity (Dove 2006: 191). Hall (2000) made this point by emphasizing that articulations shift the focus away from the idea of "identity" as a pre-existing entity and toward the process of identification as an active construction, which is always in progress and never complete (see also Butler 1993).

There have now been several high profile cases of indigenous groups that have been able to connect claims for land title or other rights with a wider set of discourses on environmental sustainability, who as a result have gained access to resources from the state, NGOs, or transnational bodies such as the United Nations and the Human Rights Commission (Avio 1994; Conklin 1997; Doane 2007; Keck 1995; Reynolds 2005; Turner 1991).

Li (2000) provides an ethnographic account of the concept of articulation that is helpful for drawing out the particularities of the Cucapá case. Li makes a comparative analysis of two sites in Indonesia to explore how, at different historical and political conjunctures, some people come to identify themselves as indigenous while other people do not. The Lauje, a relatively isolated upland group living in scattered houses with no serious competitors for their hilly terrain, have not articulated collective positions framed as "indigenous" because they have not been exposed to overtly coercive dimensions of state power. In contrast, the Lindu, another highland group, produced an identity as "indigenous" in the context of their opposition to a hydro plan with a proposed dam and the threat of forced resettlement by the state. With this comparison, Li argues that the predominance of a particular frame at a particular time does not depend on essential differences between groups but on the regimes of representation or "places of recognition" that preconfigure the formation of the groups, as well as processes of contestation and dialogue that take place on the ground (Li 2000: 154).

Li's comparison illustrates ethnographically Hall's contention that a theory of articulation is a way of asking how ideological elements *do or do not* become articulated with certain subject positions (1996: 53). Li's comparison, therefore, draws out the crucial element of contingency, the nonnecessary link that for Hall (1985) breaks with the reductionism of classical Marxist theories of ideology. By Hall's account, there is no natural fit between a social movement and its group of articulators.

However, in the case I have examined here, contingencies play out in a very different political terrain. Unlike the Lauje case examined by Li, Cucapá fishermen see themselves as indigenous but were not able to take up the reified "indigenous slot" ostensibly made available for them by the state and NGOs in relation to their fishing rights. This failure to articulate with state discourses is not just an example of the risks inherent in any attempted identification, or of the lack of "guarantees," when it comes to articulations. The Cucapá people, much like the Lindu, have been exposed to overtly coercive dimensions of state power and have had their livelihoods denied to them. This is despite the fact that by all accounts, they seem to be positioned to claim indigenous rights. There is, after all, a constitutional guarantee in Mexico that declares that the livelihood of indigenous people should be secured as well as a fully developed environmental discourse, popular in the region, that supports these indigenous claims. The Cucapá, in short, have been "languaged" (as Hall would put it) by the discourse of indigeneity and environmentalism but, as I have argued, the articulation made possible by this apparent summoning has come "unhinged." This articulation failed because of the particular way that neoliberal ideas about multiculturalism came into play in this case, which constrained the conditions under which articulations with the transnational environmental movement are possible. Thus, the fishing cooperative failed to get recognition because its members were deemed "not indigenous enough."

Therefore, the Cucapá case illustrates how contested notions of indigeneity are unevenly aligned with local, national, and transnational discourses and policies or with what Tsing has called "emergent channels of public attention" (2007: 50). As part of this unevenness, local expressions of identity failed to resonate with international environmental discourses on language, indigeneity, and nature conservation, as well as local and national stereotypes of gender inequality.

In this book, in other words, I argue that it is important to look at those cases when articulations of an identity fail or are not entirely successful in their engagements with the state. While one of the advantages of a focus on the politics of articulation is that it allows for contingency, such that no identification is inevitable, this contingency itself does not actually account for instances where some subject positions do not manage to connect to wider political historical trends. Failed articulations draw our attention to the ways that expressions of identity are bound up with very particular structures of power. They draw our attention to precisely the ways that articulations, while not natural, are powerfully determined by historical trends and political conjunctions. While Hall emphasizes the nonnecessary nature of identity articulations (the fact that there is no natural fit between a discourse and its subject positions), he also acknowledges that discourses of identity are not free floating, but are rather anchored in relation to different historical forces (Hall 1996: 54).

In emphasizing the concept of a "failed articulation" it is important to recognize that articulation is always a matter of degree. While Cucapá people are judged to be insufficiently indigenous to be granted fishing rights, we have seen that there are a myriad of contexts in which they are nevertheless recognized as indigenous in formal and informal ways and in everyday contexts. The military, as described in Doña Inez's story, quit hassling young people once they performed their indigeneity by swearing using Cucapá words. And their tracking skills were thought to be superior by local actors in the narco-networks because they have an "indigenous knowledge" of the land.

Furthermore, the Cucapá people have formal status as indigenous in a variety of contexts. For example, the village where I did my fieldwork is recognized as a "*comunidad indígena*" by the federal government and this means, as we have seen, that some Cucapá people have communal land rights. And finally, there are slews of well-meaning yet ineffectual programs implemented by NGOs that also recognize the Cucapá people as targets specifically because they are an "indigenous" population.

These kinds of recognitions, sometimes solicited and sometimes not, often seem intended to contain the more specific and political challenge represented by the Cucapá peoples' claims to direct control over their means of production in relation to fishing. For instance, both the work programs described in chapters 2 and 3 and the community mapping project examined in chapter 5 were intended to provide "alternative" forms of income to fishing. Therefore, in many cases what looks to be a recognition of a political claim to indigeneity also works to contain the more critical challenge that such a claim could pose if it were fully successful (see also Ferguson 1990; Li 2007).

For these reasons, I have emphasized that the processes that render certain enunciations of identity "inarticulate" are equally important for advancing a perspective such as that developed by Hall. The dual meaning of Hall's use of articulation has been particularly relevant in this book. The second meaning emphasizes not just conjoining positions to definite political subjects but also the way that these positions are expressed and made comprehensible and accessible to an audience. In my analysis, I have also put particular emphasis on the ways that certain discourses are often made unintelligible.

We saw how the Cucapá elders' lack of literacy with maps made their own knowledge about places untranslatable in the context of the map-making project. Their modes of understanding place were muted by the technologies and practices taken up by the project. We also saw how Cucapá people, in being primarily Spanish-speaking, are also rendered "inarticulate" in a way that resonates with work looking at the construction of inarticulateness in subordinate groups (Bourdieu 1977b; Hill 1995; McDermott 1988; Young 1983). These authors have emphasized that inarticulateness, rather than a neutral description of linguistic capacity, is an institutional and situational artifact bound up with issues of power (McElhinny 2001). By not speaking *their own* language, that is, the language that would make them authentic indigenous subjects, monolingual Spanish-speaking Cucapá people are rendered radically inarticulate.

Even more striking than failed articulations of identity are those that are locally re-articulated in ways that challenge hegemonic systems of signification. For example, we saw that despite an influx of resources made available by conservation NGOs and other work programs, some people were drawn into the drug economy because of the material and symbolic opportunities it offered. In this case, "the traditional ecological knowledge" of the Cucapá was re-articulated with the drug trade instead of with conservation projects. In this process, discourses on stewardship and conservation are de-centered in a way that challenges assumptions about indigenous knowledge as well as assumptions about local people's economic and political realities. Similarly, rather than viewing the Cucapá language as that what makes them indigenous, Cucapá youth connect their sense of collective identity to shared conditions of subordination. This move takes apart the articulation, endorsed by the neoliberal state, between the cultural identity of indigenous people and the symbolic element of language capacity.

The ways that people make sense of their historical situation and render it intelligible is not just a process of conjoining meaning with global signifiers. The fields of power within which people position themselves are also relative to dynamics within their local group. While involvement in the narco-economy fails to resonate with wider discourses on indigeneity, it also unhinges those who participate in it from other local discourses about what it means to be Cucapá. In this case, some fishermen and women reject local ideas that "the Cucapá will fish forever" and instead adamantly relinquish their nets in exchange for trafficking goods up the river. We also saw a case of a more local "dis-articulation" when Cruz's efforts to express himself as an "authentic Cucapá man" were eventually dismissed by other people in this village as aligning with mainstream Mexican machismo.

One of the most important insights that local re-articulations draw attention to is that sometimes the way that social and ethnic difference is defined and ascribed to local people is arbitrary and careless. Categories imposed to organize difference in the Colorado delta do not pay attention to the social landscape they bisect. Local people, as we have seen, are aware of the recklessness involved in such arbitrary delineations. In much the same way that the line that municipal workers painted over the dead dog on the side of the road at the beginning of this book provoked outrage because of its disregard for local life, social categories imposed with equal disregard have also created widespread discontent. They slash through local meanings, local boundaries, and local idioms of identification. More importantly, state identifications and delineations cut through local priorities and necessities and do so unapologetically.

By the same token, many Cucapá people have also challenged those lines and configurations. They have done so by subverting and reformulating hegemonic discourses about what it means to be Cucapá, what it means to be indigenous, and what it means to be poor in Mexico today. Some have bypassed local development planning and fish anyway, despite the regulations and restrictions imposed by the state. Some have further confronted their criminalization by entering the narco-economy. In doing so, they do not simply criticize the lines that both categorize them and constrain their modes of livelihood, but they also redraw these categories. And they do so, just like the state or its municipal paint-workers, unapologetically.

NOTES

Introduction

1. Colonias are neighborhoods in Mexican municipalities that have no jurisdictional autonomy or representation. In the 1990s, "colonias" also became a common American English name for the slums that developed on both sides of the US-Mexican border as a result of the surge in low-skilled jobs created on both sides of the border by the maquiladora industry (Huntoon and Becker 2001). Unless specified, I do not use the term in this sense here.

2. "El Zanjón" literally means "ditch" or "gully" in Spanish but is used by Cucapá fishers to refer to their fishing grounds, which are located in a large gully where the Gulf of California begins.

3. In the United States the term "tribe" is used to designate indigenous groups that are federally recognized by the Bureau of Indian Affairs, and as such, eligible for certain programs and services.

4. This polarization is complicated on multiple levels. For example, Indian tribes such as the Gila River reservation in Arizona have litigated—often successfully—to secure water rights and the implied authority to sell or trade those rights according to market values (Checchio and Colby 1993). During the water summit one elder from Gila River argued openly for water leasing among the tribes. It was interesting to see how his comments were dismissed in these sessions and a uniform "native" view of water as a commons was sustained over his occasional interjections. Controversies over water rights on the river have formed a small part of wider debates over whether water should be treated as a commodity, owned by individuals, or as a commons that communities have rights to (Espeland 1998; Harris 2002; Maganda 2005, 2012; Walsh 2012; Worster 1992).

5. For most of this manuscript I use the term "indigenous" to refer to the Cucapá people in Mexico. I use this particular term both because it is the generally accepted label used by international organizations such as the United Nations (at least since 2002) and because it is the closest English equivalent to the term used by Cucapá leaders in Mexico (*indígena*). One objection to the term "indigenous" is that it is an overgeneralizing referent that does not specify the people affected by European colonization during the seventeenth or eighteenth centuries and fails to recognize

many other groups as well. For this reason, when referencing indigenous people in the United States I use the term "American Indian," which is understood to mean only the peoples of the main body of the United States and according to the US Census Bureau is the preferred term to most people identifying as indigenous in the United States. It should be noted that there is no single term used to identify indigenous people that is accepted by all groups (nor, in all likelihood, by all members of the same group).

6. In the 1990s it was discovered that much of the building material donated by the government contained asbestos, and most of the residents have since removed this material.

7. Between the 1920s and the 1970s, millions of hectares of land were taken from the haciendas—Mexican and foreign-owned estates—and redistributed to peasants (Joseph and Nugent 1994). The key institution through which the Mexican state implemented agrarian reform was the postrevolutionary *ejido*. There is a vast literature on the Mexican agrarian reform and much controversy over the ejidal system (Bartra 1985; Gledhill 1991; Hamilton 1982; Nugent and Alonso 1994; Sheridan 1988). Nugent and Joseph (1994) argue that this literature falls into two categories: first, an optimistic view that agrarian reform functioned as a socially just set of brakes on the more insidious aspects of capitalist development in the countryside; and second, a more critical view arguing that by co-opting popular demands and erecting an institutional structure through which to organize the production process, the postrevolutionary state strengthened its own position at the service of capital and against peasants.

8. In the 1970s the government organized the Consejo Supremo de los Pueblos Indígenas (Supreme Council of Indigenous Peoples) at the federal level. The Consejo Supremo was constituted by Jefes Supremos (Supreme Chiefs) representing different indigenous communities from all over the country. These reforms legally reintroduced the authority figure of the *jefe tradicional* or "traditional chief" (Garduño 2003).

9. The CDI (Comisión Nacional para el Desarrollo de los Pueblos Indígenas) is the National Commission for the Development of Indigenous People. It is the federal office in charge of coordinating, evaluating, and developing programs for the implementation of indigenous rights "in conformity with article 2 of the Mexican constitution" (www.cdi.gob.mx/index.php?id_seccion=89).

10. My experiences with interviewing resonated with Briggs's (1986) exploration of how the interviewees' categorization of the interaction will profoundly influence what topics may be addressed and how information can be given.

11. The Gadsden Purchase (known in Mexico as Venta de la Mesilla) is a region of what today is southern Arizona and New Mexico that was purchased by the United States from Mexico.

12. In 2006, tribal members on the Cocopah US reservation were receiving portions of the monthly proceeds amounting to approximately seven hundred dollars a month. Among their relatives in Mexico, there has long been hope that some of these

proceeds might eventually reach them. However, a tribal member in the United States put the situation to me quite bluntly in an interview, explaining, "Any money sent to Mexico would have to come directly out of our pockets." Although the federal government requires that a certain portion of casino proceeds be donated to "community causes," the Cucapá are not US citizens and are therefore not eligible.

1. "Listen for When You Get There"

1. Established in 1902, the Bureau of Reclamation is mostly known for the dams, canals, and power plants it constructed in the western states. These water projects are considered to have promoted homesteading and the "economic development" of the West. According to their website, the Bureau of Reclamation has constructed more than six hundred dams and reservoirs, including Hoover Dam on the Colorado River and Grand Coulee on the Columbia River. They are the largest wholesaler of water in the United States and the second largest producer of hydroelectric power (www.usbr.gov/main/about/). Of the multiple entries under "reclamation" in the *Oxford English Dictionary* (2d ed.), the most relevant here are 2c, "The making (of land) fit for cultivation"; 2d, "The action or process of reclaiming used or unusable objects or materials"; and 5, "The action of claiming the return of something taken away; a claim for something."

2. Bergman points out that this is ironic because the delta was one of the first places in North America that the Spanish explored. The first written accounts of the Cucapá appear in the writings of early Spanish explorers and missionaries, including those of Hernando de Alarcón and Melchor Diaz in 1540, Juan de Oñate in 1605, Eusebio Kino in 1702, and Francisco Garces in 1776 (Alvarez de Williams 1975; Bendimez Patterson 1987). According to William Kelly (1977), beyond these irregular encounters with Europeans it was not until the establishment of a permanent American army post at Fort Yuma in 1852 that the Cucapá had significant interaction with Euro-Americans. For the next twenty-five years river boats made regular trips from the mouth of the Colorado to Fort Yuma carrying supplies, and several Cucapá men helped run the boats and barges (Kelly 1977: 9). River traffic came to an end after 1877 with the completion of the Southern Pacific Railroad into Yuma, Arizona, and the Pacific Coast. However, the discovery of gold in California in 1849 continued the western expansion as many migrants came through the area near the mouth of the Colorado River and the Grand Canyon region.

3. There is also an immense vocabulary for different kinds of water rights, such as "reserved," "perfected," "absolute," "senior," etc.

4. See Liebert 2001 for a related analysis of German metaphors for water as money, and Strang 2004 for a case in the United Kingdom.

5. See Hill 1998a, 2008, and Chavez 2001 for other examples of how stereotypes of Mexicans as lazy and incompetent have been mobilized for particularly ideological purposes.

6. In the years since the 1963 court decision, native tribes on the river have continued to increase their presence with regard to the Colorado River. At this time eleven tribes have claimed or "reserved" water rights, including the Chemehuevi Indian Tribe, the Cocopah Indian Tribe, the Colorado River Indian Tribe, the Fort Mojave Indian Tribe, the Jicarilla Apache Tribe, the Navajo Nation, the Northern Ute Tribe, the Quechan Indian Tribe of the Fort Yuma Reservation, the Southern Ute Indian Tribe, and the Ute Mountain Ute Indian Tribe (Wilkins and Tsianina Lomawaima 2001).

2. The Fishing Conflict

1. *Cachanilla* (arrowweed) is a wild, local plant that the original inhabitants of the area used in making huts.

2. See Heller 2003 for an example of the commodification of language and identity in the French Canadian context.

3. A similar ambivalence is evident in portrayals of Inuit people in Canada's ongoing controversies over seal hunting (Wenzel 1978, 1991).

4. In 1938, Mexican president Lázaro Cárdenas implemented the organization of rural fishing people into cooperatives as part of a plan to develop fishing in the region by allocating fishing rights and territories to different sectors of the population and to allow the government to regulate extraction (Cruz-Torres 2000). While cooperative organization continues up to the present, in the past few decades the fishing industry has been increasingly privatized (Cruz-Torres 2004; Vásquez León 1999).

5. While Cucapá people, Mexican state officials, and NGO workers all agree that the Cucapá are indigenous to the delta, the unit of time cited for their occupancy varies depending on who is doing the estimation. Most government officials concede the two-thousand-year figure, which has archeological traces (Flores Navarro 2004). Alvarez de Williams (1974) claims that speakers of the Yuman dialect have resided in the delta for three thousand years (see also Alarcón-Cháires 2001). The Cucapá fishing cooperative would sometimes argue that their ancestors were in the area nine thousand years ago.

6. Article 2 of the Mexican constitution uses the following criteria to define indigenous people: they must be descendants of the people that lived in the same actual territory at the beginning of colonization and preserve their own social, economic, and cultural institutions. This article also specifies that the awareness of their indigenous identity should be a fundamental criterion.

7. Discourses on "endangered languages" also draw on this argument about the interrelations between environmental and cultural preservation. For analyses of how discourses of biodiversity and linguistic diversity intersect, see Maffi 2005 and Muehlmann 2007.

8. The International Labour Organization (ILO) is the UN agency in charge of

3. "What Else Can I Do?"

1. Unless otherwise noted, all dollar figures refer to US dollars.
2. Mexico's border region has a high cost of living relative to other parts of the country. In fact, the border communities of Tijuana, Ciudad Juárez, Reynosa, and Matamoros are among the most expensive places to live in the country, with costs of living comparable to those in the United States.
3. Many who are affiliated with the "narco-world" are called "cheros" (from the word *rancheros*, "ranchers"), referring to those who dress in the clothing of northern rural Mexico. This is a significant term because of the associations between narcotraficantes and rural roots, discussed later in this chapter (see also Edberg 2004a, 2004b).
4. The terms *burrero* (mule) and *narcotraficante* both refer to those who work smuggling illicit drugs, but *narcotraficante* is also used to refer to those who sell drugs. The two terms have different connotations: *burrero* is slightly more derogatory and highlights the low status of the smuggler, whereas *narcotraficante* is more celebratory and highlights the social power associated with the role (Campbell 2005).
5. While gangs and drug traffickers are also often seen as helping their communities (see Goldstein 2003), in this case the close familial connections among residents of the village makes it harder to construe narcotraficantes as "giving to the poor" as much as simply supporting large family networks.
6. In *My Cocaine Museum*, Taussig (2004) provides an account of the process whereby Afro-Colombian gold miners are drawn into the world of cocaine production on Colombia's Pacific coast. He describes an implementation of surveillance quite similar to Alvaro's interpretation of the new regulations about fishing equipment. Taussig documents how one of the changes that shipbuilders experienced in this region was that they had to submit minutely detailed plans of every boat that was to be built, then wait half a year for approval. The idea was that if any new boat were boarded by naval patrols searching for drugs, the navy could measure off every centimeter in search of false bulkheads (2004: 223).

4. Mexican Machismo and a Woman's Worth

1. In this chapter when I refer to "Mexicans" I am referring to nonindigenous Mexicans, unless otherwise noted. As discussed in the introduction, these distinctions become particularly salient when Cucapá people are explicitly opposing themselves to nonindigenous Mexicans, which is the case for much of the ethnographic material analyzed in this chapter.

2. The terms *comadre* and *compadre* indicate the relationship of *compadrazgo* ("coparenthood") between the parents and godparents of a child. In Mexico, as in other parts of Latin America and Spain, compadrazgo is an important social institution that originates when a child is baptized.

3. The standard practice was to refer to couples living together as "married." Very few people were married legally. Don Madeleno explained that the Cucapá tend to wait twenty or thirty years into a relationship before participating in traditional marriage ceremonies and festivities to celebrate a partnership. He contrasted this to Mexican custom in which "people get married, have their celebration, and then hope that it lasts." The general trend of staying legally unmarried also reflects the economic conditions: most Cucapá people cannot afford the marriage licenses and festivities.

4. Doña Bertha's invocation of the "full-blooded Indian," which she opposes to "Mexicans," is ironic in this context, since Mexican nationalism was in fact founded on conceptions of indigenous and Mexican mixings (see Paz 1961).

5. While she does not expand on this point here, Gina often elaborated the stereotype of Cucapá men as lazy and particularly prone to substance abuse.

6. In this example Gina is opposing her own perceived immobility with my mobility, rather than a Cucapá woman's, but her comments are nonetheless revealing of the general associations between moral compromise and being out alone as a woman.

7. María was the only person who used the word *feminista* (feminist) in these interviews.

8. It is noteworthy that the kind of gender bias Don Madeleno suggests may have been manifest in these ethnographies has been discussed in anthropology as well (Keesing 1985; Weiner 1976).

9. In claiming that there were no "powerful" men, Felix was referring to the fact that men were less politically active than women. Political activity does not signal power in all social contexts (see Medicine 1987), but it was commonly invoked as a characteristic associated with power.

10. This is a common statistic mentioned on websites and blogs related to the global water crisis. For example, see the International Medical Corps website (content.imcworldwide.org/microsites/gifts/water_gifts.html). The other figure often cited is that the weight of the water the women carry is an average of twenty kilograms, the same as the average UK airport luggage allowance (see, for example, www.worldwaterworks.org/stats.html).

11. Since the fishing conflict began, with the creation of the biosphere reserve, it has been much more difficult to obtain permission for new permits. This has sustained the gender imbalance among holders.

12. Verbal assertiveness is not always a characteristic associated with powerful roles. Keenan (1974) shows how in a Malagasy-speaking village in Madagascar women are seen as more direct based on their verbal assertiveness, but this is devalued in relation to men's more "polite" indirect speech, which is highly valued.

13. Migration, organizational experience, feminist NGOs, and even official pro-

grams of development have all influenced how indigenous men and women have restructured their relations within the domestic unit and the political sphere. Indigenous women have played an active role in peasant movements for the past few decades as well as during the revolution (Olcott 2005). Changes in the domestic economy also resulted in more women involved in the informal commerce of agriculture and the informal economy more generally (Nash 1993). However, these movements forward have been concomitant with a terrifying rise in violence against women in Mexico, particularly in the northern border region. Since 1993, almost four hundred women and girls have been murdered, and more than seventy remain missing in Ciudad Juárez and Chihuahua, Mexico (Amnesty International 2005). Similar cases of systematic violence against young, often indigenous women working in the factory zone of the border have been documented in Tijuana and Mexicali. This "femicide" has been met by the systematic failure of local and international law enforcement to prevent and prosecute these crimes (Alcalá Iberri and Escalante 2005; González Rodríguez 2002; Ortega 1999; Wright 2011).

5. "Spread Your Ass Cheeks"

1. Doña Katiana, on the other hand, pointed to patterns of use, rather than economic disincentives, as a contributing factor to the loss of Cucapá. She explained that looking back she realizes that it was not possible for her children to learn to speak Cucapá because of the traditional social organization of the community ("the old ways") that persisted into their time. She remembers that it was customary for the elders to always do things separately from the younger generations. Her grandparents and parents would eat together, and the children would then eat separately. When she had her own children, eleven in all, she followed this custom. As Spanish became the dominant language, these exclusive spaces where the elders spoke were the only opportunities for the young people to learn Cucapá. Without access to these spaces, the children could not learn.

2. Laura R. Graham (2002) provides a vivid example of how dominant political groups at times deliberately manipulate indigenous monolingualism to their benefit. Graham describes how, in a dispute over the demarcation of a Waiapi reserve in Brazil, officials barred the Indians' translator from participating in a critical official meeting during the legal negotiations.

3. Thalia, at sixteen, knows more Cucapá words than her peers and her mother, has a genuine interest in learning more, and is often mentioned by other community members as the youth who is most competent in Cucapá.

4. Hill (1983) relays a similar version of boundary marking in a linguistic routine in Nahuatl, a Uto-Aztecan language of southern Mexico. She describes the rapid abandonment of Nahuatl in some communities except in limited contexts, such as cursing outsiders and toasting with pulque. Cursing outsiders takes the form of a challenge: A speaker demands, "Give me your sister." A Nahuatl speaker will know that the proper response is "No, but I will give you my brother," whereas a Spanish

speaker may merely believe he or she has been greeted and will reply, "Good morning" (Hill 1983: 266).

5. In this instance, Osvaldo uses propositional content as a way of displaying his identity to outsiders, in contrast to linguistically displaying his identity at the level of form (as occurs through the use of swearwords). Graham (2002) calls these strategies of "rhetorical engagement" and argues that learning these rhetorics enables indigenous people to engage in broader discursive contexts as well as procure resources from outside their communities.

6. An array of eco-blogs have circulated and reinforced this assertion (see, e.g., porena.blogspot.com; www.gnosticminx.blogspot.com/2007_05_01_archive .html; blog.fastcompany.com/archives/2006/08/14/innovation_and_complexity.html; blogs.salon.com/0002007/2006/08/06.html). When I presented the previous section of this chapter at a conference, the first question I received from the audience was from a linguistic anthropologist who had worked with an indigenous group in Alaska. She prefaced her question by saying: "In the indigenous language I studied, there were no swearwords." She went on to question whether the swearwords I had described were actually indigenous in origin, suggesting that perhaps they were an adaptation since colonization. I discuss the indigenous origin of Cucapá swearwords later in text. Here it is noteworthy that the researcher should express such strong doubts that swearwords would exist in Cucapá in the first place.

7. It is noteworthy that everyday practices of obscenity, as well as the specific practices of swearing I describe in this chapter, are not gendered in the ways that swearing is seen to be in much of the literature on language and gender. Men and women swear with similar prevalence and creativity. This may be related to the prominent role that Cucapá women play in every realm of decision making and as major economic contributors to the household. As we saw in chapter 4, many people explained that the central role of women is one of the characteristics that differentiated the Cucapá, as a group, from Mexicans more generally.

Conclusions

1. The environmental degradation of the delta is also linked to larger global environmental processes. Recently the links between global warming and water scarcity have also come to public attention. While global warming more commonly evokes the specter of rising oceans submerging coastal cities, the diminished supplies of fresh water might prove a far more serious problem than slowly rising seas. In an article in the *New York Times Magazine* in October 2007, Jon Gertner argued that the steady decrease in mountain snow pack (the loss of high-altitude winter snow that melts each spring) could have a catastrophic affect on the Colorado's water supply to the American West, exacerbating current conflicts. The climatology literature on melting snow-pack supports these predictions (Barnett et al. 2004; Christensen et al. 2004; Hamlet et al. 2005).

REFERENCES

Akers Chacón, Justin, and Mike Davis. 2006. *No One Is Illegal: Fighting Racism and State Repression on the U.S.-Mexico Border.* Chicago: Haymarket Books.

Alarcón-Cháires, M. C. Pablo. 2001. "Los indígenas cucapá y la Reserva de la Biosfera Alto Golfo de California y Delta del Río Colorado." In *Informe técnico para la Comisión Nacional de Derechos Humanos.* Morelia, Michoacán: Laboratorio de Etnoecología, IE-UNAM.

Alcalá Iberri, Socorro, and Lucía Escalante G. 2005. *Las muertas de Juárez.* 3rd ed. México, DF: Editorial Libra.

Alcalde, Cristina M. 2007. "'Why Would You Marry a Serrana?': Women's Experiences of Identity-Based Violence in the Intimacy of Their Homes in Lima." *Journal of Latin American and Caribbean Anthropology* 12 (1): 1–24.

Alonso, Ana Maria. 2004. "Conforming Disconformity: 'Mestizaje,' Hybridity, and the Aesthetics of Mexican Nationalism." *Cultural Anthropology* 19 (4): 459–490.

Alvarez de Williams, Anita. 1974. "Los Cucapa del delta del Rio Colorado." *Calafia* 2 (5): 40–47.

———. 1975. *Travelers among the Cucapá.* Baja California Travels Series 34. Los Angeles: Dawson's Book Shop.

American Psychiatric Association. 1994. *Diagnostic and Statistical Manual of Mental Disorders: DSM-IV-TR.* Washington, DC: American Psychiatric Association.

Amnesty International. 2005. "Mexico: Justice Fails in Ciudad Juarez and the City of Chihuahua." www.amnestyusa.org/node/55339?id=5AB197BCEE37D92D80256FB600689A74 (accessed July 18, 2010).

Anderson, Elijah. 1992. "The Story of John Turner." In *Drugs, Crime and Social Isolation,* edited by A. V. Harrell and G. E. Peterson, 147–179. Washington, DC: Urban Institute Press.

Andreas, Peter. 2000. *Border Games: Policing the U.S.-Mexico Divide.* Ithaca, NY: Cornell University Press.

Antze, Paul, and Michael Lambek. 1996. "Introduction: Forecasting Memory." In *Tense Past: Cultural Essays in Trauma and Memory,* edited by Paul Antze and Michael Lambek, xi–xxxviii. New York: Routledge.

Archibold, Randal. 2007. "In Arizona Desert, American Indian Trackers vs. Smugglers." *International Herald Tribune,* March 7.

Armstrong-Fumero, Fernando. 2009a. "A Heritage of Ambiguity: The Historical Substrate of Vernacular Multiculturalism in Yucatán, Mexico." *American Anthropologist* 36 (2): 300–316.

———. 2009b. "Old Jokes and New Multiculturalisms: Continuity and Change in Vernacular Discourse on the Yucatec Maya Language." *American Anthropologist* 111(3): 360–372.

Asad, Talal. 1993. *Genealogies of Religion: Discipline and Reasons of Power in Christianity and Islam.* Baltimore: Johns Hopkins University Press.

Astorga, Luis. 2005. "Corridos de Traficantes y Censura." *Región y Sociedad* 8(32): 145–165.

Avio, K. L. 1994. "Aboriginal Property Rights in Canada: A Contractarian Interpretation of R. V. Sparrow." *Canadian Public Policy/Analyse de Politiques* 20 (4): 415–429.

Bacon, David. 2004. *The Children of NAFTA: Labor Wars on the U.S./Mexico Border.* Berkeley: University of California Press.

Bakhtin, Mikhail M. 1994. *The Bakhtin Reader.* Edited by Pam Morris. Oxford: Oxford University Press.

Bakker, Karen. 2007. *Eau Canada: The Future of Canada's Water.* Vancouver: UBC Press.

Bamford, Sandra. 2002. "On Being 'Natural' in the Rainforest Marketplace: Science, Capitalism and the Commodification of Biodiversity." *Social Analysis* 46 (1): 35–50.

Barker, Joshua. 2005. "Engineers and Political Dreams: Indonesia in the Satellite Age." *Current Anthropology* 46 (5): 703–727.

Barnett, Tim P., Robert Malone, William T. Pennell, Detlet Stammer, Bret Semtner, and Warren M. Washington. 2004. "The Effects of Climate Change on Water Resources in the West: Introduction and Overview." *Climatic Change* 62 (1–3): 1–11.

Bartra, Armando. 1985. *Los herederos de Zapata: Movimientos campesinos posrevolucionarios en Mexico, 1920–1980.* México, DF: Ediciones Era.

Basso, Keith H. 1996. *Wisdom Sits in Places: Landscape and Language among the Western Apache.* Albuquerque: University of New Mexico Press.

Bauman, Richard. 1977. *Verbal Art as Performance.* Prospect Heights, IL: Waveland.

———. 1993. Introduction to *Folklore and Culture on the Texas-Mexican Border.* Austin: Center for Mexican American Studies, University of Texas at Austin.

Baviskar, Amita. 2005. "Adivasi Encounters with Hindu Nationalism in MP." *Economic and Political Weekly* 40 (48): 5105–5113.

Behar, Ruth, and Deborah A. Gordon. 1995. *Women Writing Culture.* Berkeley: University of California Press.

Bender, Barbara, and Margot Winer. 2001. *Contested Landscapes: Movement, Exile and Place.* New York: Bergmann.

Bendimez Patterson, Julia. 1987. "Antecedentes históricos de los indígenas de Baja California: Estudios fronterizos." *Revista del IIS* 5 (14): 11–46.

Bennett, Vivienne, Sonia Dávila-Poblete, and Nieves Rico. 2005. *Opposing Currents: The Politics of Water and Gender in Latin America.* Pitt Latin American Series. Pittsburgh: University of Pittsburgh Press.

Bergman, Charles, and Defenders of Wildlife. 2002. *Red Delta: Fighting for Life at the End of the Colorado River.* Golden, CO: Fulcrum

Bess, Jennifer. 2000. "'Kill the Indian, Save the Man!': Charles Eastman Surveys His Past." *Wicazo SA Review* 15: 7–28.

Bjornson, Marnie. 2007. "Speaking of Citizenship: Language Ideologies in Dutch Citizenship Regimes." *Focaal—European Journal of Anthropology* 49: 65–80.

Blanco, José. 2001. "La autonomía de los riesgos." *La Jornada*, April 3.

Boulder Dam Association. 1930. Untitled Pamphlet. Flagstaff, AZ: Cline Library Special Archives.

———. 1928. *The Story of a Great Government Project for the Conquest of the Colorado River.* Flagstaff, AZ: Cline Library Special Archives.

Boulder Dam Service Bureau. 1937. *Boulder Dam: Book of Comparisons.* Boulder City, NV: Bureau of Reclamation.

Bourdieu, Pierre. 1977a. *Outline of a Theory of Practice.* Cambridge: Cambridge University Press.

———. 1977b. "The Economics of Linguistic Exchanges." *Social Science Information* 16 (6): 645–668.

———. 1998. "The Essence of Neoliberalism." *Le Monde Diplomatique*, December. Electronic document, mondediplo.com/1998/12/08bourdieu (accessed March 24, 2009).

Bourgois, Philippe I. 2002. *In Search of Respect: Selling Crack in El Barrio.* Cambridge: Cambridge University Press.

Bowden, Charles, and Javier Aguilar. 1998. *Juarez: The Laboratory of Our Future.* New York: Aperture.

Boyer, Christopher R. 2003. *Becoming Campesinos: Politics, Identity, and Agrarian Struggle in Postrevolutionary Michoacán.* Stanford, CA: Stanford University Press.

Brana-Shute, Rosemary. 1980. "Lower-Class Creole Women, Clubs and Politics in Surinam." In *Women and Politics in Twentieth-Century Latin America: Studies in Third World Society*, edited by Sandra F. McGee, 33–56. Williamsburg, VA: Department of Anthropology, College of William and Mary.

Braun, Bruce. 2002. *The Intemperate Rainforest: Nature, Culture, and Power on Canada's West Coast.* Minneapolis: University of Minnesota Press.

Briggs, Charles L. 1986. *Learning How to Ask: A Sociolinguistic Appraisal of the Role of the Interview in Social Science Research.* Cambridge: Cambridge University Press.

———. 1988. *Competence in Performance: The Creativity of Tradition in Mexicano Verbal Art.* University of Pennsylvania Press Conduct and Communication Series. Philadelphia: University of Pennsylvania Press.

Briggs, Charles L., and Clara Mantini-Briggs. 2003. *Stories in the Time of Cholera: Racial Profiling during a Medical Nightmare.* Berkeley: University of California Press.

Bright, William. 1993. *A Coyote Reader*. Berkeley: University of California Press.
Brody, Hugh. 2000. *The Other Side of Eden: Hunters, Farmers and the Shaping of the World*. Vancouver: Douglas & McIntyre.
Brosius, Peter. 1997. "Endangered Forest, Endangered People: Environmentalist Representations of Indigenous Knowledge." *Human Ecology* 25 (1): 47–69.
———. 1999. "Analyses and Interventions: Anthropological Engagements with Environmentalism." *Current Anthropology* 40 (3): 277–310.
Brosius, Peter, and Diane Russell. 2003. "Conservation from Above: An Anthropological Perspective on Transboundary Protected Areas and Ecoregional Planning." *Journal of Sustainable Forestry* 17: 39–65.
Brown, David, David Farrier, Sandra Egger, and Luke McNamara. 2001. *Criminal Laws: Materials and Commentary on Criminal Law and Process in New South Wales*. Sydney: Federation.
Brysk, Alison. 2000. *From Tribal Village to Global Village: Indian Rights and International Relations in Latin America*. Stanford, CA: Stanford University Press.
Bunte, Pamela. 1980. "Birdpeople: A Southern Paiute Coyote Tale." In *Coyote Stories*, vol. 6, edited by M. B. Kendall. Chicago: University of Chicago Press.
———. 2002. "Verbal Artistry in Southern Paiute Narratives: Reduplication as a Stylistic Process." *Journal of Linguistic Anthropology* 12 (1): 2–33.
Bunte, Pamela, and Robert Franklin. 1992. "You Can't Get There from Here: Southern Paiute Testimony as Intercultural Communication." *Anthropological Linguistics* 34 (1): 19–44.
Bureau of Reclamation. 1920. *A National Menace Becomes a National Treasure*. Colorado River Project, US Department of the Interior, Cline Library Special Archives, Flagstaff, AZ.
———. 2007. "Colorado River Interim Guidelines for Lower Basin Shortages and Coordinated Operations for Lake Powell and Lake Mead." In *Executive Summary: Environmental Consequences*. Boulder, NV: US Department of the Interior.
Butler, Judith P. 1993. *Bodies That Matter: On the Discursive Limits of "Sex."* New York: Routledge.
Cameron, Deborah. 2007. "Language Endangerment and Verbal Hygiene: History, Morality and Politics." In *Discourses of Endangerment: Interest and Ideology in Defense of Language*, edited by Alexandre Duchêne and Monica Heller, 268–281. New York: Continuum International.
Campbell, Howard. 2005. "Drug Trafficking Stories: Everyday Forms of Narco-Folklore on the US-Mexico Border." *International Journal of Drug Policy* 16(5): 326–333.
———. 2008. "Female Drug Smugglers on the U.S.-Mexico Border: Gender, Crime, and Empowerment." *Anthropological Quarterly* 81: 233–267.
———. 2009. *Drug War Zone: Frontline Dispatches from the Streets of El Paso and Juárez*. Austin: University of Texas Press.
Canessa, Andrew. 2005. *Natives Making Nation: Gender, Indigeneity, and the State in the Andes*. Tucson: University of Arizona Press.

Carbaugh, Donald. 1996. *Situating Selves: The Communication of Social Identities in American Scenes.* Albany: State University of New York Press.

———. 2001. "The Mountain and the Project: Dueling Depictions of a Natural Environment." In *The Ecolinguistics Reader: Language, Ecology and Environment*, edited by F. Alwin and Peter Mühlhäusler, 124–142. London: Continuum.

Carroll, Michael P. 1981. "Levi-Strauss, Freud, and the Trickster: A New Perspective upon an Old Problem." *American Ethnologist* 8 (2): 301–313.

Cattelino, Jessica R. 2008. *High Stakes: Florida Seminole Gaming and Sovereignty.* Durham, NC: Duke University Press.

Cervone, Emma. 2002. "Engendering Leadership: Indigenous Women Leaders in the Andes." In *Gender's Place: Feminist Anthropologies of Latin America*, edited by R. Montoya, L. J. Frazier, and J. Hurtig, 179–196. Hampshire, UK: Palgrave Macmillan.

Chapin, Mac. 2004. "A Challenge to Conservationists." *World Watch*, November/December.

Chapin, Mac, Zachary Lamb, and Bill Threlkeld. 2005. "Mapping Indigenous Lands." *Annual Review of Anthropology* 34 (1): 619–638.

Chase Smith, Richard, Mario Pariona, Ermeto Tuesta, and Margarita Benavides. 2003. "Mapping the Past and the Future: Geomatics and Indigenous Territories in the Peruvian Amazon." *Human Organization* 62 (4): 357–368.

Chavez, Leo R. 2001. *Covering Immigration: Popular Images and the Politics of the Nation.* Berkeley: University of California Press.

Checchio, Elizabeth, and Bonnie G. Colby. 1993. *Indian Water Rights: Negotiating the Future.* Tucson: Water Resources Research Center, University of Arizona.

Christensen, Niklas S., Andrew W. Wood, Nathalie Voisin, Dennis P. Lettenmaier, and Richard N. Palmer. 2004. "The Effects of Climate Change on the Hydrology and Water Resources of the Colorado River Basin." *Climatic Change* 62 (1): 337–363.

Clifford, James. 1988. *The Predicament of Culture: Twentieth-Century Ethnography, Literature, and Art.* Cambridge, MA: Harvard University Press.

———. 2001. "Indigenous Articulations." *Contemporary Pacific* 13 (2): 468–490.

Clifford, James, and George E. Marcus. 1986. *Writing Culture: The Poetics and Politics of Ethnography.* Berkeley: University of California Press.

Coles, Anne, and Tina Wallace. 2005. *Gender, Water and Development.* Cross-Cultural Perspectives on Women. New York: Berg.

Colombi, Benedict. 2010. "Indigenous Peoples, Large Dams, and Capital-Intensive Energy Development: A View from Lower Colorado River." In *Indians and Energy in the Southwest: Exploitation and Opportunity*, edited by S. Smith and B. Frehner, 133–168. Santa Fe: School for Advanced Research Press.

Comaroff, Jean, and John L. Comaroff. 1999. "Occult Economies and the Violence of Abstraction: Notes from the South African Postcolony." *American Ethnologist* 26 (2): 279–303.

———. 2009. *Ethnicity, Inc.* Chicago: University of Chicago Press.

Conklin, Elizabeth. 1997. "Body Paint, Feathers, and VCRs: Aesthetics and Authenticity in Amazonian Activism." *American Ethnologist* 24 (4): 711–737.

Conklin, Elizabeth, and Laura Graham. 1995. "The Shifting Middle Ground: Amazonian Indians and Eco-Politics." *American Anthropologist* 97 (4): 695–710.

Connell, Robert. 1987. *Gender and Power: Society, the Person and Sexual Politics.* Stanford, CA: Stanford University Press.

Contreras Montellano, Oscar F. 2000. *Empresas globales, actores locales: Producción flexible y aprendizaje industrial en las maquiladoras.* México, DF: El Colegio de México, Centro de Estudios Sociologicos.

Corey, Herbert. 1923. "The Biggest Job in the World: The Story of the Colorado River Project." *American Legion Weekly*, May 11.

Crawford, James Mack. 1966. "The Cocopa Language." PhD diss., University of California, Berkeley.

———. 1983. *Cocopa Texts.* Berkeley: University of California Press.

———. 1989. *Cocopa Dictionary.* Berkeley: University of California Press.

Cronon, William. 1991. *Nature's Metropolis: Chicago and the Great West.* New York: Norton.

Cruikshank, Julie. 2005. *Do Glaciers Listen?: Local Knowledge, Colonial Encounters and Social Imagination.* Vancouver: UBC Press.

Cruz-Torres, María L. 2000. "'Pink Gold Rush': Shrimp Aquaculture, Sustainable Development, and the Environment in Northwestern Mexico." *Journal of Political Ecology* 7: 63–90.

———. 2001. "Local-Level Responses to Environmental Degradation in Northwestern Mexico." *Journal of Anthropological Research* 57 (2): 111–136.

———. 2004. *Lives of Dust and Water: An Anthropology of Change and Resistance in Northwestern Mexico.* Tucson: University of Arizona Press.

Crystal, David. 2000. *Language Death.* Cambridge: Cambridge University Press.

Culp, Peter. 2000. *Restoring the Colorado Delta with the Limits of the Law of the River: The Case for Voluntary Water Transfers.* Tucson: Udall Center for Studies in Public Policy.

Cunneen, Chris. 2001. *Conflict, Politics and Crime: Aboriginal Communities and the Police.* Sydney: Allen & Unwin.

Daly, Nicola, Janet Holmes, Jonathan Newton, and Maria Stubbe. 2004. "Expletives as Solidarity Signals in FTAS on the Factory Floor." *Journal of Pragmatics* 36: 945–964.

Dawson, Alexander S. 2004. *Indian and Nation in Revolutionary Mexico.* Tucson: University of Arizona Press.

de Barbieri, Teresita. 1990. "Sobre géneros, practicas y valores: Notas acerca de posibles erosiones del machismo en México." In *Normas y practicas: Morales y cívicas en la vida cotidiana*, edited by J. M. Ramierz Saiz, 83–105. Mexico City, Porrúa: UNAM.

de Barbieri, Teresita, and Orlandina de Oliveira. 1986. "Nuevos sujetos sociales: La presencia política de las mujeres en América Latina." *Nueva Antropología* 30: 5–29.

de Certeau, Michel. 1988. *The Practice of Everyday Life*. Berkeley: University of California Press.

de Klerk, Vivian. 1992. "How Taboo Are Taboo Words for Girls?" *Language in Society* 2: 277–289.

———. 1997. "The Role of Expletives in the Construction of Masculinity." In *Language and Masculinity*, edited by Sally Johnson and Ulrike Hanna Meinhof, 144–158. Oxford: Blackwell.

de la Cadena, Marisol, and Orin Starn. 2007. *Indigenous Experience Today*. New York: Berg.

de la Peña, Guillermo. 2005. "Social and Cultural Policies toward Indigenous Peoples: Perspectives from Latin America." *Annual Review of Anthropology* 34 (1): 717–739.

———. 2006. "A New Mexican Nationalism? Indigenous Rights, Constitutional Reform and the Conflicting Meanings of Multiculturalism." *Nations and Nationalism* 12 (2): 279–302.

de Oliveira, João Pacheco. 1999. *Ensayos en antropología histórica*. Rio de Janeiro: Universidad Federal Rio de Janeiro.

De Villiers, Marq. 1999. *Water Wars: Is the World's Water Running Out?* London: Weidenfeld & Nicolson.

Del Olmo, Rosa. 1990. "The Economic Crisis and the Criminalization of the Latin American Woman." *Social Justice* 17 (2): 40–53.

Díaz Polanco, Héctor. 1997. *Indigenous Peoples in Latin America: The Quest for Self-Determination*. Latin American Perspectives Series; no. 18. Boulder, CO: Westview Press.

Doane, Molly. 2007. "The Political Economy of the Ecological Native." *American Anthropologist* 109 (3): 452–462.

Dolan, Catherine. 2002. "Gender and Witchcraft in Agrarian Transition: The Case of Kenyan Horticulture." *Development and Change* 33 (4): 659–681.

Dove, Michael. 2006. "Indigenous People and Environmental Politics." *Annual Review of Anthropology* 35: 191–208.

Duchêne, Alexandre, and Monica Heller, eds. 2007. *Discourses of Endangerment: Interest and Ideology in the Defence of Language*. Advances in Sociolinguistics. New York: Continuum International.

DuMars, Charles T., Marilyn O'Leary, and Albert E. Utton. 1984. *Pueblo Indian Water Rights: Struggle for a Precious Resource*. Tucson: University of Arizona Press.

Dunn, Timothy J. 1996. *The Militarization of the U.S.-Mexico Border, 1978–1992: Low-Intensity Conflict Doctrine Comes Home*. CMAS Border and Migration Studies Series. Austin: CMAS Books, University of Texas at Austin.

Dwyer, Augusta. 1994. *On the Line: Life on the US-Mexican Border*. London: Latin American Bureau.

Dwyer, J. John. 2008. *The Agrarian Dispute: The Expropriation of American-Owned Rural Land in Postrevolutionary Mexico*. Durham, NC: Duke University Press.

Edberg, Cameron Mark. 2004a. "The Narcotrafficker in Representation and Practice: A Cultural Persona from the U.S.-Mexican Border." *Ethos* 32 (2): 257–277.

———. 2004b. *El Narcotraficante: Narcocorridos and the Construction of a Cultural Persona on the U.S.-Mexican Border.* Austin: University of Texas Press.

Elhance, Arun P. 1999. *Hydropolitics in the Third World: Conflict and Cooperation in International River Basins.* Washington, DC: US Institute of Peace Press.

Ellison, James. 2006. "'Everyone Can Do as He Wants': Economic Liberalization and Emergent Forms of Antipathy in Southern Ethiopia." *American Ethnologist* 33 (4): 665–686.

Environmental Protection Agency. 1998. Map of Tribal Lands.

Escobar, Arturo. 1996. "Constructing Nature: Elements for a Poststructural Political Ecology." In *Liberation Ecologies: Environment, Development, Social Movements*, edited by R. Peet and M. Wats, 46–68. London: Routledge.

———. 1999. "After Nature: Steps to an Antiessentialist Political Ecology." *Current Anthropology* 40 (1): 1–30.

Escobar Latapi, A. 1998. "Los hombres y sus historias: Reestructuración y masculinidad en México." *La Ventana* 8: 122–173.

Espeland, Wendy. 1998. *The Struggle for Water: Politics, Rationality, and Identity in the American Southwest.* Chicago: University of Chicago Press.

Etienne, Mona. 1980. "Women and Men, Cloth and Colonization: The Transformation of Production-Distribution among the Baule (Ivory Coast)." In *Women and Colonization: Anthropological Perspectives*, edited by Mona Etienne and Eleanor Burke Leacock, 518–535. New York: Praeger Security International.

Etienne, Mona, and Eleanor Burke Leacock. 1980. *Women and Colonization: Anthropological Perspectives.* New York: Praeger Security International.

Fassin, Didier. 2005. "Compassion and Repression: The Moral Economy of Immigration Policies in France." *Cultural Anthropology* 20 (3): 362–387.

Feld, Steven. 1990. *Sound and Sentiment: Birds, Weeping, Poetics, and Song in Kaluli Expression.* Philadelphia: University of Pennsylvania Press.

Fentress, James, and Chris Wickham. 1992. *Social Memory.* Cambridge: Blackwell.

Ferguson, James. 1990. *The Anti-Politics Machine: "Development," Depoliticization, and Bureaucratic Power in Lesotho.* New York: Cambridge University Press.

———. 2007. "Formalities of Poverty: Thinking about Social Assistance in Neoliberal South Africa." *African Studies Review* 50 (2): 71–86.

Field, Les W. 1999. "Complicities and Collaborations: Anthropologists and the 'Unacknowledged Tribes' of California." *Current Anthropology* 40 (2): 193–209.

———. 2008. *Abalone Tales: Collaborative Explorations of Sovereignty and Identity in Native California.* Durham, NC: Duke University Press.

Firebaugh, Luna E. 2002. "The Border Crossed Us." *Wicazo Sa Review* 17 (1): 159–181.

Fleisher, Mark S. 1998. *Dead End Kids: Gang Girls and the Boys They Know.* Madison: University of Wisconsin Press.

Flores Navarro, H. 2004. *Nuestra herencia.* 2nd ed. Recopilación Histórico-

Regional de San Luis Río Colorado. San Luis Río, CO: Comisión de Asuntos Históricos.

Foley, Douglas E. 1994. *Learning Capitalist Culture: Deep in the Heart of Tejas.* Philadelphia: University of Pennsylvania Press.

Foucault, Michel. 1995. *Discipline and Punish: The Birth of the Prison.* Translated by Alan Sheridan. New York: Vintage Books.

Fradkin, Philip L. 1981. *A River No More: The Colorado River and the West.* New York: Knopf.

Frake, Charles. 1996a. "A Church Too Far near a Bridge Oddly Placed: The Cultural Construction of the Norfolk Countryside." In *Redefining Nature: Ecology, Culture and Domestication,* edited by Roy Ellen and Katsuyoshi Fukui, 89–113. Washington: Berg.

———. 1996b. "Pleasant Places, Past Times, and Sheltered Identity in Rural East Anglia." In *Senses of Place,* edited by Steven Feld and Keith H. Basso, 229–257. Santa Fe: School of American Research.

French, Jan. 2004. "Mestizaje and Law Making in Indigenous Identity Formation in Northeastern Brazil: 'After the Conflict Came the History.'" *American Anthropologist* 106 (4): 663–674.

Fuentes, Carlos. 1972. "The Legacy of La Malinche." In *Literatura chicana: Texto y contexto / Chicano Literature: Text and Context,* edited by Antonia Castañeda Shular, Tomás Ybarra-Frausto, and Joseph Sommers. Englewood Cliffs, NJ: Prentice-Hall.

Fuller, Norma. 1996. "Los estudios sobre masculinidad en Perú." In *Detrás de la puerta: Hombres y mujeres en el Perú de hoy,* edited by P. Ruiz-Bravo. Lima, Peru: PUCP.

Gal, Susan. 1979. *Language Shift: Social Determinants of Linguistic Change in Bilingual Austria.* New York: Academic Press.

———. 1993. "Diversity and Contestation in Linguistic Ideologies: German Speakers in Hungary." *Language in Society* 22: 337–359.

———. 1995. "Language and the 'Arts of Resistance.'" *Cultural Anthropology* 10 (3): 407–424.

García, María Elena. 2005. *Making Indigenous Citizens: Identities, Education, and Multicultural Development in Peru.* Stanford, CA: Stanford University Press.

García de León, M. A. 1994. *Elites discriminadas.* Barcelona, Spain: Anthropos.

Garduño, Everardo. 2003. "The Yumans of Baja California, Mexico: From Invented to Imagined and Invisible Communities." *Journal of Latin American Anthropology* 8 (1): 4–37.

Garrett, Paul B. 2005. "What a Language Is Good For: Language Socialization, Language Shift, and the Persistence of Code-Specific Genres in St. Lucia." *Language in Society* 34 (3): 327–361.

Gaviria, Alejandro, and Daniel Mejía, eds. 2011. *Anti-Drugs Policies in Colombia: Successes, Failures and Wrong Turns.* Bogotá: Ediciones Uniandes.

Gertner, Jon. 2007. "The Future Is Drying Up." *New York Times Magazine,* October 21.

Gibler, John. 2011. *To Die in Mexico: Dispatches from Inside the Drug War*. San Francisco: City Lights.

Giddens, Anthony. 1986. *The Constitution of Society: Outline of the Theory of Structuration*. Berkeley: University of California Press.

Gifford, Edward W. 1933. "The Cocopa." *University of California Publications in American Archaeology and Ethnology* 31 (2): 257–324.

Gilmore, David D. 1990. *Manhood in the Making: Cultural Concepts of Masculinity*. New Haven, CT: Yale University Press.

Gledhill, John. 1991. *Casi Nada: A Study of Agrarian Reform in the Homeland of Cardenismo*. Studies on Culture and Society 4. Austin: Institute for Mesoamerican Studies, University at Albany. Distributed by University of Texas Press.

Goldstein, Donna M. 2003. *Laughter out of Place: Race, Class, Violence, and Sexuality in a Rio Shantytown*. California Series in Public Anthropology. Berkeley: University of California Press.

Gómez Estrada, José Alfredo. 1994. "Los Cucapa, las compañías colonizadoras y las tierras del Valle de Mexicali." *Calafia* 7 (5): 26–37.

———. 2000. *La gente del delta del Río Colorado: Indígenas, colonizadores y ejidatarios*. Colección Baja California, Nuestra Historia 15. Mexicali, Mexico: Universidad Autonoma de Baja California.

González Rodríguez, Sergio. 2002. *Huesos en el desierto*. Barcelona: Editorial Anagrama.

Gordillo, Gastón. 1999. *The Bush, the Plantations, and the "Devils": Culture and Historical Experience in the Argentinean Chaco*. Toronto: National Library of Canada.

———. 2004. *Landscapes of Devils: Tensions of Place and Memory in the Argentinean Chaco*. Durham, NC: Duke University Press.

———. 2011. "Longing for Elsewhere: Guaraní Reterritorializations." *Comparative Studies in Society and History* 53(4): 855–881.

Gordillo, Gastón, and Silvia Hirsch. 2003. "Indigenous Struggles and Contested Identities in Argentina: Histories of Invisibilization and Reemergence." *Journal of Latin American Anthropology* 8 (3): 2–30.

Gordillo, Gastón, and Juan Martin Leguizamón. 2002. *El río y la frontera: Movilizaciones aborígenes, obras publicas y mercosur en el pilcomayo*. Buenos Aires: Editorial Biblos.

Gordon, Michael. 1993. "Sexual Slang and Gender." *Women and Language* 16 (2): 16–21.

Gordon, Raymond G., Jr. 2005. *Ethnologue: Languages of the World*. 15th ed. Dallas: SIL International. Available at www.ethnologue.com.

Graham, Laura. 2002. "How Should an Indian Speak? Amazonian Indians and the Symbolic Politics of Language in the Global Public Sphere." In *Indigenous Movements, Self-Representation, and the State in Latin America*, edited by Kay Warren and Jean Jackson, 181–228. Austin: University of Texas Press.

Gray, Andrew. 1996. *The Arakmbut of Amazonian Peru*. Providence, RI: Berghahn Books.

Greenough, Paul R., and Anna Lowenhaupt Tsing. 2003. *Nature in the Global South: Environmental Projects in South and Southeast Asia*. Durham, NC: Duke University Press.

Grounds, Richard A., George E. Tinker, and David E. Wilkins. 2003. *Native Voices: American Indian Identity and Resistance*. Lawrence: University Press of Kansas.

Gupta, Akhil. 1998. *Postcolonial Developments: Agriculture in the Making of Modern India*. Durham, NC: Duke University Press.

Gupta, Akhil, and James Ferguson. 1992. "Beyond 'Culture': Space, Identity, and the Politics of Difference." *Cultural Anthropology* 7 (1): 6–23.

Gustafson, Bret D. 2009. *New Languages of the State: Indigenous Resurgence and the Politics of Knowledge in Bolivia*. Durham, NC: Duke University Press.

Gutmann, Matthew. 1993. "Los hombres cambiantes, los machos impenitentes y las relaciones de genero en México en los noventa." *Estudios Sociológicos* 11 (33): 725–740.

———. 1996. *The Meanings of Macho: Being a Man in Mexico City*. 10th anniversary ed. Berkeley: University of California Press.

———. 1997a. "The Ethnographic (G)Ambit: Women and the Negotiation of Masculinity in Mexico City." *American Ethnologist* 24 (4): 833–855.

———. 1997b. "El machismo." In *Masculinidad/es: Poder y crisis*, edited by T. Valdéz and J. Ovarría. Santiago, Chile: Internacional/FLACSO.

Haenn, Nora. 1999. "The Power of Environmental Knowledge: Ethnoecology and Environmental Conflicts in Mexican Conservation." *Human Ecology* 27 (3): 477–491.

———. 2002. "Nature Regimes in Southern Mexico: A History of Power and Environment." *Ethnology* 41 (1): 1–26.

Hale, Charles. 2002. "Does Multiculturalism Menace?" *Journal of Latin American Studies* 34 (3): 485–524.

———. 2005. "Neoliberal Multiculturalism: The Remaking of Cultural Rights and Racial Dominance in Central America." *Political and Legal Anthropology Review* 28 (1): 10–28.

Hall, Stuart. 1983. "The Problem of Ideology: Marxism without Guarantees." In *Marx: A Hundred Years On*, edited by B. Matthews, 25–46. London: Lawrence and Wishart.

———. 1985. "Signification, Representation, Ideology: Althusser and the Post-Structuralist Debates." *Critical Studies in Mass Communication* 2 (2): 91–114.

———. 1991. "The Local and the Global: Globalization and Ethnicity." In *Culture, Globalization and the World-System: Contemporary Conditions for the Representation of Identity*, edited by Anthony D. King, 19–40. Binghamton: SUNY Press.

———. 1996. "On Postmodernism and Articulation: An Interview with Stuart Hall by Lawrence Grossberg." *Journal of Communication Inquiry* 10: 45–60.

———. 2000. "Who Needs 'Identity?'" In *Identity: A Reader*, edited by P. Gay, J. Evans, and P. Redman, 15–30. London: Sage.

Hamilton, Nora. 1982. *The Limits of State Autonomy: Post-Revolutionary Mexico.* Princeton, NJ: Princeton University Press.

Hamlet, Alan F., Philip W. Mote, Martyn P. Clark, and Dennis P. Lettenmaier. 2005. "Effects of Temperature and Precipitation Variability on Snowpack Trends in the Western United States." *Journal of Climate* 18 (21): 4545–4561.

Hanks, William F. 1990. *Referential Practice: Language and Lived Space among the Maya.* Chicago: University of Chicago Press.

——. 1999a. "The Five Gourds of Memory." In *Intertexts: Writings on Language, Utterance, and Context,* 197–217. Lanham, MD: Rowman & Littlefield.

——. 1999b. "Intertextuality of Space in Yucatan." In *Intertexts: Writings on Language, Utterance, and Context,* 249–271. Lanham, MD: Rowman & Littlefield.

Harris, Leila M. 2002. "Water and Conflict Geographies of the Southeastern Anatolia Project." *Society & Natural Resources* 15 (8): 743–759.

Harrison, K. David. 2007. *When Languages Die: The Extinction of the World's Languages and the Erosion of Human Knowledge.* New York: Oxford University Press.

Harvey, David. 2005. *A Brief History of Neoliberalism.* Oxford: Oxford University Press.

Harvey, Neil. 1998. *The Chiapas Rebellion: The Struggle for Land and Democracy.* Durham, NC: Duke University Press.

Harvey Pearce, Roy. 1953. *The Savages of America: A Study of the Indian and the Idea of Civilization.* Baltimore: John Hopkins University Press.

Hathaway, Michael. 2010. "The Emergence of Indigeneity: Public Intellectuals and Indigenous Space in Southwest China." *Cultural Anthropology* 25 (2): 301–333.

Hecht, Susana, and Alexander Cockburn. 1990. *The Fate of the Forest: Developers, Destroyers and Defenders of the Amazon.* New York: Verso.

Heilpern, David. 1999. "Judgment: Police v. Shannon Thomas Dunn, Dubbo Local Court." *Alternative Law Journal* 24 (5): 238–242.

Heller, Monica. 2003. "Globalization, the New Economy, and the Commodification of Language and Identity." *Journal of Sociolinguistics* 7 (4): 473–492.

Herlihy, Peter H., and Gregory Knapp. 2003. "Maps of, by, and for the Peoples of Latin America." *Human Organization* 62 (4): 303–314.

Hernández Castillo, Rosalva Aída. 1998. "Between Hope and Despair: The Struggle of Organized Women in Chiapas since the Zapatista Uprising." *Journal of Latin American Anthropology* 2 (3): 77–99.

——. 2001. "La antropología aplicada al servicio del estado-nación: Aculturación e indigenismo en la frontera sur de México." *Journal of Latin American Anthropology* 6 (2): 20–41.

——. 2002. "Indigenous Law and Identity Politics in Mexico: Indigenous Men's and Women's Struggles for a Multicultural Nation." *PoLAR* 25 (1): 90–107.

Heyman, Josiah M. 1999. *States and Illegal Practices.* Oxford: Berg.

Hill, Jane H. 1983. "Language Death in Uto-Aztecan." *International Journal of American Linguistics* 49 (3): 258–276.

——. 1995. "The Voices of Don Gabriel: Responsibility and Self in a Modern Mexicano Narrative." In *The Dialogic Emergence of Culture*, edited by Dennis Tedlock and Bruce Mannheim, 97–147. Chicago: University of Illinois Press.

——. 1998a. "Language, Race, and White Public Space." *American Anthropologist* 100: 680–689.

——. 1998b. "'Today There Is No Respect': Nostalgia, 'Respect,' and Oppositional Discourse in Mexicano (Nahuatl) Language Ideology." In *Language Ideologies: Practice and Theory*, edited by Bambi Schieffelin, Kathryn Woolard, and Paul Kroskrity, 68–86. Oxford: Oxford University Press.

——. 2002. "'Expert Rhetorics' in Advocacy for Endangered Languages: Who Is Listening, and What Do They Hear?" *Journal of Linguistic Anthropology* 12 (2): 119–133.

——. 2003. "What Is Lost When Names Are Forgotten?" In *Nature Knowledge*, edited by G. Ortalli. Providence, RI: Berghahn.

——. 2008. *The Everyday Language of White Racism*. Chichester, UK: Wiley-Blackwell.

Hinton, Leanne, and Kenneth L. Hale. 2001. *The Green Book of Language Revitalization in Practice*. San Diego: Academic.

Ho, Stephanie. 2007. "Report: Iraq Most Dangerous Country for Journalists in 2006." *Boxun News*, February 7.

Hobsbawm, Eric. 1969. *Bandits*. New York: Delacorte.

Holston, James. 2008. *Insurgent Citizenships: Disjunctions of Democracy and Modernity in Brazil*. Princeton, NJ: Princeton University Press.

Huntoon, Laura, and Barbara Becker. 2001. "Colonias in Arizona: A Changing Definition with Changing Location." In *Memoria of a Research Workshop, "Irregular Settlement and Self-Help Housing in the United States,"* 3438–3441. Cambridge, MA: Lincoln Institute of Land Policy.

Iglesias Prieto, Norma. 1997. *Beautiful Flowers of the Maquiladora: Life Histories of Women Workers in Tijuana*. Translations from Latin America Series. Austin: University of Texas Press, Institute of Latin American Studies.

Inoue, Miyako. 2007. "Language and Gender in an Age of Neoliberalism." *Gender and Language* 1 (1): 79–91.

Irwin, Robert McKee. 2003. *Mexican Masculinities*, vol. 11 of *Cultural Studies of the Americas*. Minneapolis: University of Minnesota Press.

Jackson, Jean E., and Kay B. Warren. 2005. "Indigenous Movements in Latin America: Controversies, Ironies, New Directions." *Annual Review of Anthropology* 34 (1): 549–573.

Jenkins, Matt. 2007. "The Efficiency Paradox." *High Country News* www.hcn.org/issues/339/16808 (accessed July 5, 2011).

Joseph, Gilbert M., and Daniel Nugent. 1994. *Everyday Forms of State Formation: Revolution and the Negotiation of Rule in Modern Mexico*. Durham, NC: Duke University Press.

Juffer, Jane. 2006. *The Last Frontier: The Contemporary Configuration of the U.S.-Mexico Border*. Durham, NC: Duke University Press.

Kaus, Andrea. 1993. "Social Realities of Environmental Ideologies: A Case Study of the Mapimí Reserve." *Culture and Agriculture* 13 (45–46): 29–34.

Kearney, Michael. 1991. "Borders and Boundaries of State and Self at the End of Empire." *Journal of Historical Sociology* 4: 52–74.

Keck, Margaret. 1995. "Social Equity and Environmental Politics in Brazil: Lessons from the Rubber Tappers of Acre." *Comparative Politics* 27 (4): 409–424.

Keenan, Eleanor. 1974. "Norm-Makers, Norm-Breakers: Uses of Speech by Men and Women in a Malagasy Community." In *Ethnography of Communication*, edited by Richard Bauman and Joel Sherzer, 125–143. Cambridge: Cambridge University Press.

Keesing, Roger. 1985. "Kwaio Women Speak: The Micropolitics of Autobiography in a Soloman Island Society." *American Anthropologist* 87 (1): 27–39.

Kelly, William. 1977. *Cocopa Ethnography*. Tucson: University of Arizona Press.

King, Anthony. 2000. "Thinking with Bourdieu against Bourdieu: A 'Practical' Critique of the Habitus." *Sociological Theory* 18 (3): 417–433.

Kingfisher, Catherine. 2002. *Western Welfare in Decline: Globalization and Women's Poverty*. Philadelphia: University of Pennsylvania Press.

Kiy, Richard, and John D. Wirth. 1998. *Environmental Management on North America's Borders*. Environmental History Series, No. 14. College Station: Texas A&M University Press.

Knight, Alan. 1990. "Racism, Revolution, and Indigenismo: Mexico, 1910–1940." In *The Idea of Race in Latin America, 1870–1940*, edited by Richard Graham, 71–113. Austin: University of Texas Press.

Kopinak, Kathryn. 1998. *Desert Capitalism: Maquiladoras in North America's Western Industrial Corridor*. Tucson: University of Arizona Press.

Krauss, Michael. 1992. "The World's Languages in Crisis." *Language* 68 (1): 4–10.

Krauze, Enrique. 1997. *Mexico: Biography of Power: A History of Modern Mexico, 1810–1996*. New York: HarperCollins.

Krech, Shepard. 1999. *The Ecological Indian: Myth and History*. New York: W. W. Norton.

———. 2005. "Reflections on Conservation, Sustainability, and Environmentalism in Indigenous North America." *American Anthropologist* 107 (1): 78–86.

Kulick, Don. 1992. *Language Shift and Cultural Reproduction: Socialization, Self, and Syncretism in a Papua New Guinean Village*. Studies in the Social and Cultural Foundations of Language, No. 14. Cambridge: Cambridge University Press.

———. 1995. "Speaking as a Woman: Structure and Gender Arguments in a New Guinea Village." *Cultural Anthropology* 8 (4): 510–541.

———. 1998. "Anger, Gender, Language Shift, and the Politics of Revelation in a Papua New Guinean Village." In *Language Ideologies: Practice and Theory*, edited by Bambi Schieffelin, Kathryn Woolard, and Paul Kroskrity, 87–102. Oxford: Oxford University Press.

Kuper, Adam. 2003. "The Return of the Native." *Current Anthropology* 44 (3): 389–402.

Labov, William. 1966. *The Social Stratification of English in New York City*. Washington, DC: Center for Applied Linguistics.
———. 1972. *Sociolinguistic Patterns*. Philadelphia: University of Pennsylvania Press.
Lakoff, Robin Tolmach. 1975. *Language and Woman's Place*. New York: Harper & Row.
Lambek, Michael. 1996. "The Past Imperfect: Remembering as Moral Practice." In *Tense Past: Cultural Essays in Trauma and Memory*, edited by Paul Antze and Michael Lambek, 235–254. New York: Routledge.
Lancaster, Roger N. 1992. *Life Is Hard: Machismo, Danger, and the Intimacy of Power in Nicaragua*. Berkeley: University of California Press.
Langton, Marcia. 1988. "Medicine Square." In *Being Black: Aboriginal Culture in "Settled" Australia*, edited by I. Keen, 201–226. Canberra: Aboriginal Studies Press.
Laurie, Nina, Robert Andolina, and Sarah Radcliffe. 2002. "The Excluded 'Indigenous'? The Implications of Multi-Ethnic Policies for Water Reform in Bolivia." In *Multiculturalism in Latin America: Indigenous Rights, Diversity and Democracy*, edited by Rachel Sieder, 252–276. New York: Palgrave Macmillan.
Leacock, Eleanor Burke. 1977. "Women in Egalitarian Societies." In *Becoming Visible: Women in European History*, edited by Renate Bridenthal and Claudia Koonz, 15–38. Boston: Houghton Mifflin.
———. 1980. *Myths of Male Dominance: Collected Articles on Women Cross Culturally*. New York: Monthly Review Press.
Lefebvre, Henri. 1991. *The Production of Space*. Cambridge, MA: Blackwell.
Lévi-Strauss, Claude. 1963. *Structural Anthropology*. New York: Basic Books.
Levinson, David. 1989. *Family Violence in Cross-Cultural Perspective*, vol. 1 of *Frontiers of Anthropology*. Newbury Park, CA: Sage.
Li, Tania Murray. 2000. "Articulating Indigenous Identity in Indonesia: Resource Politics and the Tribal Slot." *Comparative Studies in Society and History* 42 (1): 149–179.
———. 2007. *The Will to Improve: Governmentality, Development, and the Practice of Politics*. Durham, NC: Duke University Press.
Liebert, Wolf. 2001. "The Sociohistorical Dynamics of Language and Cognition: The Emergence of the Metaphor Model 'Money Is Water' in the Nineteenth Century." In *The Ecolinguistics Reader: Language, Ecology and Environment*, edited by A. Fill and Peter Mühlhäusler, 101–108. London: Continuum.
Limón, José Eduardo. 1994. *Dancing with the Devil: Society and Cultural Poetics in Mexican-American South Texas*. New Directions in Anthropological Writing. Madison: University of Wisconsin Press.
Lippi-Green, Rosina. 1997. *English with an Accent: Language, Ideology, and Discrimination in the United States*. London: Routledge.
Maffi, Luisa. 2001. *On Biocultural Diversity: Linking Language, Knowledge, and the Environment*. Washington, DC: Smithsonian Institute Press.
———. 2005. "Linguistic, Cultural and Biological Diversity." *Annual Review of Anthropology* 34 (1): 599–617.

Maganda, Carmen. 2005. "Collateral Damage: How the San Diego-Imperial Valley Water Agreement Affects the Mexican Side of the Border." *The Journal of Environment & Development* 14 (4): 486–506.

———. 2012. "Border Water Culture in Theory and Practice: Political Behavior on the Mexico-U.S. Border." *Journal of Political Ecology* 19: 81–93.

Malinowski, Bronislaw. 1922. *Argonauts of the Western Pacific: An Account of Native Enterprise and Adventure in the Archipelagoes of Melanesian New Guinea*. Studies in Economics and Political Science, No. 65. London: G. Routledge; New York: E. P. Dutton.

Malotki, Ekkehart, and Michael Lomatuway'ma. 1985. *Gullible Coyote: A Bilingual Collection of Hopi Coyote Stories = Una'ihu*. Tucson: University of Arizona Press.

Mani, Lata. 1998. *Contentious Traditions: The Debate on Sati in Colonial India*. Berkeley: University of California Press.

Marcus, George E., and Michael Fischer. 1986. *Anthropology as Cultural Critique: An Experimental Moment in the Human Sciences*. Chicago: University of Chicago Press.

Marx, Karl, Friedrich Engels, and David B. Riazanov. 1963. *The Communist Manifesto of Karl Marx and Friedrich Engels*. New York: Russell & Russell.

Marosi, Richard. 2006. "U.S. Crackdown Sends Meth Labs South of Border." *Los Angeles Times*, November 26.

Martin, Joann. 1990. "Motherhood and Power: The Production of a Women's Culture of Politics in a Mexican Community." *American Ethnologist* 17 (3): 470–490.

Martinez Novo, Carmen. 2006. *Who Defines Indigenous? Identities, Development, Intellectuals, and the State in Northern Mexico*. New Brunswick, NJ: Rutgers University Press.

Mathews, Andrew S. 2008. "State Making, Knowledge, and Ignorance: Translation and Concealment in Mexican Forestry Institutions." *American Anthropologist* 110: 484–494.

———. 2009. "Unlikely Alliances Encounters between State Science, Nature Spirits, and Indigenous Industrial Forestry in Mexico, 1926–2008." *Current Anthropology* 50: 75–101.

McCay, Bonnie J. 1984. "The Pirates of Piscary: Ethnohistory of Illegal Fishing in New Jersey." *Ethnohistory* 31 (1): 17–37.

McClusky, Laura J. 2001. *"Here, Our Culture Is Hard": Stories of Domestic Violence from a Mayan Community in Belize*. Louann Atkins Temple Women and Culture Series, No. 2. Austin: University of Texas Press.

McDermott, David Hughes. 2005. "Third Nature: Making Space and Time in the Great Limpopo Conservation Area." *Cultural Anthropology* 20 (2): 157–184.

McDermott, Gerald. 1994. *Coyote: A Trickster Tale from the American Southwest*. San Diego: Harcourt Brace.

McDermott, Ray. 1988. "Inarticulateness." In *Linguistics in Context: Connecting Observation and Understanding*, edited by Deborah Tannen, 37–68. Norwood, NJ: Ablex.

McElhinny, Bonnie. 2001. "See No Evil, Speak No Evil: White Police Officers' Talk about Race and Affirmative Action." *Journal of Linguistic Anthropology* 11 (1): 65–78.

———. 2003. "Theorizing Gender in Sociolinguistics and Linguistic Anthropology." In *The Handbook of Language and Gender*, edited by B. Myerhoff and J. Holmes, 21–42. Oxford: Blackwood.

———. 2006. "Written in Sand: Language and Landscape in an Environmental Dispute in Southern Ontario." *Critical Discourse Studies* 3 (2): 123–152.

———. 2007. "Language, Gender and Economies in Global Transitions: Provocative and Provoking Questions about How Gender Is Articulated." In *Words, Worlds, Material Girls: Language and Gender in a Global Economy*, edited by Bonnie McElhinny, 1–38. Berlin: Mouton de Gruyter.

McGee, William J. 1901. "Man's Place in Nature." *American Anthropologist* 3 (1): 1–13.

Medicine, Bea. 1987. "The Role of American Indian Women in Cultural Continuity and Transition." In *Women and Language in Transition*, edited by Joyce Penfield, 159–166. Albany: State University of New York Press.

Miller, Bruce G. 2003. *Invisible Indigenes: The Politics of Nonrecognition*. Lincoln: University of Nebraska Press.

Mohanty, Chandra Talpade, Ann Russo, Lourdes Torres, and American Council of Learned Societies. 1991. *Third World Women and the Politics of Feminism*. Bloomington: Indiana University Press. Available at link.library.utoronto.ca/eir/EIRdetail.cfm?Resources__ID=362238&T=F.

Mola, Carlos Loret De. 2001. *El negocio: La economía de México atrapado por el narcotráfico*. Barcelona: Grijalbo Mondadori SA.

Mondaca Cota, Anajilda. 2004. *Las Mujeres También Pueden: Género y Narcocorrido*. Culiacán: Universidad de Occidente.

Montechino, S. 1991. *Madreys huachos: Aegorías del mestizaje chileno*. Santiago, Chile: Editorial Cuarto Propio/CEDEM.

Montoya, R., L. J. Frazier, and J. Hurtig. 2002. *Gender's Place: Feminist Anthropologies of Latin America*. Hampshire, UK: Palgrave Macmillan.

Moore, Donald S. 1998. "Subaltern Struggles and the Politics of Place: Remapping Resistance in Zimbabwe's Eastern Highlands." *Cultural Anthropology* 13 (3): 344–381.

Moore, Robert E. 2006. "Disappearing, Inc.: Glimpsing the Sublime in the Politics of Access to Endangered Languages." *Language and Communication* 26: 296–315.

Mota, Vivian M. 1980. "Politics and Feminism in the Dominican Republic: 1931–1945 and 1966–1974." In *Sex and Class in Latin America*, edited by June Nash and Helen Icka Safa, 265–278. New York: J. F. Bergin.

Muehlmann, Shaylih. 2007. "Defending Diversity: Staking Out a Common, Global Interest?" In *Discourses of Endangerment: Interest and Ideology in the Defence of Language*, edited by Alexandre Duchêne and Monica Heller, 14–34. New York: Continuum International.

———.Forthcoming. *When I Wear My Alligator Boots: Life at the Edges of the War on Drugs*. Berkeley: University of California Press.

Muehlmann, Shaylih, and Alexandre Duchêne. 2007. "Beyond the Nation-State: International Agencies as New Sites of Discourses on Bilingualism." In *Bilingualism: A Social Approach*, edited by Monica Heller, 96–110. New York: Palgrave Macmillan.

Mufwene, Salikoko S. 2001. *The Ecology of Language Evolution*. Cambridge Approaches to Language Contact. Cambridge: Cambridge University Press.

Mühlhäusler, Peter. 1996. *Language Change and Linguistic Imperialism in the Pacific Region*. London: Routledge.

Mühlhäusler, Peter, and Adrian Peace. 2006. "Environmental Discourses." *Annual Review of Anthropology* 35: 457–479.

Myerson, George, and Yvonne Ryden. 1996. *The Language of Environment: A New Rhetoric*. London: University College of London Press.

Nader, Laura. 1972. "Up the Anthropologist—Perspectives Gained from Studying Up." In *Reinventing Anthropology*, edited by Dell Hymes, 284–311. New York: Pantheon.

Nash, June C. 1993. *Crafts in the World Market: The Impact of Global Exchange on Middle American Artisans*. Albany: State University of New York Press.

Navarro Smith, Alejandra. 2008. "Cucapás, derechos indígenas y pesca: Dilemas del sistema productivo pesquero vis-à-vis las políticas de conservación de las especies en el Golfo de California." *Revista Chilena de Antropología Visual* 12 (2): 172–196.

———. 2010. "Cucapás y reconocimiento de sus derechos como pueblo indígena." In *Diversidad cultural, racismo, exclusión y xenofobia en la frontera norte México-Eeuu*, edited by Alejandra Navarro Smith and Carlos Velez-Ibañez, 87–117. Mexicali: Cuadernos del CIC-Museo.

Navarro Smith, A., A. Tapia, and E. Garduño. 2010. "Navegando a contracorriente: Los Cucapás y la legislación ambiental." *Culturales* 6 (12): 43–74.

Negron, Sito. 2007. "Activists, Mayors Protest U.S.-Mexico Border Wall." *Reuters*, August 25.

Nelson, Diane M. 1999. *A Finger in the Wound: Body Politics in Quincentennial Guatemala*. Berkeley: University of California Press.

Nettle, Daniel, and Suzanne Romaine. 2000. *Vanishing Voices: The Extinction of the World's Languages*. New York: Oxford University Press.

Niezen, Ronald. 2003. *The Origins of Indigenism: Human Rights and the Politics of Identity*. Berkeley: University of California Press.

Nugent, Daniel, and Ana Maria Alonso. 1994. "Multiple Selective Traditions in Agrarian Reform and Agrarian Struggle: Popular Culture and State Formation in the Ejido of Namiquipa, Chihuahua." In *Everyday Forms of State Formation: Revolution and the Negotiation of Rule in Modern Mexico*, edited by Gilbert M. Joseph and Daniel Nugent, 207–246. Durham, NC: Duke University Press.

Nye, David. 1994. *American Technological Sublime*. Cambridge: MIT Press.

O'Neil, Patrick H. 2007. *Essentials of Comparative Politics*. 2nd ed. New York: W. W. Norton.
Obando, Ana Elena. 2003. *Women and Water Privatization: Women's Human Rights*. Association for Women's Rights in Development (AWID). www.awid.org/Library/Women-and-Water-Privatization (accessed July 28, 2011).
Olcott, Jocelyn. 2005. *Revolutionary Women in Postrevolutionary Mexico*, Next Wave. Durham, NC: Duke University Press.
Ortega, Gregorio. 1999. *Las muertas de Ciudad Juárez: El caso de Elizabeth Castro García y Abdel Latif Sharif Sharif*. México, DF: Fontamara.
Ortner, Sherry. 1974. "Is Female to Male as Nature Is to Culture?" In *Woman, Culture, and Society*, edited by Michelle Zimbalist Rosaldo, Louise Lamphere, and Joan Bamberger, 68–87. Stanford, CA: Stanford University Press.
———. 1984. "Theory in Anthropology since the Sixties." *Comparative Studies in Society and History* 26: 126–166.
———. 1995. "Resistance and the Problem of Ethnographic Refusal." *Society for Comparative Study of Society and History* 37 (1): 173–193.
———. 2000. *The Fate of "Culture": Geertz and Beyond*. Berkeley: University of California Press.
———. 2006. *Anthropology and Social Theory*. Durham, NC: Duke University Press.
Pagán, José A. 2004. *Worker Displacement in the US/Mexico Border Region: Issues and Challenges*. Cheltenham, UK: Edward Elgar.
Palma, M. 1990. *Malinche: El malinchismo o el lado femenino de la sociedad mestiza*. In *Simbólica de la feminidad*, edited by M. Palma, 13–39. Quito, Ecuador: Ediciones Abya-Yala.
Paredes, Américo. 2003. "The United States, Mexico, and *Machismo*." In *Perspectives on las Américas: A Reader in Culture, History and Representation*, edited by Matthew C. Gutmann, Félix V. Matos Rodríguez, Lynn Stephen, and Patricia Zavella, 329–341. Oxford: Blackwell.
Paredes, Américo, and Richard Bauman. 1993. *Folklore and Culture on the Texas-Mexican Border*. Austin: CMAS Books, Center for Mexican American Studies, University of Texas at Austin.
Payan, Tony. 2006. *The Three U.S.-Mexico Border Wars: Drugs, Immigration, and Homeland Security*. Westport, CT: Praeger Security International.
Paz, Octavio. 1961. *The Labyrinth of Solitude: Life and Thought in Mexico*. New York: Grove.
Peluso, Nancy. 1995. "Whose Woods Are These? Counter-Mapping Forest Territories in Kalimantan, Indonesia." *Antipode* 27 (4): 383–406.
Pemberton, John. 1994. *On the Subject of "Java."* Ithaca, NY: Cornell University Press.
Perramond, Eric. 2004. "Desert Traffic: The Dynamics of the Drug Trade in Northwestern Mexico." In *Dangerous Harvest*, edited by M. Steinberg, J. Hobbs, and K. Mathewson, 209–217. Oxford: Oxford University Press.
Peters, Michael A. 2001. *Poststructuralism, Marxism, and Neoliberalism*. Lanham, MD: Rowman & Littlefield.

Postero, Nancy Grey. 2007. *Now We Are Citizens: Indigenous Politics in Postmulticultural Bolivia.* Stanford, CA: Stanford University Press.

Povinelli, Elizabeth A. 2002. *The Cunning of Recognition: Indigenous Alterities and the Making of Australian Multiculturalism, Politics, History, and Culture.* Durham, NC: Duke University Press.

Powell, John W. 1888. "From Barbarism to Civilization." *American Anthropologist* 1 (2): 97–123.

Pronatura. 2005. *Elaboración de dos programas de desarrollo comunitario sustentable (pdcs) en zonas Costeras (Ejidos López Aceves, López-Collada y Salinas de Gortari) y de Humedales (Comunidad Indígena Cucapá, Ejidos Oviedo Mota-El Indiviso, Mesa Rica y Luis Encinas Jonson) de la Reserva de la Biosfera (RB) del Alto Golfo de California y Delta del Río Colorado: Final Report for the National Commission on Natural Protected Areas.* San Luís Río Colorado: Pronatura.

Pyne, Stephen J. 1999. *How the Canyon Became Grand: A Short History.* New York: Viking.

Ramírez, Arturo. 1990. "Views of the Corrido Hero: Paradigm and Development." *Americas Review* 18 (2): 71–79.

Ramírez, Santiago. 1959. *El Mexicano: Psicologia de sus motivaciones.* Mexico City: Editorial Pax-México.

Ramírez Paredes, Juan Rogelio. 2002. *Nunca más sin nosotros: Evolución histórica del proyecto del ezln.* México, DF: Ediciones y Gráficos Eón.

Ramos, Alcida R. 1994. "The Hyperreal Indian." *Critique of Anthropology* 14 (2): 153–171.

———. 1995. *Sanumá Memories: Yanomami Ethnography in Times of Crisis.* Madison: University of Wisconsin Press.

Ramos, Samuel. 1962. *Profile of Man and Culture in Mexico.* Austin: University of Texas Press.

Reisner, Marc. 1993. *Cadillac Desert: The American West and Its Disappearing Water.* Vancouver: Douglas & McIntyre.

Reynolds, James I. 2005. "The Impact of the Guerin on Aboriginal and Fiduciary Law." *Advocate* 63: 365–372.

Richland, Justin B. 2008. "Sovereign Time, Storied Moments: The Temporalities of Law, Tradition, and Ethnography in Hopi Tribal Court." *PoLAR: Political and Legal Anthropology Review* 31 (1): 8–27.

———. 2011. "Beyond Listening: Lessons for Native/American Collaborations from the Creation of the Nakwatsvewat Institute." *American Indian Culture and Research Journal* 35 (1): 101–111.

Roig-Franzia, Manuel, and Juan Forero. 2007. "U.S. Anti-Drug Aid Would Target Mexican Cartels." *Washington Post,* August 8.

Roseberry, William. 1989. *Anthropologies and Histories: Essays in Culture, History and Political Economy.* New Brunswick, NJ: Rutgers University Press.

Sánchez, Yolanda Olgas. 2000. *A la orilla del Río Colorado.* Mexicali: Colonia Pro-Hogar.

Sanday, Peggy Reeves. 1981. *Female Power and Male Dominance: On the Origins of Sexual Inequality.* Cambridge: Cambridge University Press.

Schatzki, Theodore. 1997. "Practices and Action: A Wittgensteinian Critique of Bourdieu and Giddens." *Philosophy of the Social Sciences* 27 (3): 283–308.

Schegloff, Emanuel A. 1997. "'Narrative Analysis' Thirty Years Later." *Journal of Narrative and Life History* 7 (1–4): 97–106.

Scheper-Hughes, Nancy. 1992. *Death without Weeping: The Violence of Everyday Life in Brazil.* Berkeley: University of California Press.

Schmink, Marianne. 1981. "Women in Brazilian Politics." *Signs* 7 (1): 15–134.

Schneider, Jane, and Peter Schneider. 2005. "Mafia, Antimafia, and the Plural Cultures of Sicily." *Current Anthropology* 46 (4): 501–520.

Scott, James C. 1992. *Domination and the Arts of Resistance: Hidden Transcripts.* New Haven, CT: Yale University Press.

———. 1998. *Seeing Like a State: How Certain Schemes to Improve the Human Condition Have Failed.* Yale Agrarian Studies. New Haven, CT: Yale University Press.

Scott, Joan. 1988. "Deconstructing Equality vs. Difference." *Feminist Studies* 14: 33–50.

Segal, Robert. 2000. *Hero Myths: A Reader.* Oxford: Blackwell.

Seligson, Mitchell A., and Edward J. Williams. 1981. *Maquiladoras and Migration: Workers in the Mexico-United States Border Industrialization Program.* Austin: Mexico-U.S. Border Research Program, University of Texas.

Server, John. 1949. "The Colorado Is Flowing Merrily out to the Sea While Arizona and California Play Tweedle-Dum and Tweedle-Dee." *Western Construction News*, April 15.

Sheridan, Thomas E. 1988. *Where the Dove Calls: The Political Ecology of a Peasant Corporate Community in Northwestern Mexico.* Tucson: University of Arizona Press.

Shiva, Vandana. 2002. *Water Wars: Privatization, Pollution and Profit.* Cambridge, MA: South End.

Sidnell, Jack. 1997. "Organizing Social and Spatial Location: Elicitations in Indo-Guyanese Village Talk." *Journal of Linguistic Anthropology* 7 (2): 143–165.

———. 2000. "Primus Inter Pares: Storytelling and Male Peer Groups in an Indo-Guyanese Rumshop." *American Ethnologist* 27 (1): 72–99.

Sieder, Rachel. 2002. *Multiculturalism in Latin America: Indigenous Rights, Diversity and Democracy.* New York: Palgrave Macmillan.

Siegel, James T. 1986. *Solo in the New Order: Language and Hierarchy in an Indonesian City.* Princeton, NJ: Princeton University Press.

Skutnabb-Kangas, Tove. 2000. *Linguistic Genocide in Education—or Worldwide Diversity and Human Rights?* New York: Routledge.

Skutnabb-Kangas, Tove, Luisa Maffi, and David Harmon. 2003. *Sharing a World of Difference: The Earth's Linguistic, Cultural and Biological Diversity.* SUNESCO, Terralingua, and World Wide Fund for Nature. Paris: UNESCO.

Smith, Gavin. 1999. *Confronting the Present: Towards a Politically Engaged Anthropology.* Oxford: Bergmann.

Smythe, William. 1900. "An International Wedding: Tale of a Trip on the Borders of Two Republics." *Sunset*, October, 286–300.

Solis, Elvia. 2005. "Tensión en el Alto Golfo de California." *El Mexicano*, April 24.

Sonoran Institute. 2007. *The Colorado Delta Land of the Kwapa*. www.sonoran institute.org/library/recoreading/doc_download/613-kwapa-map-english.html (accessed August 1, 2011).

Speed, Shannon. 2005. "Dangerous Discourses: Human Rights and Multiculturalism in Neoliberal Mexico." *PoLAR: Political and Legal Anthropology Review* 25: 29–51.

Spielberg, Joseph. 1974. "Humour in Mexican-American Palomilla: Some Historical, Social, and Psychological Implications." *Revista Chicano-Requeña* 2: 41–50.

Stephen, Lynn. 1997. "Redefined Nationalism in Building a Movement for Indigenous Autonomy in Southern Mexico." *Journal of Latin American Anthropology* 3 (1): 72–101.

———. 2002. *Zapata Lives! Histories and Cultural Politics in Southern Mexico*. Berkeley: University of California Press.

Stern, Steve J. 1995. *The Secret History of Gender: Women, Men, and Power in Late Colonial Mexico*. Chapel Hill: University of North Carolina Press.

Strang, Veronica. 2004. *The Meaning of Water*. Oxford: Berg.

Streicker, Joel. 1995. "Policing Boundaries: Race, Class and Gender in Cartagena, Columbia." *American Ethnologist* 22 (1): 54–74.

Sundberg, Juanita. 2004. "Identities in the Making: Conservation, Gender and Race in the Maya Biosphere Reserve, Guatemala." *Gender, Place and Culture: A Journal of Feminist Geography* 11 (1): 43–66.

Sutton, Laurel A. 1995. "Bitches and Shankly Hobags: The Place of Women in Contemporary Slang." In *Gender Articulated: Language and the Socially Constructed Self*, edited by Kira Hall and Mary Bucholtz, 560–572. New York: Routledge.

Suzman, James. 2003. "Comments: The Return of the Native." *Current Anthropology* 44 (3): 398–400.

Taussig, Michael T. 1993. *Mimesis and Alterity: A Particular History of the Senses*. New York: Routledge.

———. 2004. *My Cocaine Museum*. Chicago: University of Chicago Press.

Terdiman, Richard. 1993. *Present Past: Modernity and the Memory Crisis*. Ithaca, NY: Cornell University Press.

Tiano, Susan. 1994. *Patriarchy on the Line: Labor, Gender, and Ideology in the Mexican Maquila Industry*. Philadelphia: Temple University Press.

Tisdale, Shelby Jo-Anne. 1997. *Cocopah Identity and Cultural Survival: Indian Gaming and the Political Ecology of the Lower Colorado River Delta*. Tucson: University of Arizona Press.

Toussaint, Sandy. 2008. "Climate Change, Global Warming and Too Much Sorry Business." *Australian Journal of Anthropology* 19 (1): 84–88.

Trudgill, Peter. 1972. "Sex, Covert Prestige and Linguistic Change in the Urban British English of Norwich." *Language in Society* 1: 179–196.

Tsing, Anna Lowenhaupt. 1993. *In the Realm of the Diamond Queen: Marginality in an Out-of-the-Way Place*. Princeton, NJ: Princeton University Press.

———. 2000. "The Global Situation." *Cultural Anthropology* 15 (3): 327–360.

———. 2007. "Indigenous Voice." In *Indigenous Experience Today*, edited by Marisol de la Cadena and Orin Starn, 33–67. New York: Berg.

Turner, Terence. 1991. "Representing, Resisting, Rethinking: Historical Trans-Formations of Kayapo Culture and Anthropological Consciousness." In *Colonial Situations: Essays on the Contextualization of Ethnographic Knowledge*, edited by George W. Stocking Jr., 285–313. Madison: University of Wisconsin Press.

United Nations Office on Drugs and Crime (UNODC). 2010. World Drug Report. www.unodc.org/documents/wdr/WDR_2010/World_Drug_Report_2010_lo-res.pdf. New York: United Nations (accessed July 28, 2011).

Valdéz, T., and J. Ovarría. 1997. *Masculinidad/es poder y crisis*. Santiago, Chile: Internacional/FLASCO.

Valenzuela Arce, Javier Manuel. 2002. *Jefe de Jefes: Corridos y Narcocultura*. Barcelona: Random House Monadori.

Vásquez León, Marcela. 1999. "Neoliberalism, Environmentalism and Scientific Knowledge: Redefining Use Rights in the Gulf of California Fisheries." In *States and Illegal Practices*, edited by Josiah Heyman, 233–260. New York: Berg.

Viqueira, Juan Pedro. 2001. "Los usos y costumbres en contra de la autonomía." *Letras Libres* 27: 30–36.

Viveros, Mara V. 1997. "Los estudios sobre lo masculino en América Latina: Una producción teórica emergente." *Nómadas* 6: 55–67.

———. 2001. "Contemporary Latin American Perspectives on Masculinity." *Men and Masculinities* 3 (3): 237–260.

Waisman, Lic, Victor Lichtinguer, and Sr. Javier Bernardo Usabiaga Arroyo. 2002. *Caso de los habitantes de la comunidad indígena Cucapá: Comision Nacional de los Derechos Humanos*. www.cndh.org.mx/recomen/2002/008.htm (accessed July 28, 2011).

Walden, Andrew. 2007. "Mexico: The Next Colombia?" *FrontPageMagazine.com*, September 6. http://archive.frontpagemag.com/readArticle.aspx?ARTID=27860 (accessed September 30, 2012).

Walley, Christine. 2004. *Rough Waters: Nature and Development in an African Marine Park*. Princeton, NJ: Princeton University Press.

Walsh, Casey. 2012. "Introduction: Mexican Water Studies in the Mexico-US Borderlands." *Journal of Political Ecology* 19: 50–56.

Ward, Evan. 2001. "The Twentieth-Century Ghosts of William Walker: Conquest of Land and Water as Central Themes in the History of the Colorado River Delta." *Pacific Historical Review* 70 (3): 359–385.

Weiner, Annette B. 1976. *Women of Value, Men of Renown: New Perspectives in Trobriand Exchange*. Austin: University of Texas Press.

———. 1988. *The Trobrianders of Papua New Guinea: Case Studies in Cultural Anthropology*. New York: Holt, Rinehart and Winston.

Weismantel, Mary J. 2001. *Cholas and Pishtacos: Stories of Race and Sex in the Andes*. Women in Culture and Society. Chicago: University of Chicago Press.

Wenzel, George W. 1978. "The Harp-Seal Controversy and the Inuit Economy." *Arctic* 31 (1): 2–6.

———. 1991. *Animal Rights, Human Rights: Ecology, Economy, and Ideology in the Canadian Arctic*. London: Belhaven.

West, Paige. 2005. "Translation, Value, and Space: Theorizing an Ethnographic and Engaged Environmental Anthropology." *American Anthropologist* 107 (4): 632–642.

———. 2006. *Conservation Is Our Government Now: The Politics of Ecology in Papua New Guinea*. Durham, NC: Duke University Press.

West, Paige, James Igoe, and Dan Brockington. 2006. "Parks and Peoples: The Social Impact of Protected Areas." *Annual Review Anthropology* 35 (2006): 251–277.

White, Rob. 2002. "Indigenous Young Australians, Criminal Justice and Offensive Language." *Journal of Youth Studies* 5 (1): 21–35.

Whorf, Benjamin Lee. 1964. *Language, Thought, and Reality: Selected Writings*. Cambridge: MIT Press.

Wilkins, Lomawaima, and K. Tsianina Lomawaima. 2001. *Uneven Ground: American Indian Sovereignty and Federal Law*. Norman: University of Oklahoma Press.

Willis, Paul. 1981. *Learning to Labour: How Working Class Kids Get Working Class Jobs*. New York: Teacher's College Press.

Windsor, Mulford. 1969. *The Menace of the Colorado*. Phoenix: Cline Library.

Wolmer, William. 2003. "Transboundary Conservation: The Politics of Ecological Integrity in the Great Limpopo Transfrontier Park." *Journal of South African Studies* 29: 261–278.

Wood, Dennis, and John Fels. 1992. *The Power of Maps*. New York: Guilford.

Woodbury, Anthony. 1993. "A Defense of the Proposition, 'When a Language Dies, a Culture Dies.'" SALSA: *Texas Linguistic Forum* (33): 101–129.

Woodbury, David. 1941. *The Colorado Conquest*. New York: Dodd, Mead.

Woolard, Kathryn. 1985. "Language Variation and Cultural Hegemony: Toward an Integration of Sociolinguistic Theory and Social Theory." *American Ethnologist* 12 (4): 738–748.

Worster, David. 1992. *Rivers of Empire: Water, Aridity, and the Growth of the American West*. New York: Oxford University Press.

Wright, Melissa. 2011. "Necropolitics, Narcopolitics, and Femicide: Gendered Violence on the Mexico-U.S. Border." *Signs* 36(3): 707.

Wyler, Grace. 2011. "The Mexican Drug Cartels Are a National Security Issue." *Business Insider*. June 13. www.businessinsider.com/why-the-us-needs-to-stop-fighting-the-drug-war-and-start-fighting-the-cartels-2011-6 (accessed July 13, 2011).

Yashar, Deborah J. 1998. "Contesting Citizenship: Indigenous Movements and Democracy in Latin America." *Comparative Politics* 31 (1): 23–42.

Yeh, Emily T. 2007. "Tibetan Indigeneity: Translations, Resemblances and Uptake." In *Indigenous Experience Today*, edited by Marisol de la Cadena and Orin Starn, 69–97. New York: Berg.

Young, Donna J. 1996. "Remembering Trouble: Three Lives, Three Stories." In *Tense Past: Cultural Essays in Trauma and Memory*, edited by Paul Antze and Michael Lambek, 25–44. New York: Routledge.

———. 2005. "Writing against the Native Point of View." In *Auto-Ethnographies: The Anthropology of Academic Practices*, edited by Donna Jean Young and Anne Meneley, 203–216. Peterborough, OT: Broadview.

Young, Michael. 1983. "'Our Name Is Women; We Are Bought with Limesticks and Limepots': Autobiographical Narrative of a Kalauna Woman." *Man* 18 (3): 478–501.

Zerner, Charles. 2000. *People, Plants and Justice: The Politics of Nature Conservation*. New York: Columbia University Press.

INDEX

activism: environmental, 66–71; fishing, 116, 150; indigenous, 6, 13; linguistic, 147
Agua del Coyote, 49
alliances, 57–60, 69, 73, 82; ambivalence of, 69
alligator boots, 84, 106
Americans, 2; gringos, 92, 118, 153
American West, 30, 190
amnesia, 19, 121–123, 141
Arizona v. California, 42
Arizona Water Summit, 4, 15
arrowweed, 56, 184n1
articulation, 6–7, 14, 60, 73, 78–79, 99, 117–118, 147–177; disarticulation, 7, 175–178; as enunciation and expression, 7, 146–148, 178; failure of, 6, 77; inarticulate, 7, 178
assimilation, 12, 13, 56, 126, 148–150
authenticity, 7, 18–19, 56–61; authenticators, 157, 161, 166–167; and fishing practices, 68, 76, 78, 120, 148–151; and language, 157–168, 171–174

barbarism, 40
Basso, Keith, 49–50, 52–53
Bechtel Corporation: privatization of water in Bolivia, 14. *See also* privatization; water
binational water agreements, 6
biomedicine, 122, 142. *See also* amnesia
biosphere, 3, 4, 55, 64–65, 73, 76, 82, 92, 186n11

blankness, 28
boats: painting of, 114; registration of, 16, 96; smuggling with, 96
border: antagonism, 96, 106; economy of, 100; folklore of, 107–111
Boulder Dam, 30, 33–37. *See also* Hoover Dam
boundary marking, 134, 148, 155–156, 187n4
Bourgois, Philippe, 111, 138
Braun, Bruce, 67
Briggs, Charles, 50, 182n10
Bureau of Reclamation, 4, 15, 28–31, 35–38, 45–46, 185. *See also* reclamation
burrero, 85, 101, 187. *See also* mules

cachanilla, 56, 184n1
Campbell, Howard, 95, 185n4
campesinos, 12
canals, 27, 185; Panama, 36; Suez, 36
capitalism, 60, 66, 69, 111
Cárdenas, Lázaro, 10, 184n4
cartels, 85–86, 95, 116
Center for Biological Diversity, 45
Centro de Investigación y Estudios Superiores de Ensenada, 66
Cerro Prieto, 2, 26, 47
chakira, 88, 123, 125, 132
cheros, 107, 184n2
chief: gender of, 134; Supreme Chiefs, 182n8; traditional chief, 10, 153, 182n8
civilization, 32, 39–41, 44

class: -based organizing, 12, 76–77; hierarchy, 5; Mexican working, 96, 122, 165–166; and narco-culture, 107–110; and women's rights, 137–138
Clifford, James, 78
climate change. *See* global warming
Cocopah, 7, 15, 22, 42, 48, 53, 133, 182n12, 184n6; casino, 1, 22, 53, 183n12
colonialism, 27, 68, 117, 127, 137, 142, 144, 167
colonias, 2, 26–27, 84, 93, 127, 182n1
Colorado compact, 31, 161
Colorado River and Hardy River Water Users' Association, 79, 83, 85, 89–91
Colorado River Land Company, 10
comisario, 10, 125, 153
Comisión Nacional para el Desarrollo de los Pueblos Indígenas, 11, 182n9
Commision for Indigenous Development (CDI), 62, 90–91
comunidad indígena, 176
conquest: of the Colorado River, 32, 34, 36, 39–42; of indigenous people, 25, 41, 107, 142
Consejo Supremo de los Pueblos Indígenas, 182n8
Conservation International, 66
Corey, Herbert, 36, 39
corvina, 56, 61, 64–65, 71–72, 79, 81, 111, 140
covert prestige, 154
coyote, 47, 49
creation myth: Cucapá, 2, 27, 47
criminalization: of fishing, 6, 18, 25, 82, 117, 179; of identity, 84–85, 96
crisis of masculinity, 135
cristal. *See* crystal meth
Cruikshank, Julie, 52
crystal meth, 9, 88–89, 124, 132
cultural performance theory, 111–113
cultural recovery, 51, 58, 148
cultural restoration projects, 158

Defenders of Wildlife, 45, 70
Department of the Interior, 28, 30, 46
depression: Great Depression, 37; symptom of withdrawal, 89
discrimination: cultural and linguistic, 149, 169; environmental, 73, 81–82, 99; gendered and ethnic, 101–102, 104, 112, 114
domestic violence, 61, 131–132
Drug Enforcement Agency, 95, 103, 107, 109
drugs: cocaine, 84, 95, 109; marijuana, 88
drug trade, 84–86, 94, 97, 105–107, 117, 178

earthquakes, 8
ecotourism, 66, 69, 77, 85, 92, 158
ejido, 10, 93, 153, 182n7
elders: on Cucapá language, 156, 165, 187; on maps, 50–54; on swearwords, 165
endangerment: of culture and language, 141–149, 184n7; of species, 43–46, 61, 70
engineers: dam construction, 43, 47–49; waterspeak, 31
environmental degradation, 10, 30, 61, 70, 90, 136, 171, 188n1; gendered effects, 136
environmental discourses, 18, 57, 60–61, 66–69, 82, 171, 176
environmental impact: of burning garbage, 61; of fishing, 65, 71
environmental movements, 13, 45–46, 56, 60, 67–69, 159, 171, 174
essentialism: strategic, 69, 78
ethnography: access and methodology, 15–17; of conflicting accounts, 120; of Cucapá, 132; of illegal activities, 16–17, 85, 99; of language, 152; of lines, 22; of place, 46; reversal of, 140–145
expletives. *See* swearwords

femicide, 186–187n13
feminism: classic liberal feminism, 140; perception of Cucapá women, 129–130. *See also* independence: women's
fishing conflict, 61; cooperatives, 15, 18, 51, 55, 62–82, 85, 93, 114, 118, 126, 134, 137, 184n4; permits, 55, 74–76, 81, 86, 113, 119, 137
folklore, 84, 104, 107, 142
Foucault, Michel, 22
free trade, 27, 58, 84

Gadsden Purchase, 21, 182n11
giants, 27, 47–48
Gila River, 181n4
Glen Canyon Dam, 36, 39
global warming, 188n1
Gordillo, Gaston, 43
Graham, Laura, 187n2, 188n5; and Conklin, Beth, 67
Grand Canyon, 1, 43–45
Grand Coulee, 183n1
groserías. *See* swearwords
Gulf of California, 1, 3, 35, 43, 45, 57, 84, 87, 88, 95, 181n2
Gutmann, Mathew, 122, 134, 143

haciendas, 183
Hale, Charles, 58–59, 76–77, 148
Hall, Stuart, 6, 7, 77–78, 144, 147–148, 175–178
Hardy River, 3, 8, 70, 83, 90, 124
hegemony, 56, 73, 111–112; discourses, 177–179
Hill, Jane H., 151, 156, 166, 183n5
Hobsbawm, Eric, 110–111
Hoover Dam, 26, 31, 35–39, 43–45. *See also* Boulder Dam
Hopi, 4
houses: cleaning, 101, 103; that Cruz built, 123; in Las Pintas, 27, 47; of mud, 56; in village, 8

Human Rights Commission, 3, 63–64, 68, 115, 135, 174
Hutpa Niuaha, 48–49

identity: formation, 78–79, 119, 173–178; oppositional, 63, 69, 143
ideology: of gender, 14, 118, 129; of language, 147, 156, 168; of work, 187
illegality: economy, 112–115. *See also* criminalization: of fishing
Immigration and Naturalization Service, 21, 107
Imperial Valley, 1
independence: Ana's, 139; indigenous groups, 59; Latin American, 13; women's, 122, 128–129, 140, 143
International Monetary Fund, 13
interviews, 50, 159, 165; about Cucapá language, 151–152, 165; elicitation techniques, 50, 151; methodological problems, 16; as pathways of communication, 15–16, 130, 138; about place/maps, 25–26, 159

Kiliwa, 71
knowledge: of drug trade, 86, 116, 178; ecological, 41; versus gossip, 141; of language, 151, 162
Kulick, Don, 164, 166
Kuper, Adam, 80

land: communal, 10; connection to, 25–27; reform, 10, 182; rights to, 10–13
language: competency, 158; and culture, 148; endangerment of, 43, 146–147; revitalization projects, 158
Las Pintas, 25, 46–49
Law of the River, 31, 41–42, 46
lawyers: arguing with, 149; fishing cooperative lawyer, 55–56; water-speak, 31
laziness. *See* ideologies of work

Lee's Ferry, 1
legibility, 167; incomprehensibility, 146, 161, 167
Li, Tania, 78–79, 174–177
Limón, José, 165–166
lines, 180; bisected dog, 20–21, 95, 131, 179; línea de compactación, 2, 21; territorial lines, 3, 9–10, 14, 18, 27, 86, 118, 186
literacy: with government, 114; with maps, 177
Living Rivers, 45

machismo, 14, 18, 105, 119, 122–123, 128, 134, 142–143, 178
Malverde, Jesús, 84, 109–110
Mapeo Comunitario, 50–52
maps: absences from, 44; blankness beneath the border in, 42; as instruments of persuasion, 31; of paper, 52; political efficacy of, 52–53; as representations of land and water, 28–30
maquiladoras, 2, 58, 109
marriage, 186; mixed, 79, 149
Martínez Novo, Carmen, 59–60, 77
memory, 120, 122, 141–144. *See also* amnesia
mestizaje, 126
metaphors: as a commodity, 5, 33; as sacred, 5; as wasteful, 32–39; of water, 33, 39–40; as a weight, 133–137; as a wild Indian, 40–42
methamphetamine. *See* crystal meth
Mexicali, 55, 62, 65, 71, 87–89, 93, 95, 97, 101–102
Mexicali Valley, 3, 7, 10, 21
Mexican Federal Agency for Environmental Protection, 65, 68, 110
Mexican Revolution, 10, 96, 143
Mexican saltwater sea bass. *See* corvina
military, 3, 86–88, 95–96, 109, 176
mimesis, 161
mobility: women's, 126–129

mules, 85–86, 100, 106
multiculturalism, 4, 12–13, 58–60, 76–77, 79, 82, 175
Murrieta, Joaquín, 96
mutual intelligibility, 53

narco-corridos, 83, 110
narco-economy, 83–87; criticisms of, 100, 114
narcotraficante: celebration of, 106
National Irrigation Congress, 33
nationalism, 17, 37–39, 44, 117, 142–143; dams as national projects, 33–39
neoliberalism, 13, 58–59, 68, 77
nets: confiscation of, 110; for fishing, 65, 70, 74
noble savage, 60, 67, 76, 157, 164
nondenotational significance, 157, 168
non-governmental organizations, 18, 60–61, 67, 69, 73, 79, 84, 89–92, 174–178; language revitalization, 154–158; and work, 115, 119, 124
North American Free Trade Agreement (NAFTA), 58, 84, 93, 108–109. *See also* free trade
nostalgia: of Cruz and Ana's marriage, 123; of gender equality, 126–127; of language, 156; of past, 156; of river, 49, 54, 100. *See also* romanticization
nuclear zone. *See* Zanjón
Nye, David, 37–38

obscene: sociality of, 164–165. *See also* swearwords
oral history. *See* stories
Ortner, Sherry, 112, 134, 147

Pancho Villa, 96
paper rights, 41
Paz, Octavio, 165–166
People, Conservation, and Nature, 159
performing indigeneity, 14, 56, 88, 123
pino salado. *See* tamarisk

places on or off of maps, 46; listening for places, 54; place making, 27, 51–52; place names, 49–51
pointing: fingers at men, 134; at places not on maps, 25
police, 8, 108; conflicts with indigenous people, 163
poverty: the culture of, 97, 99; and the fishing conflict, 5, 61; and the narco-economy, 89, 92, 96, 98, 110
Pozo de Coyote, 25
prison, 106, 170
privatization, 58; of fishing cooperatives, 184n4; of land, 11; of public sector utilities, 6; of water, 33, 184n4
profanity. *See* swearwords
Pronatura, 93
prostitution, 129
Pyne, Stephen, 43–44

reclamation, 40–42. *See also* Bureau of Reclamation
resistance, 87; "hidden transcript," 161; internal to group politics, 112–115; against the state, 18, 98, 100–112, 160. *See also* Scott, James
romanticization: and the environment, 68, 117; of indigenous people, 61, 117; of narco-culture, 106, 111. *See also* nostalgia

salinity: of land, 1; of water, 8
San Andrés Fault, 8
Sánchez, Yolanda, 132, 151
San Felipe, 2, 71, 95
savagery: of the Colorado River, 34, 39, 41, 43; of Indians, 40–41. *See also* noble savage
Scott, James, 130, 161, 167
Sea of Cortez. *See* Gulf of California
second river, 42
sexuality, 130, 155
shrimping, 79, 80, 107

smuggling, 19, 87, 89, 95, 106–108, 157, 185n4
Smythe, William, 33
social bandit, 110–111
songs. *See* narco-corridos
Speed, Shannon, 58–59
stories: about the drug trade, 85–92; about places, 26–27, 48–54; about swearwords, 152–156
structure and agency debate: 19, 96–100, 111, 182; structuration, 98
sublime: the technological, 37–38
sustainable development, 66–67, 69, 117
Sustainable Water Project, 45
swearwords, 152, 154, 155, 167; chingar, 165–166; use versus meaning, 152, 165

tamarisk, 83–84, 92, 124
tides: fishing by the, 71–72, 139
Tohono O'odham, 86, 95, 151
tourist camps, 87, 90, 94, 97, 101, 150
traditional ecological knowledge. *See* knowledge
travel: alone as a woman, 129–130; of the giant, 47–49; through the desert, 86
tributary: of the Colorado River, 3
Tsing, Anna, 27, 129, 176

unemployment, 5, 84, 93–94, 98, 172
Universidad Nacional Autónoma de México, 66
Upper Gulf of California Biosphere Reserve, 57

Valle de Guadalupe, 26
Venta de la Mesilla. *See* Gadsden Purchase
violence: of drug war, 85, 95, 106; against fisherman, 181; in the village, 131–132; against women, 61, 187n13, 132. *See also* domestic violence

wages, 37, 77, 84, 91, 93–97, 110, 128
war on drugs, 19, 86, 106, 107
water compacts, 28
water: different kinds of rights, 183n3; tribal rights to, 41, 181n4; water scarcity, 3, 6, 21, 25, 45, 84, 136–137, 172
waterspeak: beneficial use, 26, 31–32, 41, 43
Willis, Paul, 111
Wishpa, 49

Woodbury, David, 34–36, 39
World Bank, 13
World Water Forum, 16

Yaqui, 126, 128

Zanjón, 3, 26, 64–65, 71, 79, 181n2; nuclear zone, 57, 65, 75–76, 84, 138, 171
Zapatista, 14, 58, 119

Made in the USA
San Bernardino, CA
25 August 2017